Henry Howard,
Earl of Surrey

Twayne's English Authors Series

Arthur F. Kinney, Editor

University of Massachusetts, Amherst

TEAS 429

Tho Howard   E: of Surrey.

HENRY HOWARD, EARL OF SURREY (1517–1547)
After Holbein. Copyright reserved. Reproduced
by gracious permission of Her Majesty Queen
Elizabeth II, the Royal Library, Windsor Castle

Henry Howard, Earl of Surrey

By William A. Sessions

Georgia State University

Twayne Publishers
A Division of G. K. Hall & Co. • Boston

Henry Howard, Earl of Surrey

William A. Sessions

Copyright © 1986 by G.K. Hall & Co.
All Rights Reserved
Published by Twayne Publishers
A Division of G.K. Hall & Co.
70 Lincoln Street
Boston, Massachusetts 02111

Copyediting supervised by Lewis DeSimone
Book production by Elizabeth Todesco
Book design by Barbara Anderson

Typeset in 11 pt. Garamond
by Modern Graphics, Inc., Weymouth, Massachusetts

Printed on permanent/durable acid-free paper
and bound in the United States of America

Library of Congress Cataloging in Publication Data

Sessions, William A.
  Henry Howard, Earl of Surrey.

  (Twayne's English authors series; TEAS 429)
  Bibliography: p. 165
  Includes index.
  1. Surrey, Henry Howard, Earl of, 1517?–1547—
Criticism and interpretation. I. Title. II. Series.
PR2373.S47   1986   821'.2   86–4773
ISBN 0–8057–6920–X

Contents

Editor's Note

This new life and study of the works of Henry Howard, the Poet Earl of Surrey, is a deeply informed and highly informative book. William Sessions untangles all the various Plantagenet and Tudor strands in the web of the poet earl's ancestry and the family marriages and alliances in his lifetime, showing how his political, social, and lyric songs, sonnets, satires, elegies, translations, and paraphrases all comment, directly or indirectly, on his Catholic alliances at court or—more surprisingly—his latter-day hints of Calvinistic thought. Howard was a remarkable poet: his ten brief years made more history for English poetry than any other poet in English, for he not only introduced classical forms to English but forged as well the first English sonnets and the first blank verse. Sessions argues this was a natural outcome for a poet whose entire body of poetry was a deliberate and sophisticated series of verbal explorations, employing the rhetoric, logic, and philosophy of humanism to a degree unmatched before or since. By painstakingly showing the various layers and resources—notably Vergil and Chaucer—that lie directly (and referentially) behind the deftness of these poems, Sessions also shows conclusively that Surrey was a poet of intertextuality, a poet who took the humanist concern with *imitatio* to its highest and its farthest reaches. This study of Surrey, both introductory and comprehensive, will be a useful guide for years to come.

—ARTHUR F. KINNEY

About the Author

William A. Sessions is Professor of English at Georgia State University. He received his undergraduate degree from the University of North Carolina at Chapel Hill, where he was the first editor of the *Carolina Quarterly*, and received his doctorate from Columbia University. He was a Fulbright Scholar in Germany. As an editor and founder of *Studies in the Literary Imagination*, he has edited volumes on Sidney, seventeenth-century English prose, and Bacon, the latter considered a standard work on the subject. He has published in classical studies and in modern literature, both European and American, and on modern poetry. His major work has been in the Renaissance where he has published more than twenty-five essays in *Milton Studies*, *English Literary Renaissance*, *Renaissance Papers*, and other journals and in four books, ranging from studies of Milton to the seventeenth-century lyric and Herbert. His monograph on Spenser and Vergil, *Spenser's Georgics*, has been widely acclaimed and demonstrates his particular interest in the effects of classical culture on the Renaissance. He has also published two books, an anthology and commentary on forms of poetry and an introduction to *Romeo and Juliet*. As a poet, he is the author of works in the *Southern Review*, *California Quarterly*, *Georgia Review*, and other periodicals. He is presently Director of the Georgia State University Poetry Series in Atlanta.

Preface

Henry Howard, the Poet Earl of Surrey (1517–47), has suffered in the twentieth century a lack of general audience. He has made the anthologies, but he has only just made them, and until recently few literary critics could find in his texts enough material for any theory to justify either further reading of his work or even learning just what the works are. The purpose of this study is to offer the general reader a comprehensive view of Surrey's poetry lacking until now that will provide a basis for further study of Surrey. In fact, only through such a comprehensive view can the recovery of Surrey's stature as poet begin. Without such a general survey of Surrey's canon as this study offers, criticism of Surrey, no matter how good, will always remain incomplete. To accomplish this purpose of a full critical introduction, I have thus aimed in method toward directness and simplicity, working from larger contexts of literary theory, philosophy, history, and anthropology (wherever relevant) to specific exercises in practical criticism. Because Surrey was revolutionary in style, inventing many forms, not least the English sonnet and blank verse, such exercises in criticism provide a good means for any beginning student to enter the texts of Surrey. There a reader new to the texts can discover not only Surrey's remarkable poetic strategies but his technical prowess, if not genius, as it functions in terms of larger contexts.

Toward this aim of practical analysis, I have chosen to divide this study into a kind of *enumeratio*, a figure Surrey obviously loved, of the actual forms he used and, in the case of blank verse, invented. Immediately such an organization of the book serves the purpose of emphasizing the formal basis of Surrey's whole view of art, which a number of recent studies, notably Jentoft's, have skillfully demonstrated. It also reflects what is possibly the earliest ordering of Surrey's texts, that in the Arundel Harington manuscript. Most of all, it will direct the general reader toward the complexity and depth of Surrey's art that in his brief life and brief writing career (hardly more than ten years) always began with experimentation in form. Such an organization may well serve a variety of audiences beyond the general reader and beginning student, for, as any student of

Surrey quickly learns, trying to interpret these texts, with their formal demands, inevitably leads to the critical controversies of interpretation in the Renaissance and in our own time.

For these reasons analysis by forms seems the best method to turn to Surrey's texts themselves, especially in their own opening toward decorum, Milton's "grand masterpiece to be observed," which is exactly where any humanist poet such as Henry Howard, Earl of Surrey, would start. Thus, after the biographical introduction, I have introduced, in my second chapter, some theoretical conceptions for approaching Surrey's poetry in general and then used, as an illustration in practical criticism for the whole study, a contextual analysis of one song. In the following chapters, divided according to Surrey's main literary forms, I have generally followed the same procedure, opening with general background on the form and its relevance followed by specific analyses. Thus the divisions that mark the ensuing chapters, on the sonnets, songs, Poulter's measure and biblical paraphrases, elegies, and blank verse (Aeneid), support a logical method of moving from the general form to the individual text—which in the Renaissance often reflects a mysterious and compelling whole in itself. Questions of interpretations, given such textual wholes, can hardly be avoided in such a method. Thus the problem of analyzing Surrey necessarily entails answering and dealing with modern criticism of the Renaissance that tends to exclude Surrey from any serious interpretation at all. Although I respond often and explicitly to misunderstandings, as I see them, of Surrey, primarily I have responded to such criticism implicitly, by showing texts that prove just the opposite of attacks from critics who often do not know the original text or, more likely, do not know its place in Surrey's larger context of works.

Because Surrey can best be approached by understanding the special place of holistic structure in his work, I have particularly emphasized formal devices such as figures of speech because they are one specific means by which to develop and enhance that perception of structure. Of course, any response to or interpretation of a text merely begins in such awareness of grammar-school figures and techniques, but, as of all major Renaissance poets, so of Surrey no full interpretation is possible without recognition of the place such formal devices hold in artistic strategy. I have by no means exhausted the analysis of such devices in any single poem; I have simply wanted to indicate the larger strategies at work. The more

advanced student may want to work from these rudimentary analyses and bring current, more comprehensive studies of such devices to bear on the various texts.

But what is new and original in what follows is an analysis of every poem we can be certain that Surrey wrote. Whatever the limitation of attempting to be comprehensive in presentation, the method does serve the special need of introducing Surrey to a modern audience. Such an audience has little if any knowledge of his work because Surrey's anthologized pieces often appear as fragmented and as separate as his own severed head. In part, this need to be comprehensive arises from the fact that we have no full text of Surrey's work in this century and at the moment no edition in print at all. There is thus a clear need for a general critical introduction. This is not to say that—despite the fact that Surrey's text has been problematic from the beginning because we lack any holograph of his poems—we have not had some superb charting of the various manuscripts, with their variant readings, notably by Hughey, Eckert, and Ridley. We have also had well-developed, if critically limited, editions of Surrey.

For purposes of this study I have used the Clarendon edition edited by Emrys Jones, supplementing it, when analyzing poems not in Jones, by reference to the Padelford edition, the standard edition of Surrey for most of this century. For Wyatt poems I have referred to his *Collected Poems,* edited by Kenneth Muir and Patricia Thomson (Liverpool: Liverpool University Press, 1969). I have numbered each poem according to its sequence in all these editions, the first letter of the editor's name indicating the edition. One of the recent blessings for Surrey students has been Jentoft's reference guide to Wyatt and Surrey, which provides, at least until the late 1970s, annotated comments on Surrey bibliography and texts.

Finally, I acknowledge my indebtedness to Professor Arthur F. Kinney, whose encouragement stimulated the research and the discoveries of this book from the very start. Among students, I wish to thank for specific readings Beverly Langford, Alice Gambrell, and John Correll. I wish particularly to thank the Dean of the College of Arts and Sciences, Clyde F. Faulkner, and the Georgia State University Research Council for further research funding which allowed me to travel to England. I am especially grateful for the assistance of Mrs. Sara Rodger at Arundel Castle during my research

there and also the encouragement of His Grace, the Duke of Norfolk, the direct descendant of Henry Howard, the Earl of Surrey.

In personal acknowledgment I want to thank Ernestine Little for her gift of teaching me the first lessons of language, a gift from a very generous nature. My wife, Zenobia Urania, has provided an atmosphere of beauty, intellectual and physical, which has made possible whatever work I have been able to finish. Most of all, I dedicate this book to Lee Cooper Sessions, who not only first gave me books but taught me what grand realities exist within their covers.

William A. Sessions

Georgia State University

Chronology

1517   Born probably in late winter or early spring at Kenninghall Palace in Norfolk, East Anglia, first child to Thomas Howard, third Duke of Norfolk and Elizabeth Stafford, daughter of the Duke of Buckingham and descendant of Edward III, John of Gaunt, and the Percys.

1524   Death of grandfather, the "Flodden Duke," with elaborate state funeral at Framlingham Castle and Thetford Priory; given the courtesy title of Earl of Surrey.

1527   Education probably under John Clere (and possibly John Skelton and Stephen Gardiner); also trained in *ars belli,* practice in tilting yard, and in riding and hunting.

1529   First public appearance at a dinner with Norfolk and the Prior of Bartley; marriage suggested between Surrey and first cousin Anne Boleyn and later between Surrey and Princess Mary.

1531   At Windsor Castle with the young Duke of Richmond, Henry Fitzroy.

1532   Marriage contract with Lady Frances de Vere, daughter of the Earl of Oxford, concluded and marriage celebrated in spring; does not live with wife but travels with Richmond in entourage of Henry VIII and Anne Boleyn to France.

1533   Winter and spring in Paris and Fontainebleau with Richmond as members of the Dauphin's household and then in summer in entourage of Francis I to Provence; returns to England and possibly attends in September Princess Elizabeth's christening; on 26 November Richmond and Surrey's sister, Elizabeth, married at Hampton Court; Surrey lives with wife for the first time.

1536   First son Thomas born 12 March; Anne Boleyn beheaded 19 May, and Henry marries Jane Seymour on 5 June; Duke of Richmond dies in July and is buried at Thetford Priory, later transferred to Framlingham; destruction of monasteries begins.

1537   Imprisonment at Windsor Castle where he probably com-
        poses first sonnet and elegy on Richmond; one of chief mour-
        ners at funeral of Jane Seymour on 14 October.

1540   Granted reversion and rents reserved on lease of the house
        and lands of Wymondham, Norfolk; Cromwell arrested on
        10 June and beheaded on 28 July; Henry marries Catherine
        Howard; Surrey and father appointed to the Stewardship of
        Cambridge University; continues his translation of the *Aeneid.*

1541   Knighted early in year and given the Order of the Garter;
        to Calais with Earl of Southampton and Lord Russell to
        study war in France; in May returns to Windsor for cele-
        bration of Feast of Saint George and formal initiation into
        the Order of the Garter; Catherine Howard accused of adul-
        tery (high treason).

1542   On 13 February, witness to execution of Catherine Howard;
        sent to prison for second time on 13 July; by 1 August fights
        in Scotland with father; on 11 October Sir Thomas Wyatt
        dies.

1543   In April imprisoned for rioting in London, released in few
        weeks; goes to the Continent where Wallop admits him to
        council of war; received by the Grand Master in the Spanish
        lines and by Charles V who writes Henry praising him; in
        winter created Cup Bearer to the King.

1544   Contract drawn between the king and Norfolk that Surrey,
        his heir, receive Saint Leonard's Hill overlooking Norwich
        in Norfolk, now renamed Mount Surrey; Surrey begins to
        build his palace there; in London acts as King's Welcomer,
        greeting the Spanish Dukes of Najera and Alburquerque; in
        June, in France with Imperial and English forces; made
        Marshal of the Field; with Henry VIII at siege and capture
        of Boulogne in September.

1545   Aide-de-camp to Henry and sent to Portsmouth to attend
        naval defense under Lord Lisle; on 31 August Privy Council
        gives Surrey command of Boulogne over Grey; made Lieu-
        tenant General of the King on Sea and Land for all Conti-
        nental possessions of England, his highest military honor.

1546   Skirmish near Boulogne with severe losses made issue at
        court by Seymour and other enemies; Surrey recalled and

coldly received at court although Henry gives him confiscated monastery; in August last court function in entertainment of the French Ambassadors at Hampton Court; imprisoned in December for threatening letter to Blage; trial before Wriothesley, Seymour, and other members of the Privy Council; Norfolk arrested in December; Surrey charged by Council with treason for using royal arms on his escutcheon and other personal effects and plotting to interfere with the succession of Prince Edward.

1547 Norfolk confesses to the charges on 12 January; Surrey tried by common-law jury from Norfolk on 13 January (he was not a peer); passionately maintains innocence but found guilty and sentenced to be hanged, drawn, and quartered; sentence commuted to beheading; beheaded on 19 January and immediately buried in All-Hallows Barking near the Tower of London.

Chapter One

The Life of Henry Howard, Earl of Surrey

Birth

Henry Howard, by courtesy titled Earl of Surrey and later styled the Poet Earl of Surrey, was born probably in 1517 and was beheaded by direct order of Henry VIII on 19 January 1547. He was the eldest child of Thomas, the third Duke of Norfolk and his wife, the Lady Elizabeth Stafford. His entire life was spent under the reign of Henry VIII, the old king dying only eight days after Surrey's execution. The only evidence for his birthdate appears in an inscription on Surrey's last portrait painted in either late summer or early autumn 1546: "ANNO DNI 1546 AETATIS SVE 29."[1] There seems to have been no birth record and, oddly, no indication of his christening; the fact that Surrey's Christian name had not been used before in the Howard family suggests the possibility that Henry VIII may have been his intended godfather although no record or allusion to such a relationship exists. If later, as many commentators argue, Henry and his court provided models for Surrey's figure of the corrupt Sardanapalus and his court in one of Surrey's most powerful sonnets, the early relationship, if it existed at all, provides one of those ironic perspectives that haunted the brief life of the young earl.

There had been, in fact, an earlier family connection with Henry VIII, the king who would later marry Henry Howard's first cousins Anne Boleyn and Catherine Howard. Thomas Howard, the Earl of Surrey when his first son, Henry, was born, was the uncle of Henry VIII, having as his first wife Henry's aunt, the sister of Queen Elizabeth and the daughter of Edward IV, the Lady Anne Plantagenet. This marriage produced no surviving children, and when the Lady Anne died, Thomas Howard, already in his forties, married Elizabeth Stafford, the teenage daughter of the richest man in England, the Duke of Buckingham. Both the royal connection and

the rich wife exemplified the extraordinary resourcefulness of this third Duke of Norfolk whose long life spanned more monarchs (Edward IV to Mary Tudor) than almost any other leading peer in English history. If this Howard epitomized the strategies of his contemporary Machiavelli (but without the Italian idealism), Holbein's famous portrait of Thomas Howard in 1539 reveals the realism of a survivor in a world that began in the Middle Ages and ended in the birth throes of the modern world.

Richard III had made Surrey's great-grandfather, John, the first Howard Duke of Norfolk, the climax of the slow rise of the Howard family beginning in the thirteenth century "in a dull and windswept part of North Norfolk."[2] Despite the rather grandiose chivalric, even Anglo-Saxon, Howard origins probably believed by Surrey, the rise of these merchants and lawyers was much simpler. It followed the main routes to nobility in medieval England: law, warfare, and marriage, the most famous being that of John's father Robert, a hero who may have fought under Henry V at Agincourt. He had married the daughter of Thomas Mowbray, then the Duke of Norfolk, the Earl Marshal of England, and the great-grandson of Edward I, whose fate Shakespeare dramatizes at the opening of *Richard II*. This same John, offspring of Robert and the Mowbray heiress, and Surrey's great-grandfather, gained the support of Richard III to the title and indeed, as Shakespeare dramatizes in *Richard III*, died for the hunchbacked king at Bosworth, leaving son and grandson facing disaster. It was not until Surrey's grandfather's great victory over the Scots at Flodden Field in 1513, that the young Tudor king Henry VIII, now a drinking companion of young Thomas, gave "The Flodden Duke," as Surrey's grandfather would henceforth be called, his peerage, creating him as the second Duke of Norfolk, and naming Thomas, the father of the poet, by courtesy the new Earl of Surrey.

Thomas Howard's marriage in 1513 with the young Elizabeth Stafford was not a happy one. She was herself the daughter of the most splendid and arrogant nobleman of the day, the third Duke of Buckingham, who in 1521 would be the first of the political beheadings of the reign of Henry VIII (his grandson, Henry Howard, would be the last). Through her mother Elizabeth Stafford was the descendant of Hotspur and the Percys. Years later, in the middle 1530s, she would write to Thomas Cromwell, then Chancellor, and complain that she was forced into the marriage by deceptions of

Norfolk.[3] Henry was the first of their three children. The child received the courtesy title Earl of Surrey when his grandfather, the "Flodden Duke," died at eighty in 1524 and his father Thomas became the third Duke of Norfolk. Of the two other children, Mary became the wife of Surrey's beloved friend, Henry Fitzroy, the Duke of Richmond, who was the natural son of Henry VIII; widowed in her teens, after an unconsummated marriage, she never married again and died childless. The younger son Thomas survived the arrest of his father and brother, and on her accession Elizabeth made him Viscount Bidon; his granddaughter became the subject of Spenser's elegy *Daphnaida*. The marriage of Surrey's parents finally collapsed in 1534 when the Duchess of Norfolk separated herself from the duke's household. By then the duke had taken a mistress, Elizabeth Holland, from his own household at Kenninghall palace in East Anglia.[4] What the young boy Henry must have heard was constant bickering and fighting, after presumably halcyon years earlier when among other things, as the intellectual Countess of Surrey, his mother perhaps inspired John Skelton to write *Garlande or Chapelet of Laurell*.[5] When the break came, the children sided with the father. The estrangement never ended; the duchess accused her children in frantic letters; ironically she outlived almost all her family.

Childhood

Whatever the domestic violence in his immediate family, the little boy Henry Howard grew up as the center of a vast household, a little kingdom by twentieth-century standards. His father was frequently away on the king's business, either at Westminster or Windsor or Hampton Court or in Ireland, France, or even Rome. Surrey's birth, christening, and early childhood took place in that string of Howard castles and palaces that lined Norfolk and Suffolk in East Anglia. The most important were Framlingham, with its ancient Mowbray fortress and superbly moated landscape, and Kenninghall, Thomas Howard's own embellished favorite, on the site of an old royal Anglo-Saxon crowning place, which he enlarged to a magnificence his increasing wealth could afford. At one time it may have rivaled Hampton Court.[6] Because Norfolk was absent so much on state business, the young Howard, as his father's heir, was the center of all domestic activities such as meals, morning Mass,

evening prayer, evening musical entertainments, and even events such as hunting and hawking that he learned early. In later years (August 1539) a Calvinist dean attacked this scion of the peer who supported the Catholic wing of the English religious settlement and called Surrey "the most folish prowde boye that ys in Englande."[7] It is a wonder, given the circumstances of his life and heredity, that the young Henry Howard was not more proud or arrogant, if indeed the Calvinist dean's canard is true. No event could have impressed the enormous Howard prestige on the boy more than the funeral in 1524 of his famous grandfather who had defeated the Scots in the great victory at Flodden in 1513. It was a Catholic ceremony with the highest panoply of the Middle Ages—possibly the last such elaborate public event in England.[8]

Against such public ceremonies the private life of the boy developed. It was a dichotomy that would mark the almost thirty years of Henry Howard's life, extending to his last weeks in the Tower when he wrote his biblical paraphrases. His inner life was doubtless stimulated by the most profound discovery of his early years: the world of language newly opened by humanism. Whoever his private tutor, whether John Clerke, the Poet Laureate John Skelton, or the eminent and powerful cleric Stephen Gardiner,[9] young Henry Howard had the very good fortune to discover through classical texts and their new interpretations, largely from Italy, a world of letters and literature. Besides Latin, possibly some Greek, and certainly the dominant modern foreign languages, Surrey's curriculum also consisted of philosophical disciplines like logic, still grounded firmly in the old Scholastic methods although newly interpreted into forms like Agricola's place-logic, which were really stratagems of language. By Surrey's twelfth birthday, Norfolk had already begun to boast of his son's unusual linguistic talents and typically planned to make use of them. He wanted his son to become "preceptor and tutor" to the king's bastard son, the Duke of Richmond, a year younger than Surrey, who had become increasingly important in view of Catherine of Aragon's failure to produce a male heir.[10]

Norfolk's scheming reminds the modern reader of a startling fact: such linguistic prowess as Surrey was showing was rare among the governing class of England. For this reason it counted as nothing in Norfolk's humanistically untrained eyes unless it could be used, as all talents at court had to be, for a political purpose. Certainly

for a high aristocrat to write poetry or invent literary forms was almost unknown in English, with some remarkable exceptions. In fact, the Earl of Surrey marks a major change in social history of the English-speaking world, the transformation of governing classes (even on bureaucratic levels) by ideals of language rather than by sheer utility or power. Surrey provides the first real instance of an English aristocrat adapting fully to the new civilization of the Renaissance, from literary form to sartorial design.[11] In fact, the whole of Surrey's work attests to his absorption of Renaissance culture with its basis in humanism. The habits of reading and interpretation, the writing that must have begun in the still points of inner life in his violent world, never left him. In the one book we have from Surrey's library, an Aldus 1541 copy of Castiglione's *Cortegiano,* Surrey appears to have been a reader like Virginia Woolf, pen or pencil in hand.[12]

Youth

Thus the boy who came to the English court at Windsor in 1530 to be the companion of Henry VIII's first son and possible heir apparent had a highly developed linguistic and even literary sensibility. He there found a world in which to develop his talents and native genius. Away from the bleak windswept plains and fens of East Anglia, Surrey found himself at one of the enlightened courts of Europe, the result of at least two decades of carefully cultivated Renaissance tastes. Chivalric sports, music, dancing, Continental food and wines, the languages of the civilized world, as well as the new painters and musicians and renowned humanists at Henry VIII's court, all of these must have enchanted the fourteen-year-old boy; their effects can be found in Surrey's later elegy on the Duke of Richmond. At the center of Surrey's courtly life was his developing close friendship with the twelve-year-old Henry Fitzroy, the illegitimate son of Henry VIII. Like Surrey, the young Duke of Richmond had also known domestic turmoil and the demands of a public arena.

From Windsor the two boys were plunged into the very heart of the European Renaissance, light-years from the gloomy castles of East Anglia into the luminous galleries of Fontainebleau. In autumn of 1532, wishing to introduce Anne Boleyn to the French king Francis I and thereby gain public esteem for his forthcoming plans,

Henry VIII journeyed to France with Anne, Henry Fitzroy, and the Earl of Surrey. Gaining Francis's agreement in Calais and Boulogne to press Henry's divorce with the pope, Henry left Richmond and Surrey as a further gesture of their unity, to sojourn and be "brought up with the King's children," as the Grand Master Montmorency reported.[13] After a trip to Paris, the boys journeyed with the French court to Fontainebleau, where they viewed innovative architectural wonders found nowhere else north of the Alps. They also discovered the most complete display of Renaissance culture in any one place in Europe. Francis's own splendid libraries were being assembled under the direction of Guillaume Budé; the king's own collections of art soon to be the basis of the Louvre were also there (as decorations for the baths!); Italian humanist artists, poets, and scholars, who had begun to migrate north at the beginning of Francis's reign (and including Leonardo da Vinci), influenced the intellectual life. Even though Surrey never traveled abroad again except as soldier in northern France, his exposure in Fontainebleau to Italian humanist culture and avant-garde art forms completed his education. In May of 1533 the two boys traveled with Francis I and his sons and entourage to meet the pope in Provence, the historic land of the troubadours. The meeting never took place, and in a few months the boys returned to England. In their absence the English court had drastically changed: Catherine of Aragon had been divorced; Thomas More had resigned; and Anne Boleyn already pregnant was married to Henry by the new Archbishop of Canterbury, Cranmer. The split between England and Catholic Europe had begun.

Before he had left England in 1532, Surrey had married but, deemed too young to live with his wife, he had remained with the Duke of Richmond. Now, on their return, the fifteen-year-old Surrey proceeded to live with his bride, Lady Frances de Vere, daughter of the Earl of Oxford. At the same time Richmond married Mary, Surrey's sister, although he did not live with her for the same reason of age. Surrey's wife, younger than he, was an heiress, although, commented Chapuis to his royal master Charles V, "la fille n'est de grands biens ne grands alliance."[14] The Imperial Ambassador was quite wrong about her wealth and her connections; and her looks, if we judge by the Holbein drawing, are far from unattractive, if not grand. Her features are certainly not "characterless."[15] Most important, what began as an arranged marriage turned, through the loving natures of these two young aristocrats, into one of the

happiest of court marriages during a period of remarkable infidelity and adultery, led notoriously by Henry himself. On 12 March 1536 the first of their children, Thomas, was born, to the delight of the older Thomas, the grandfather third Duke of Norfolk, as well as of the nineteen-year-old father. This son would be the fourth Duke of Norfolk and would follow his father to the block at the Tower, accused by his cousin Elizabeth of conspiring with Mary Queen of Scots. A second son was born in 1538, named Henry for his father, much later created Earl of Northampton by James I (after a long suppression under Elizabeth). This son took his father's remains from a grave near the Tower and in 1614 moved the bodies of both his parents to Saint Michael's church at Framlingham where he built an elaborate tomb to their memory. Three daughters followed this son: Jane, called "one of the most learned ladies of a learned age,"[16] who became the Countess of Westmoreland and was praised by John Foxe for her linguistic abilities in Latin and Greek; Catherine, also renowned for her scholarship, who married Baron Berkeley; and a child born a few months after Surrey's execution, Margaret, who married Baron Scrope. On the beheading of their father in 1547, the children were taken from their mother and given to their aunt the Duchess of Richmond, who had become an ardent Protestant, and who chose John Foxe as their tutor.

1536

Despite the birth of his son and the beginning of his family, the year 1536 was a year of great sorrow for Surrey, both public and private. In May his cousin the Queen Anne Boleyn was tried and beheaded, and on the very day of her execution Cranmer granted a special license for Henry to marry Jane Seymour. The latter event marked the entrance into power of Surrey's mortal enemy Edward Seymour, brother of the new queen. Seymour was immediately created Viscount Beauchamp, later the Earl of Hertford, and then— after Henry's death and Surrey's beheading, when he was sole Protector and the most powerful figure in England—Duke of Somerset, a royal title formerly associated with Henry VII and the Tudors themselves. Shortly after this marriage Surrey's beloved half uncle Thomas Howard was imprisoned in the Tower and died there because he had secretly married Margaret Douglas, one of the few legitimate heirs to the English throne and the grandmother of James I through

her late marriage to Darnly. The greatest tragedy of all for Surrey
occurred on 22 July 1536, when Richmond died. He was buried
with the Howards at Thetford Abbey. Surrey's grief marked a clear
change in his social personality.

In the next year Surrey suffered the first of his imprisonments,
each the result of temper and wrong use of gesture and language.
In this case, if Edmond Bapst's conjecture is correct,[17] the imprisonment was caused by a physical attack on Edward Seymour himself
by the young Surrey within the park of Hampton Court. Because
physical violence within the precincts of the court constituted a
threat to the dignity and safety of the king, the penalty was severe:
loss of the right hand, imprisonment, and confiscation of possessions. Surrey was fortunately spared, no doubt through his powerful
father's intercession. He was sentenced to Windsor Castle as a prisoner during a period when the court was not there, likely during
the late spring and summer months of 1537. When Queen Jane,
who had delivered a boy Edward shortly before her death, was buried
in early November, Surrey was already freed, and participated in
the funeral services as "assistant about the corpse and chair."[18]

In the four years that followed, Surrey led a quiet life, always in
the public arena of the court but now also as an aristocratic country
gentleman. It is probably during this period that Surrey began to
develop his poems. Outside the Howard palaces and castles in East
Anglia and houses in London, the ferment of revolution was dis-
mantling the old medieval civilization, and its main agent was
Thomas Cromwell, the patron of Surrey's older friend Sir Thomas
Wyatt.

By 1540 Cromwell and the Reformers had effectively destroyed
all monastic life in England but their momentum had been checked
by Norfolk and Gardiner in the Act of Six Articles, which brought
certain Catholic principles back onto the religious scene, marking
the Church of England forever. Cromwell thus maneuvered to find
a Protestant queen for Henry in Anne of Cleves, who to Henry's
disgust did indeed turn out to be "the Flanders mare." Before
Cromwell's death for this fatal error, one of the events held in honor
of the new queen was a tournament held on 1 May 1540. Such a
reconstruction of the chivalry that had clearly passed in the ideo-
logical bloodshed of recent years merely emphasized Henry's illusion
that he was a figure like the other Henry who conquered at Agincourt.[19] For Surrey such rituals, as he showed in his elegy at Wind-

sor, not only revitalized the past but gave direction and meaning to a chaotic present. They were clearly one more aspect of that stylization and self-representation that Castiglione had described in the courtier. Surrey's chief challenger here was Dudley, the father of the Earl of Leceister, the future grandfather of Sir Philip Sidney, and a new Tudor man like Seymour, who would condemn Surrey at his trial and beheading and later, having destroyed Seymour, would try to make his daughter-in-law Lady Jane Grey queen instead of Mary Tudor. Within three months of this elaborate event Cromwell was dead, Henry had divorced Anne of Cleves, and a new queen, a girl of seventeen, a Howard, Surrey's own first cousin, had appeared. Old Norfolk had discovered in the country of East Anglia another niece, who was much more orthodox religiously than her cousin Anne but hardly in any other way, least of all sexually.

Triumph and Imprisonment

In the fifteen months of the reign of his cousin Catherine Howard, Surrey gained his greatest political power. First he was dubbed a knight in the spring of 1541, and then his greatest honor: on Saint George's Day, 23 April, he was elected to be Knight of the Garter at the annual chapter. In this halcyon time it is probable that Surrey began the plans for his grand home, a Renaissance palace remembered, even twenty-five years after its destruction, for its splendor. Surrey did not actually acquire the site for this palace until 14 January 1544, when the Duke of Norfolk received from the king the old abbey of Saint Leonard's on a hill overlooking the city of Norwich. The fact that Surrey chose the celebrated Dutch humanist Hadrian Junius as the tutor for his children and that the poet Thomas Churchyard as a very young man served in his household affirms that Surrey may have envisioned for his new Surrey House an English version of the French and Italian circles that he had himself known. Because this structure and its gardens were used in Kett's Rebellion of 1549 as a command post for outlaws and even earlier emptied of its superb interiors, especially its tapestries, by Seymour and his henchmen in December 1546,[20] what remained of Surrey's dream was likely abandoned by the end of the century. Surrey House simply disappeared.

After the execution of Catherine Howard in the winter of 1542, the young Henry Howard became increasingly involved with vio-

lence, at least in the public scene. In this period, Surrey, in his midtwenties, was imprisoned twice. On 13 July 1542, the Privy Council sent an order to the Warden of the Fleet prison "to receyve therle of Surrey" and keep him prisoner "during the Kinges plesor" with only two servants and none of the entertainment of friends which aristocrats commonly provided while in prison.[21] Surrey had issued a challenge to one John à Leigh, possibly because this Leigh, accused of association with Cardinal Pole, Henry's cousin and his bitterest enemy in Rome, may have tried to insinuate a relationship between the Howards and Pole, a charge that appears again in Surrey's trial more than four years later. It is possible that the silent enemy behind the whole fabric was Edward Seymour who perhaps knew then, as he certainly learned later, how to bait the highly sensitive descendant of the Howards, Buckingham, and Hotspur. In any case, the event produced a letter from Surrey, one of the few places where Surrey explains his motives, albeit here written for the eyes of the Privy Council and so a very special kind of linguistic display.[22] Receiving the letter, the council immediately acted to free Surrey, and the reason was likely not only his father's influence but also the need to have Surrey at the Scottish front to aid his father, who was in command of the English army, in the new outbreak. Within a month, Norfolk, with Surrey beside him, invaded Scotland with an army of twenty thousand soldiers. It was the kind of attack that Surrey had begun to excel in, a series of raids, and, as we know from his later sonnet-elegy on his squire Thomas Clere, the two of them watched Kelsal burn to the ground.

Returning to London, on leave with his friends Thomas Wyatt Junior, Clere, and others, Surrey was arrested again. Beginning as a prank in a tavern during the Lenten season, the episode spread into violence, which played into the hands of Seymour and Surrey's enemies at court. This time the council was not so forgiving and into their evidence were woven the first hints of the treason for which Surrey would later be charged: his pretension to the throne (from a housemaid's remarks) and the question of the resemblance of Surrey's personal coat of arms to the king's (again based on a maid's comment).[23] Surrey's response this time to his accuser was not an abject apology, although officially he no doubt showed the same requisite obeisance as before. Instead he penned a fierce satire attacking London itself. He used in English for the first time formal Roman satire modeled not on Horace, as Wyatt's satire, but on

Juvenal. The result is a prophetic voice speaking its own modern jeremiad. Henry's London is a collapsing Babylon.

"Lieutenant General of the King on Sea and Land"

At this moment in his public life Surrey found a means to gain the honor he felt he had increasingly lost in the radical political and social changes of the last years of the reign of Henry VIII: he went to France in the service of the realm. By 1543 England and the empire had allied themselves against France, and on 1 October Surrey was commended by Henry VIII to Charles V as a "knight of his Order [of the Garter] who desires to see the Emperor's camp . . . hoping that by experience of war he may succeed to the honorable qualities of his relatives."[24] Released from his third imprisonment probably in late spring, Surrey had spent the summer and early autumn with his growing family, either at Kenninghall or Surrey House overlooking Norwich, one of the few respites in his last years. Now, after translating the *Aeneid* into the most modern style and language of his time, Surrey would actually live the life of "arms and the man."

Arriving in France, Surrey went immediately to the front. Here Wallop, the head of the English expeditionary force supporting the emperor in northern France, took the young nobleman and his entourage, including Clere, through the trenches before Landrecy. Fascination with new technology characterized all of Surrey's military leadership, and shortly thereafter Wallop wrote Surrey's father: "my lord of Surrey hath lost no time since his arrival at the army; for he visiteth all things that be meet for a man of war to look upon his learning."[25] Twice the Holy Roman Emperor Charles V, the most powerful single monarch in Europe, met Surrey and sent special letters to Henry praising him. Surrey arrived back in England in time to attend the 1543 Christmas eve Chapter of the Order of the Garter at Hampton Court, and for the winter he stayed comparatively free, with a few court duties but otherwise supervising the building of his mansion and the training of his young children.

By early summer Surrey was back in France again, having been appointed by the king as Marshal of the Field, a tribute for a young man twenty-seven years old. It was a job requiring extraordinary executive control. In fact, the dexterity that Charles V had earlier

commended in Surrey now demonstrated itself in his supervising activities of encampment, supplying of food and ordnance, key planning of all transportation, as well as acting as judge of all legal proceedings behind the lines and in the camps.[26] The most important event during this period occurred in September 1544 when Henry VIII himself came to France and, with Surrey at his side, entered Boulogne, with all the pomp of another Henry V at Agincourt. In reality, although Henry and Surrey together had watched the engineers blow up the castle (the work of which Surrey had no doubt prepared), the real defeat of the French probably came from a secret deal worked out between its commandant De Vervin and Edward Seymour. The aging Henry was nevertheless given his theatrical moment. He could leave the scene and having expended his forces on Boulogne, Henry did not care about reinforcements for the siege of Montreuil where Norfolk and Surrey were in charge and which finally had to be abandoned. In the spring Surrey had returned to England as a kind of aide-de-camp to the king. In fact, in July 1545 Surrey was sent on an errand to Portsmouth. There he joined Dudley for a series of naval maneuvers and may have watched the *Mary Rose* sink with seven hundred men on board. By August Surrey was back in France, commanding a force of eight thousand men "in consideracion of the desyre he hath to se and serve," as Paget, the King's Secretary, wrote.[27] After the death of the two chief English commanders in France, Surrey was suddenly given his greatest assignment and the highest military honor of his short life. He was made commander of Boulogne and entitled "Lieutenant General of the King on Sea and Land." It was an unusual honor for someone so young, a recognition of Surrey's natural ability to organize and direct men in the field as well as of his personal courage and sense of heroic challenge. This kind of young daring martial figure, like Vergil's Pallas or Achilles, directly appealed to the aging Henry caught in his lifelong illusion of conquering France as his ancestors had.

It was precisely here that Surrey's problem and the seeds for his downfall lay: the level at which Surrey acted as surrogate for the youthful dreams of the wasted old king. The whole narrative of this struggle can be found in Surrey's letters and dispatches, virtually all we have of his correspondence.[28] They painfully detail the refusal of the Privy Council to provide adequate supplies, soldiers, or fortifications for Surrey's defense of Boulogne, which he kept secure

even after his recall in spring of 1546. In contrast, his father and the other members of the Privy Council warn the young general of twenty-eight that he is encouraging the old man in a foolish enterprise for which the English nation has no money. Norfolk also warned his son directly and by secret message that he was allowing himself to be trapped by their enemies at court. Furthermore, an intimate relationship between the two Henrys, however constructed of illusion and dream, could not be tolerated by Seymour, Dudley, and Paget, the most powerful of the new Tudor men at court. Nor, they felt, could funds be wasted on such an atavistic dream. These new Tudor men waited their moment, confusing Surrey wherever possible with switches of command and with insufficient men and funds (and Surrey, with his own debts in England mounting, was paying out of his own pocket). At the same time, Surrey, always the chivalric leader, continued to pour forth appeals for the men under him describing their noble exploits in superb narrative scenes.

Finally the moment came for Surrey's enemies. Early in January 1546 Surrey had his only failure as a military leader. Learning that the French were bringing reinforcements to their army besieging Boulogne, Surrey sent cavalry and foot soldiers to prepare an ambush on a hill outside the walls of the city. After an immediate success, the English second line suddenly began to retreat from the fray, abandoning the first line, which held some of the most distinguished officers in the English army, including friends of Henry VIII. A slaughter and rout of the English forces followed. A later account of the English debacle by a Welsh officer depicts a Surrey near lunacy and suicide as, charging with his horse through the retreating lines, he tried to make his men hold firm.[29] The immediate result was that Surrey became the pawn of the new Tudor men who were his enemies. He had failed Henry's impossible dream of conquest and therefore lost the king's support. From this point on, the letters from the council became cooler. Finally by March Paget advised him, in a series of letters and with presumed friendship, to accept the fact that he was to be demoted to a position under the general command of Seymour, who would henceforth lead in France.

Return and Rage

By April 1546 Surrey was back in England and coldly received at court. Old Norfolk had correctly read the political signs and was

attempting to reach some kind of settlement with Seymour in order to consolidate the two powerful houses through marriage. The old duke had proposed, without telling his son, that his widowed daughter should marry Seymour's brother Thomas (who would later marry the widowed Queen Catherine Parr) and that Surrey's own children be betrothed to Seymour's, allowing ancient Howard blood to be mixed with that of the new Tudor men. Learning this strategy while at court, Surrey became violent. His rage found its moment in a scene in front of witnesses with his sister Mary in an anteroom of the palace. The incident became a major part of evidence against him at his trial. Surrey accused his sister, who was attracted to the handsome Thomas, of really desiring to whore for the corpulent diseased Henry: "You should become the Royal Mistress and play the part in England that is held in France by the Duchess d'Etampes," Surrey proclaimed loudly to his sister comparing her to the mistress of Francis I whom Surrey had known at Fontainebleau.[30]

After this episode, Surrey's own actions became more erratic— or so the new Tudor men wanted them to appear. Surrey's last important court function occurred on 24 August 1546, the result of the English capitulation of Boulogne to France in the treaty of peace, an humiliating enough event in itself for the brave defender of Boulogne. The king ordered a lavish display as the French Ambassadors Extraordinary arrived in England for the ratification of the treaty. The magnificence was such that the very torch bearers were arrayed in cloth of gold. Four persons from the entire realm were selected to provide horses, with footstools, for the French admiral: Henry himself, Cranmer, Norfolk, and Surrey. In the order of precedence for the nobility, Surrey ranked with the Princess Mary and his cousin the Princess Elizabeth, so that in the line of peers the eldest son of a duke outranked even the first of the earls, Hertford, Edward Seymour who was Lord High Chamberlain.

The first months of autumn 1546 moved quietly with Surrey in East Anglia. At Surrey House with his family he writes Paget in October to secure lands for the belfrey and dormitory of a nearby monastery recently despoiled. By November, however, the situation of the old king had worsened. The question of the proper regent for the young Edward became the central gossip of the court, discussed with an intensity never before felt. As with most struggles after 1530 in the English Renaissance, the religious question intensified the political. The leading candidates were either the How-

ards and Gardiner, or Seymour with his brother and the other new Tudor men, most of whom represented the Protestant faction of Henry's religious settlement. Evidence at Surrey's trial from various sources definitely places Surrey as planning for a role in this transfer of power. He saw himself as a guide to the young king, as years before he had guided Edward's half brother the Duke of Richmond. In the meantime, first as almost innocent doodling,[31] Surrey began a design of his coat of arms, the heraldic blazon that asserted the most public identity of self. It would be part of a series of self-representations by which Surrey clearly hoped to impress the court with his own place in the new scheme of things.[32] His last portrait, probably painted by William Scrots (Stretes) in late summer and early fall 1546, was the most explicit of these representations,[33] but Surrey's redesigning of his coat of arms was the most notorious. It may be true that in the larger context of his time, Surrey marks a transition between medieval forms of knighthood and the stylizations of Castiglione.[34] If so, such Renaissance forms as painting and visual design were natural modes for Surrey to define himself, caught as he was between two worlds, in heightened self-consciousness.

In Henry's court, such representations became the very basis of Surrey's final indictment for treason, indeed the only factual basis. In major evidence at his trial, his cousin and former friend Richard Southwell (whose cold gaze dominates Holbein's famous portrait) declared, in effect, that Surrey presumed a legal right to the throne because of his own royal ancestry, as a descendant of English kings. The proof, Southwell said, was the recent change of design in Surrey's coat of arms. Most significantly, the young earl had placed in the first quarter of his shield the royal arms of England ascribed to Edward the Confessor. This was the native English saint, the last of the Anglo-Saxon saints, on whose vigil day the young Edward, the heir to the Tudor throne, had been born. The body and shrine of this saintly king in Westminster Abbey remained the only relics of a Catholic saint not destroyed by the forces of Cromwell and Henry VIII. The implications of Surrey's act in inventing such a design were greater, of course, than the actual event, which was trivial in itself. In fact, Surrey had every right to bear such arms; his Mowbray ancestors had always borne them. Furthermore, as even Southwell admitted, Surrey had distinguished the arms by "three labels silver" to show their place.[35] Even here Southwell used the distinction against Surrey, obviously according to a carefully or-

chestrated plot set by Seymour and the others. He claimed such labeling was the prerogative of the heir presumptive, Prince Edward, and that Surrey did not have the permission of the king to use it. Indeed the king had not given, nor would be inclined to give, such permission. Surrey's rather fantastic self-glorification on silver, linen, escutcheon, or even in his portrait may have affirmed for Surrey his own existence and right to power and glory at the Tudor court, but members of that court did not acknowledge such emblems or symbols to be his.

Thus the trap for Surrey had been set. Old Norfolk must have warned his reckless son time after time, but the two men appear long since to have ceased to understand each other. Surrey, with his youth and brilliance, visual and intellectual, was the truly continental Renaissance gentleman and courtier, who naturally attracted the malevolent forces ruling the English court, their tongues like those of Spenser's Blatant Beast. Even the brother of the poet George Herbert, Edward Lord Herbert of Cherbury, writing almost one hundred years later, was amazed at the persecution of Surrey, especially the vindictiveness of the old king toward the passionate young courtier: "it was notorious how the King had not only withdrawn much of his wonted favour, but promised impunity to such as would discover anything concerning him."[36] Indeed of all the major witnesses against Surrey, almost all were knighted or received titles or acquired new possessions when in the following months Seymour gained absolute power over the realm as Protector of the new boy king, his nephew Edward.

Last Days

Surrey was arrested in early December 1546 ostensibly for writing a threatening letter to a former friend George Blage, who had registered violent Protestant objections to the possible Howard tutelage of the young Edward.[37] Surrey was at Whitehall finishing his midday meal when a captain of the guard with halberdiers waiting in a nearby hall said that his father wanted to see him. A Spanish merchant in the English court at the time witnessed the event in which Surrey disappeared forever from public life. He went down sidestairs to a waiting boat that conveyed him instantly to Lord Chancellor Wriothesley's house in Holborn.[38] Hearing of his son's arrest, Norfolk made the mistake of writing to Bishop Gar-

diner; the system of espionage that Seymour had established inter-
cepted it and used it as an excuse to arrest the old duke himself.
On Sunday, 12 December 1546, Surrey was made to walk alone
through the streets of London to the Tower. Although interpretations vary, it is probably true that his cries of anger and outrage
were voluble and loud and that the crowds themselves lamented,
the opposite effect of what the council had expected and wanted.[39]

His enemies miscalculated nothing else. With genuine shock
tactics, Southwell and a deputized group of Seymour's agents raced
to East Anglia to seize all the wealth and goods of the Howards
before any protest or reaction could follow. Arriving at Kenninghall
before daybreak the following Tuesday, 14 December, they fright-
ened the three women there, the Duchess of Richmond, Bess Holland, and the Countess of Surrey, who was seven months pregnant.

In the legal system of this period the real investigation of justice
came with the informal sessions of examination before the main trial
by which time the verdict was generally already decided. Thus
shortly after his arrest, Surrey was faced with Southwell and his
evidence of treason (evidence at the heart of Surrey's condemnation
that, within six months after his beheading, had completely disappeared). So hurt and stunned was Surrey by Southwell and his
attacks that he offered to fight him "in his shirt," a chivalric gesture
of knighthood that was prelude to a violent altercation.[40] The tes-
timonies that began to emerge were all circumstantial, based on
interpretations of remarks and innuendoes, themselves interpretations of actions Surrey had taken. Without any real evidence except
the heraldic design and Surrey's portrait, the proof took the form
of a rhetorical strategy. Surrey's enemies attempted to establish an
ethos for their opponent, in this case a reckless bad nature. From
heralds to glassmakers to friends and even relatives, entanglements
of a conspiracy on Surrey's part were made to appear. There was no
objective evidence. No cross-examinations were allowed, only Surrey's own penetrating responses. His sister in particular gave damaging evidence, which derived, however distantly, from a fact. Her
brother had found in an old French romance *Lancelot du Lac* heraldic
arms that he had put in his own coat of arms. She also declared
that he had put above his own fantastic escutcheon the royal emblems
of the Cap of Maintenance and the Crown of England in the guise
of a crest. Either from malice or ignorance, Surrey's sister omitted
the fact that such a cap was the simple ermine crest of the Howards

and the crown merely the Scottish crown granted to the Howards after the Flodden victory.[41] Far more damaging, however, if not finally fatal, were interpolations in a state paper which were the foundation of charges against Surrey. These insertions were printed in small capitals by a shaking hand and were made by Henry VIII himself. Henry's underlining and comments revealed what deeply he must have felt: he saw Surrey as a threat to dynasty and his young son. For Henry these were, after all, the same Howards who had supported Richard III against his father and who might start another War of the Roses. For the king who sought the old grandeur of Crecy, Poitiers, and Agincourt, the crass ambition of the new Tudor men counted for nothing against the Howard threat to his son, or so he had come to believe. "If a man cummYING OF THE COLLATERALL LYNE TO THE HEYRE OFF the crown, who ought NOT to beare thArmes of England BUT ON the seconde quarter" begins Henry's first bitter comment remarking on the question of proper heraldic design, emphasizing the error of using "THE VERY PLASE only of the Heir Masle Apparant." The first comment ends with the question "HOW THYS MANS INTENT IS TO BE JUGGYD; AND WHETHER THYS importe any daunger, peril, or slaundre to the title of the Prince, or very Heire Apparant."[42] As the king himself knew well, Richard II had given Surrey's Mowbray ancestors the right to wear such arms. The implicit threat, however, in Surrey's indiscretion and impoliteness in not asking the king's permission to make such a change in his heraldic design remained. If Henry VIII's interpolations have a final cold fury, the dying old king is thinking at every moment of his own guileless son Edward.

Surrey's official trial was held in London in the great hall of the Guildhall on 13 January 1547. Lord Herbert of Cherbury who had records no longer available has given the best account of Surrey's defense, which was a long oration that began at nine in the morning and ran until five in the afternoon by which time it was already dark. It was primarily a defense based on linguistic and rhetorical strategies, although it was unlikely anyone could change the will of the dying king or the powerful forces of the Privy Council. Surrey's bravura graphically showed itself when an obviously suborned witness repeated his own supposed sarcastic taunt to Surrey. The young Henry Howard turned at that moment to the jury, made up of Norfolk men who, because Surrey was not a peer, were to judge him. "I leave it to your judgment," said Surrey calmly, "whether

it were probable that this man should speak thus to the Earl of Surrey and he not strike him."[43] In the seventeenth century, Edward Herbert summed up the rhetorical and linguistic strategies Surrey used during his ordeal: "He was of a deep understanding, sharp wit, and deep courage, defended himself many ways: sometimes denying their accusations as false, and together weakening the credit of his adversaries; sometimes interpreting the words he said in a far other sense than in that in which they were represented."[44] Only a poet like Lord Herbert of Cherbury could perhaps understand the levels of language and metaphor in Surrey's defense. In fact, Surrey's is the only confrontation in the English Renaissance where an important poet goes on trial and himself confronts the powers of an absolute state with his own powers of language. It is one of the very few instances not only in English literature but in Western civilization.

The jury deliberated much later than Paget and the other members of the council had wanted—so much so that Paget had to slip out and bring back the king's threat against the jurors if they did not bring in the verdict already decided on in the earlier examinations.[45] The jury soon returned with a verdict of guilty. Six days later, 19 January 1547, in the last of the executions by Henry VIII, Henry Howard, Earl of Surrey, was led out of the Tower to the scaffold at Tower Hill. There in his thirtieth year he was killed, his head severed from his body.

Chapter Two
Introduction to the Works

Surrey as Humanist

Surrey's conception of poetic art.   If the life of Henry Howard has elements of romance, the poetry of the Earl of Surrey reveals itself as a product of deliberate invention and craftsmanship. Surrey's perception of his art arose from the teachings of humanism, which he learned early and never ceased to develop in his poetry. The humanist movement was already flowering in England in the Tudor court and at most levels of religion and education when Surrey's art began as its offspring. This meant for the Poet Earl of Surrey an imitation of literary forms derived primarily from Italy and France and interpreted and informed by early English humanists and by first experimenters in poetic adaptations of the new learning like Wyatt. As with other Tudor humanists, Surrey shared the exuberant sense that his work was new, original, completely modern, and capable of changing his English world, especially the language it spoke. Indeed by 1537, a probable date for the inception of Surrey's literary career, humanism offered, both officially and unofficially, not only a curriculum of languages but a program precisely for the refinement of the English language itself.[1]

Thus, far from perceiving his poems as only personal inventions, Surrey sought, even more than Wyatt, a civic and communal purpose for his art. Such purpose explains the general context for all his poetry, especially the translations from Vergil. In this sense Surrey was a true Howard scion because he was redeeming, by reshaping it for his own time, the language of his ancestors. If Surrey had any formal intention for writing poetry beyond the general purpose of humanism, he probably held, as the young Milton did later, the dream of bringing through poetic art a glory to England as full as that of King Arthur and his chivalric knights. Like Milton, who would develop Surrey's invention of blank verse to its highest epic form, such a dream called for a special sense of election and vocation. It meant a special awareness of self operating in time and history,

a self-perception Surrey the man already had, as we have seen. Indeed, in all Surrey's texts, the interplay between his life, his self-perception, and the formal resources of the communal language he is reshaping give the structures of his texts, at their best, a special tension and vitality. Like the great classical models before him, his art develops from a sense of the poet's particular time and history, not least in Surrey's most inventive forms.

It was natural, therefore, that Surrey would find more in humanism than simple civic duty, and that he would bring to his art that opening humanism had given to new conceptions of self. These entailed not only deeper understanding of the individual self but significantly the relationship of that self to court and society. What Surrey never ceased to explore, generally in forms more public than Wyatt's introspective lyrics, was the Renaissance sense of self integrity, an ideal Surrey found fully and graphically revealed in Castiglione's *Courtier,* a work he knew well. Because the Renaissance after Petrarch had posited in so many of its forms a special relationship of the self to the texts of its past, integrating those texts with their human experiences into the total experience of the particular self, communal as well as private, became, as much as anything else, a method of translation.

It was a method that ended in a new text where the integrated self found its own language. Translation had its own Orphean music, to use a familiar Renaissance image for such a process of harmonious intertextuality. The Renaissance humanists thus taught Surrey how a new text was a work of art emanating from a reintegrated self, which might reveal indeed a translation so new as to be startlingly original. Wholeness and integrity through text and textuality, the synthetic work of translation or adaptation of forms, could lead the Renaissance artist or thinker to a new self-definition in the new text. In this way the formal integrity of the new text could not be separated from, nor conceived without, self-expression and the special voice in the text.

This process A. Bartlett Giamatti demonstrates in the myth of a resurrected Hippolytus whose severed body is healed by Aesculapius. Term and figure here symbolize an act of unity found through reintegration and translation of old texts, an integrity of self rising as new art or new thought. Explicating the Roman myth of Hippolytus, Giamatti defines this dialectic of self which leads from old texts to new text: "The humanist's supreme reaction is finally his

own sense of himself; his crucial composition is the reconstruction of self out of what the past has given him—a sense of self that is defined by the activity of making up the self. The humanist is Aesculapius to his own Hippolytus, restorer of himself out of the fragments old and new of his own humanity."[2]

In fact, in the Vergilian retelling of the Hippolytus story, in book 7 of the *Aeneid,* Greek Hippolytus, reborn in Italy and father of sons, becomes Latin Virbius or "twice man," a literal rebirth through translation. What this composite figure, the new young man, mirrored in Vergil's text was the progression of Aeneas himself from cultural and personal dismemberment toward the ultimate wholeness of his destiny Rome. Here was a cosmic reintegration of self. Such hope of cultural unity may indeed have been the first level of meaning in the *Aeneid* that drew the Poet Earl of Surrey to his most ambitious task, turning the *Aeneid* into his own modern English for the Tudor court.

Indeed, whatever the problematic of defining the self through a reading of texts from the past and present, it remains a social and cultural act. In the Renaissance to translate on any level, to make and invent (even to read) a work of art, was for the realizing self to recognize an audience whose center, certainly in Tudor England, was the court. However fully the new work of art might give the reading of past texts or of the poet's self-perception, its assembled text could be nothing but a process of studied proportions for an audience like the Tudor court, proportions of language and music. The Renaissance court was in fact the center of social reality; it was the only place where humanist poets could find an audience who could adequately respond to their texts and translations. Certainly in 1537 the court of Henry VIII was the heart of English political and cultural reality and provided the only audience who would understand Surrey's new lyrics and translations.

Thus the humanist dynamic of self, text, and court led to a grand concept of poetic art as translation as well as precise practice, an idea that motivated generations of poets, scholars, and critics. Such a concept fueled humanism as it came to England from Italy and France. What Giamatti defines as its formulaic proportions actually states the functioning terms of humanism for Surrey and his master Wyatt, as they reshaped English poetry. Theirs was a special moment of revolution when the English language itself was developing its own brave new texts. This revolution was only possible because

of its being posited on a humanist dialectic that naturally led to new forms.

"**The first English classical poet.**"   By no accident, therefore, Surrey in his own time was perceived as a humanist, one who specifically used the language of poetry in one more act of recovery and discovery. In both the general and exact conceptions of translation, Surrey's personal invention, his art, was perceived as serving a greater community, even implementing the dream of most English humanists of founding the new Rome in England. As Ruth Hughey surmises,[3] it was likely Sir John Cheke who wrote the earliest tribute, although unpublished, to Surrey. Having left his post as Regius Professor of Greek and Public Orator at Cambridge in 1544 to become tutor to the young Prince Edward, Cheke could hardly have been sympathetic to what he probably perceived as the traitorous attempt by Surrey to usurp the rights of his young pupil to the English throne. Yet in this same period, Cheke called the severed head of Surrey "The happie head of witt," its "tongue well sett to speak . . . / a subtill toole to fyle the rowghe hewen to the best, / of style a Streame to flowe. . . . "[4] Cheke died in September 1557, three months after the first appearance of *Tottel's Miscellany,* and it may have been that the praise of Cheke and others encouraged Richard Tottel to center his volume around the already legendary figure of Henry Howard. In fact, as John M. Berdan has shown, it was the humanist program of such intellectuals as Cheke at Cambridge and Grimald at Oxford, and the currents of learning that they stirred throughout England, that "prepared the educated reader to applaud" Tottel's volume with its lyrics of Surrey and, a few days later in the same June 1557, Tottel's volume of Surrey's translations from the *Aeneid.*[5]

Cheke's tribute to Surrey in English hexameters, a new form Surrey had used for his paraphrase of Psalm 55, likely reflected a tribute to Surrey's own daring new experiments and texts.[6] Such imitation by a renowned Protestant humanist was tribute indeed to young Henry Howard, who at twenty-nine had left fifty-eight poems that most modern editors definitively accept as his (excluding his translations of the *Aeneid,* books 2 and 4). All of these were unpublished, except for his tribute to Wyatt, which appeared probably in 1542 shortly after Wyatt's death. This canon, preserved in *Tottel's Miscellany* and in seven manuscripts, presents difficult textual problems and, in the case of Tottel, contains outright corrections of

Surrey's text.[7] Furthermore, both before and after Tottel, these unpublished poems were copied in manuscripts probably from original texts, the holographs of which are lost.[8] These manuscripts circulated widely among the intellectual leaders of the nation, whether at court, cathedral, or university (a typical procedure for any poet's work in the Renaissance), but for some, given the legendary circumstances surrounding Surrey's life and death, the manuscripts were perhaps especially treasured.

In fact, just how popular these manuscripts were can be judged by Tottel's preface in June 1557. Tottel congratulates himself that to the glory of his nation and his language, he has brought forth these poems from restricted private sources, who in hoarding are not so aristocratic or "gentle" after all: "It resteth nowe (gentle reder) that thou thinke it not euil doon, to publish, to the honor of the Englishe tong, and for profit of the studious of Englishe eloquence, those workes which the vngentle horders vp of such treasure haue heretofore enuied thee."[9] The reputation of Surrey's work and possibly his legend show in the very setting of Tottel's title page. Giving the impression that the whole volume belongs to Surrey, it reads: "SONGES AND SONETTES, written by the ryght honorable Lorde Henry Haward late Earle of Surrey, and other."[10]

Such early recognition of Surrey as the first truly humanist English poet not only prepared for Tottel's emphasis but enhanced the literary stature of Surrey until the twentieth century. Praised by the leading classical scholar of his day, Surrey was recognized at once in the sixteenth century, as Thomas Warton noted two centuries later, as "the first English classical poet." Warton was emphasizing Surrey's continuity, not merely in the invention of new specific forms out of old texts but in the outstanding achievements of his total form: "his justness of thought, correctness of style, and purity of expression."[11] These are terms that might well fit the texts of Vergil and, mutatis mutandis, may even be applied to the texts of a twentieth-century poet such as John Ashbery. Originality and classicism in this sense are not mutually exclusive. In fact, because Surrey wrote in a period that profited from almost two centuries' (mainly in Italy) of redefinition of language and texts, he learned from humanism the value and meaning of poetic continuity, no matter how surprising and original the poem's surface. At its best, Surrey's poetry had and has continuity with what the contemporary American poet A. R. Ammons calls "the whole body of the an-

thology,"[12] that is, the best of the past. Surrey's strategies of accommodation make this past, the ancient texts, "relevant and available," in Frank Kermode's terms.[13] Surrey's work of translation, of literally bringing over, is, in this sense, a classic text, however new, because he has translated old texts for his time.

One might argue, as H. A. Mason does with Wyatt,[14] that Surrey's best work develops out of this humanist mode of translation. Such a mode moves from a residual, if primitive, method of translation, like that prescribed by Ascham in his *Scholemaster* as the "double translation,"[15] and rises to the emulation of the greatest of all literary forms (at least as the Italians and Sidney proclaimed it), the heroic poem, the Vergilian epic. Although Mason himself has quite a different judgment on Surrey's achievement,[16] this method of seeing all literary writing as an act of translation reveals points of development in Surrey's brief poetic career, just as Mason argues it does with Wyatt's. Indeed one can argue that these points, when fully developed and exampified as texts, produced the archetypal works in Surrey's canon that Tottel and the Elizabethans Gascoigne, Ascham, and Sidney recognized as landmarks of continuity in the development of English poetic language.

Surrey's new texts thus presented to the Renaissance the inventions of blank verse and an English form of the sonnet, both direct results of his working method of translation, and more, a conception of the lyric in English as truly classical, in the terms and context defined above. Such classicism evinced itself first of all in a masterly control of structure. It was not that the ingredients of this structure—Surrey's diction, syntax, and general musicality—were new; they obviously derived, as editors and critics for four centuries have shown, from texts older than Surrey's. What was new in Surrey was the value of classical control of form for his lyric texts and their subjects. The humanist texts from the past had provided Surrey with the resources he needed to understand such integrity and control of form. The humanist poets of Italy and more particularly, as Patricia Thomson has shown,[17] Petrarch and the followers of *petrarchismo,* trained Surrey (and Wyatt before him) to use classical control, with the most complex modern sources, to shape poetic structure in the Renaissance. Through all these Italian sources and subtexts, the Renaissance texts themselves derived in form from the classical. Through them Surrey learned to control the strategic elements in a text so as to give the reader an impression of wholeness.

This is the integrity of form for which Surrey is famous. C. S. Lewis finds it a special evidence of his superiority,[18] and this control and form no doubt immediately attracted Surrey's many readers in the sixteenth century. Not only did a minor poet like Thomas Churchyard, who began his life as an apprentice in Surrey's household and lived long enough to be acknowledged by Spenser in his 1596 *Colin Clouts Come Home Againe,* proclaim Surrey "a Tully for his tongue,"[19] but Ben Jonson in the next century defined Surrey with Wyatt as the very source of English eloquence, both poets "for their times admirable: and the more, because they began Eloquence with us."[20] Ironically, in his inventions for his courtly audience, in one sense forms of self-aggrandizement like his portraits, Surrey became representative of the age, even in development of the common language.[21]

Reform of language, in the greater sense of enhancing its eloquence, could only have been possible in texts where a self-conscious poet had a recognized control of linguistic forms, born of earlier texts but certainly not of "spontaneous overflow." At their best, Surrey's lyrics contain a fully dramatized, even self-perceiving voice within the text. This voice is almost always subsumed into the totality of the text, Surrey's varied formal structures of language made visible and musical as his text rises from earlier texts. This merging of voice and identity into the structure of the text has been far less interesting to twentieth-century readers than, for example, Wyatt's attractive ironic persona, which we tend to see and hear as an earlier Donne, while ignoring Wyatt's own multileveled structures of language. In fact, even in Surrey's seemingly most intimate lyrics (more often elegies than love poems), the emotion is fully dramatized in the text. Indeed, the dramatized emotion is itself often rendered in terms of a subtext of which it is in effect a translation. The tension between these texts, at its best, reveals dramatized structure within the living voice speaking or singing the text. Thus, imitating texts, which the humanists understood as a mode of translation that carried with it a whole vision of civilization, was not just a matter of technical devices alone, even though poets could only begin and end with these. For Surrey as humanist poet such a conception of poetry implied a civilizing task that involved the Vergilian task of invention, the making of a new classic for his time.

With this conception of translation, Surrey wrote his lyrics and his two books from the *Aeneid*. His formal training in classical and European languages and his close reading of Chaucer's language (nearer to his own but already crucially different) prepared him for a task of translation that was, in the end, his own self-invention. To take a text, with its structure of ideas and words, and turn it into another text with an idiom of his own linguistic making was Surrey's method. At its best Surrey's text reflected his perceptions and reading of that first text, in the way Aesculapius transmuted the fragmented Hippolytus, in Vergil's myth, into Roman integrity. Surrey's literary career was hardly more than ten years but in that Tudor and Continental world, which everywhere was answering Erasmus's call "ad fontes" (to the sources), the mode of translation must have appeared to him inevitable. Translating, he could not only turn classical texts into his own language and thus redeem and renew his world, but invent new lyrics as well to establish his own self-integrity.

Example of Surrey's Conception of Translation

Sources and resources for translation. A lyric of Surrey's "When ragyng love with extreme payne" (J1) illustrates this conception of translation. E. M. W. Tillyard called this poem by Surrey "his best lyric."[22] The love poem combines the motifs of Petrarch with the myths of the Trojan war to produce an original text. Inventive filtering of standard European *petrarchismo* through a network of classical themes is a special characteristic of Surrey's work. Furthermore, structuring a Petrarchan subject within a network of allusions, almost all historical and Vergilian rather than Ovidian, is a technique that had seldom appeared before, certainly not so positively in English or Continental love poetry. In "When ragyng love," the ancient myth of Troy—itself translated for Surrey through Homer, Vergil, and Chaucer—is made contemporary because its universal themes are related to the immediate voice of a male persona. This male voice in turn appropriates a popular and established form, the love complaint, and uses its psychological shifts to dramatize a human condition whose universality the voice illustrates in the myth of the Trojan war. The result of these strategies of accommodation is a lyric, new and different in England, and soon

to be very popular throughout Renaissance England both as lyric and as professional ballad.

The Chaucerian figure who most embodied the Trojan myth for Surrey's time was Troilus in the narrative romance *Troilus and Criseyde*. In him Surrey found a popular figure who combined myth and the medieval love complaint. Troilus was likely the prototype for this voice in Surrey's poem—and for all such voices in all Surrey's love complaints. Indeed Troilus may have been the model for the love complaint for the whole of the English Renaissance; if Sidney's digression in his *Defense of Poesie* is any true indication, he was Chaucer's greatest invention for this period. The distinguished and widely read Thynne edition of Chaucer, appearing first in 1532 when Surrey was beginning his most intense intellectual explorations, had given even more authority to Chaucer's popular work. *Troilus* had another appeal for Surrey. As Thomson has shown,[23] this realistic narrative, the equivalent of a modern novel, was freed from a medieval allegorizing technique and had a psychological atmosphere very appealing to Surrey, who was himself, like Wyatt, disposed to the realism of northern humanists like Erasmus and More. The English Troilus was thus as much Surrey's contemporary as the Petrarchan lovers, a fact not too surprising when we realize that it is the voice of Chaucer's Troilus that presents the first translation of Petrarch in English (bk. 1, ll. 400–20).

As a result, in constructing "When ragyng love with extreme payne," Surrey simply translates Chaucer, Vergil, and the Homeric story with that same sense of contemporaneity by which the medieval mind had also seen England as Roman England, Venus as Dame Venus, and the lines of continuity between past and present as living and unbroken. The distances between the voices of Vergil and Chaucer and Surrey himself were not the chasms of time a more scientifically oriented generation would envision. A living past, in the Renaissance a tradition that interpreted present through past, had a sense of continuity and anthology not always found in modern interpretation.[24] This continuity sometimes involves musical subtexts as well as linguistic. The primary mode of performance in this lyric is the dramatized voice, as even a silent reading will show, and so its lyric text might easily be adapted to music and sung. In the Renaissance the musical possibility added to its contemporaneity and made universal themes more accessible to a popular courtly audience. Surrey did, in fact, model his poem on an Italian song

form familiar from the musical renderings of Petrarch and the Pe-
trarchans: the *frottola,* tetrameter lines rhyming in stanzaic form
a b a b c c and resembling the ballad.[25] Surrey's text of experience,
both personal and communal, thus drew on subtexts he saw as
contemporary having the simplicity and lightness of a popular musical form.

> When ragyng love with extreme payne
> Most cruelly distrains my hart;
> When that my teares, as floudes of rayne,
> Beare witnes of my wofull smart;
> When sighes have wasted so my breath
> That I lye at the poynte of death:
>
> I call to minde the navye greate
> That the Grekes brought to Troye towne,
> And how the boysteous windes did beate
> Their shyps, and rente their sayles adowne,
> Till Agamemnons daughters bloode
> Appeasde the goddes that them withstode.
>
> And how that in those ten yeres warre
> Full manye a bloudye dede was done,
> And manye a lord, that came full farre,
> There caught his bane, alas, to sone,
> And many a good knight overronne,
> Before the Grekes had Helene wonne.
>
> Then thinke I thus: sithe suche repayre,
> So longe time warre of valiant men,
> Was all to winne a ladye fayre,
> Shall I not learne to suffer then,
> And thinke my life well spent to be
> Servyng a worthier wight than she?
>
> Therfore I never will repent,
> But paynes contented stil endure:
> For like as when, rough winter spent,
> The pleasant spring straight draweth in ure,
> So after ragyng stormes of care
> Joyful at length may be my fare.

This poem appears early in Tottel's text entitled: "The louer comforteth himself with the worthinesse of his loue." The poem was registered as a ballad three times within the next five years; more than ten years later, as proof of its continued popularity, a "moralization" came out.[26] The close relationship of the *frottola* form to the popular ballad that Surrey knew from both folk and medieval courtly sources was no doubt a factor that helped to determine Surrey's choice of form. Its popularity led to critical acclaim in 1589, at the very beginning of the richest period of the English Renaissance, when George Puttenham used this poem three times as an illustration in *The Arte of English Poesie* of the very best practice in all English poetic art. Puttenham established poetic standards in his enormously influential *Arte* using, as his editors remark, "the early-Tudor courtly makers." His essential "textbook" *Tottel's Miscellany* provided copious illustrations. Each of Puttenham's references to "When ragyng love" occurs significantly in his long section called "Of Proportion" where Surrey is praised for his control of rhythm and caesura and diction, and "this ditty of th'Erle of Surries" called "passing sweete and harmonical."[27]

Its smoothness is directly related to the poem's larger context of musicality. It is probable that Surrey understood quite well such musical possibilities for his poems and even possible that Surrey sang and accompanied himself on a musical instrument.[28] What is more important than Surrey's actual musical training is his exposure to the new musical forms, not least in the Tudor court itself where Italian forms had appeared certainly as early as Castiglione's visit to England in 1506,[29] and then, more significantly for Surrey, at the French court. Arriving there in 1532 with the Duke of Richmond and actually staying in the apartments of the dauphin, Surrey had the opportunity to hear musicians among the best in Europe.[30] At these courts, Surrey would have heard many *frottole* whose chief motif, as Alfred Einstein notes, is love "as understood in a very definite social sphere,"[31] love music as part of the ritual of love. With its light rhythm, such a form could absorb almost any species of Renaissance song lyric, including the courtly sonnet.

By no accident, therefore, the structure of Surrey's thirty-line poem is quite similar to that of the sonnet. Although the iambic tetrameter stanzas of "When ragyng love" have a rhyme scheme *a b a b c c* similar to Chaucer's rhyme royale in *Troilus,* in his poem Surrey has set up a double structure like the sonnet. The first three

of his five six-line stanzas perform the function of the octet in the sonnet form; the last two of the six-line stanzas answer and respond as though a sestet in a sonnet. The resultant pattern is very simple but very powerful. "The completeness, the shape" that Lewis admires[32] in all Surrey's lyrics is exemplified by this poem of thirty lines reduced, in superb proportion, to three sentences.

Translation as rhetoric, logic, and myth. What Surrey is offering in this poem as a new model for future Renaissance poets is a complete strategy, a rounded harmonious shape. This desire for completeness characterizes an impulse of the Renaissance poet often missed in certain modern criticism which demands asymmetry in a poetic text and disdains harmony. In contrast, the Renaissance poet may sustain the objective arrangement of the arguments completely and logically to the end, a special characteristic even of late Renaissance poets like the Metaphysicals. As Maurice Evans notes,[33] Surrey's "unhurried precision" in his best work occurs in "a form entirely suited to its contents." Its objectivity never pretends "to more feeling then the occasion deserves." For Evans such art is new, "occasional, classical, and urbane" and there is "nothing comparable until Ben Jonson." At the same time, as Jonson's own art reminds us, this simplicity can be deceptive. In fact, Surrey's structure in "When ragyng love" is one of the earliest to embody the same strategy as the first sonnet of Sidney's *Astrophil and Stella* and, in varying modes, the religious lyrics of Herbert: building simple statement out of complex materials. This is a classical achievement reflecting Horace's dictum of "multum in parvo" and, like Horatian texts, belying its own complexity of strategies. Harmonious, if deceptive, simplicity may also be for Surrey the result of his desire as Renaissance courtier for urbane art, the ideal Castiglione defines as *sprezzatura* or "true art [that] . . . does not seem to be art."[34]

One may even argue that the larger simplicity of structure in "When ragyng love" is itself the kind of graceful gesture only a "courtly maker," as Puttenham calls Surrey, would make. His Tudor court audience would have noticed at once not only the very modern and very stylish Petrarchan surface of the poem but the older popular courtly love complaint. The opening battle metaphor, for example, with its lamenting knight wounded "all for love," and its retrospective frame, would have recalled Chaucer and earlier courtly singers. The almost suicidal note in the opening lines differs, however, from such cries either in Chaucer or in *petrarchismo* because of

its concision. Here, as elsewhere in his work, Surrey reduces the Chaucerian or medieval conventions to smaller scale, making a new Renaissance lyric out of traditional forms like the complaint.

The Tudor reader beginning the poem would have felt the power of this reduction and concision. The Tudor courtier would have felt the sophisticated structural progression of the poem. What readers were really responding to, of course, was not only a grammatical series of subordinate clauses in the first stanza but a rhetorical device. It was one Surrey could have learned in the first days of his humanist training, the *hirmus,* or long periodic sentence most evident in translating an author he knew well, Cicero. Surrey has three such Ciceronian sentences to mark his structure in "When ragyng love" (Tottel's punctuation at the end of stanza two is arbitrary). The first of these builds to a crescendo shortly after its center, falling to a cadenced conclusion in its focus on the figure and name of "Helene." Within this larger rhetorical device of the first three stanzas, Surrey incorporates other technical forms learned from the handbooks of rhetoric. These rhetorical techniques serve to dramatize the pressing argument of his voice. Thus the grammatical figure of *anaphora* is employed from the very beginning. In fact, the repetition of "when" sets up the first stanza into neat units of two lines each; in the last two lines, the neat epigrammatic couplet, with its insistent rhymes, dramatizes the opening pressing terror of the lover: "breath"/"death." In these units the whole range of Petrarchan clichés is rendered, first, in the actual translation of Petrarch's first two lines from *Sonneto in vita 13*[35] and then, more significantly, in the voice speaking the poem.

The voice here is the echo of a male refugee from the world of *petrarchismo,* which had had by Surrey's time well over a hundred years of literary descendants and artificialities. The figure that emerges, almost suicidal in his rage of love, also anticipates Romeo. Consequently, at the very start of the poem the male rage of love is not joined with just any kind of pain but "extreme payne"; his heart is "Most cruelly" dis-trained because of this rage.[36] There is the further implication that "love" here is not only the lover's personal emotion but the impersonal god Cupid, not the cherubic child but the Ovidian master of Petrarch's *Trionforo d'amore* and Chaucer's *Romaunt of the Rose* and the later terrible figure in Spenser's *Maske of Busyrane* in the Legend of Chastity of *The Faerie Queene.* As this Petrarchan catalogue continues, the tears are floods and,

true to the cliché, they are as vast as rain and give legal witness of his woe and his "smart." Then completing the shorthand *petrarchismo,* the lover in the first stanza describes his sighs as slowly choking him, driving him toward what Surrey has been aiming at all along, the dramatic crisis, in this case, the standard Petrarchan "point of death."

As a good artist, Surrey knew from the start that he must dramatize this possible moment of death in order to make the logical structure of his argument credible. He has built to this moment through shrewd artifice. The lover is led to the moment near death through a series of signs, *petrarchismo* so quickly and easily accessible by the 1530s that Surrey has only to give the minimum for his Tudor audience to understand the whole. The Petrarchan concept thus becomes a means to an end, a specific means to dramatize quickly the personal voice and lead to the real experience being recounted in the poem, the real subject of the lyric. For this cataloguing of signs, Surrey uses a popular rhetorical figure *amplificatio,* a device he uses in almost all his poems. As a popular legacy from the medieval texts, *amplificatio* makes the Petrarchan experience of the lover dramatic and accessible to Surrey's particular Tudor audience.

The result of such artifice and dramatization within the lyric is to set the structure toward universalizing the emotion in it. Indeed, if Surrey is developing (as contrasted to merely accepting) anything in the Petrarchan subtext, it is probably not so much the superstructure of *petrarchismo* he found in Europe and learned from Wyatt but Petrarch's own subtext of Saint Augustine's *Confessions*[37] found in his sonnets and elsewhere. Although on a greatly reduced scale and with radically inverted terms (set by Petrarch himself), "When ragyng love" may also be interpreted as a structure of language in which Augustinian self-perception in a painfully ambiguous world provides a method for self-invention, for (unlike Hamlet) gaining the name of action or expression, so that finally the self can arrive at endurance and hope, the attitude expressed at the poem's closure.

The second stanza enlarges the terms of the terrible dilemma of human existence set in the first stanza. How can the lover even attempt to love in such a world and survive? Immediately continuing the confessional Petrarchan mode, the "I" in the poem calls "to minde," after the subordinate clauses of distrained "hart," "wofull smart," and "poynte of death," the original grand disaster of classical

culture. This was the bloody destruction of Troy. Surrey lingers over this scene, with vivid narrative details: "the navye greate"; "Troye towne," with its use of the Chaucerian double syllable for Troy; "boysteous windes" that "beate" and "rente"; and "sayles" that are "adowne." This precise realistic rendering of myth demonstrates Surrey's seemingly anachronistic perception of Troy. Indeed, with its medieval sense of continuity, this stanza could well have been written in the fifteenth century; there are no historical distinctions, at least as we understand them.[38] Past is present. Even Surrey's choice of archaic diction is not just nostalgia or a sense of the past as lost but a type of modern inventiveness called for by Castiglione.[39] It too adds to the kind of contemporary urgent realism of event that serves Surrey's artistic needs here.

What this realistic evocation of myth leads to, in the next lines, is the first use of proper names. This artifice is a consequence of the vividly depicted scene and provides a structural climax for which the reader has been carefully prepared through such exact realism. In this naming Surrey resorts to a favorite periphrastic figure *antonomasia,* and the terrible myth of Iphigenia is reduced to the concise "Agamemnons daughters bloode." Furthermore, the figure of *metonymy* used in this phrase, blood for murder and for the war itself, becomes a means in the next stanza to reduce the whole effect of the ten-years' war to a few phrases. Therefore, at once, in the logic of the poem, the first unjust murder is necessary for an unjust war to proceed, and a goddess must be appeased who with frightening reality (using a strong Anglo-Saxon verb in an incisive epigrammatic couplet) "them withstode."

All this violence has been called to mind by the lover-speaker, and so the third stanza merely repeats the initial bloodletting. Here the insistent figure of *anaphora* picks up the narrative once more with its series of "and how" phrases.[40] The *anaphora* continues with variations on "manye a" and metrical variations of this repeating phrase, all of which suggest the total devastation of the war. A last example of *anaphora* moves from simple blood to the death of a lord who so poignantly "came full farre" (a universal lament in all wars) and "caught" his destruction too soon. Now, for the first time, the voice comes downstage, as it were, for an outburst "alas," only to return in the narrative to the worst of all these deaths: the "good knight overronne." At this climactic moment of the stanza, when the knight, the best of all social types (a literary fact from Chaucer

on), is destroyed, the real cause of this central tragedy of the Western world is disclosed. Helen herself is the figure whose beauty caused this cycle of blood in which the first effect was the murder of another woman, an innocent girl. Establishing Helen as cause, Surrey has completed the first mode of progression within his poem. Its rhythm has developed largely through parallel phrasal units, often in antitheses, controlling the long complex sentence.

Yet the headlong motion of these tetrameters and their quick echoing rhymes plunging forward on the stream of the rising Ciceronian period have led to a moment of logic. Indeed such structure is suited to the argumentative frame of the poem, for now the progressive argument can define that moment exactly. The dying self, as first dramatized through the convenience of *petrarchismo,* has recalled in myth (for two stanzas after setting the dilemma in the first stanza) the greater destruction of Homeric Troy. This is the primal myth used by Vergil and Chaucer, Surrey's greatest literary masters. Then, at the end of two stanzas memorializing the bloodshed that marked the beginning of the Western world, the voice has recalled its single cause, a woman, Helen. Now, in this mythic contrast, the lover's own personal destruction by a woman finds a greater context. Indeed the lover now has the logic of history itself. The voice's individual private dilemma is thus given universal meaning. By a ritualizing of myth the textual voice is placed in the context of the tradition of Western history, through bloody catalogues of love beginning with the Trojan war. Furthermore, in the murder of the young innocent girl at the end of stanza two, Surrey had developed the figure of *paradigma* for the lover's own potential self-slaughter in a rage of love.

In the fourth stanza, the linguistic structure of the poem repeats the mental act that led to the second stage of the poem. "Then thinke I thus:" says the voice almost meditatively and starts the last phase of the poem. The lover-speaker now invents an argument to give him a solution out of his ambiguous situation. This situation has been so fully dramatized within the universalizing structure of the poem that the lover now sees his dilemma as but one more reflection of a larger human dilemma. The result is to give him the hope of survival, even of action, and the ability to endure his situation because history tells him he is not alone in his suffering; there is a larger community in which the lover-speaker's own action can find meaning. In the clearest Aristotelian sense, therefore, this

action has risen from the structure of the poem, from the text itself. Indeed Surrey's lyric has become a special kind of drama, with its own *peripeteia,* as Walter R. Davis notes: "So vivid has been his sense of the past that it has changed his lament into a firm resolution."[41]

The central place of dramatic action, change of lament into resolution, arises from the carefully calculated structure in Surrey's lyric. It results from the articulation of logical devices, notably a syllogism. As C. W. Jentoft has demonstrated,[42] "When ragyng love" utilizes for its structure the methods learned in the humanist grammar schools (or in Surrey's case, from his private tutors). These techniques involved forms of logic as well as rhetoric, in both cases primarily as defined by Aristotle. For example, when the last stage of action in the poem begins in the fourth stanza, Surrey introduces the topics of invention of comparison and similarity. These topics have a special force and meaning coming immediately after the ending of the first long *hirmus.* At this point the persona's situation has been fully dramatized and enlarged through two sets of mythology, one Petrarchan and Renaissance, and the other, the Trojan, oldest in the Western world. In a second Ciceronian period, therefore, the lover asks the rhetorical question that will turn the progression of the poem.

That turn in the fourth stanza is based upon a topic of comparison. If knights and "valiant men" fought a war for such a long time "all to winne a ladye fayre," can he "not learne to suffer" and "thinke" his life well spent serving a lady much worthier than the adulterous if beautiful Helen? The epigrammatic couplet at the end of the fourth stanza emphasizes this logical topic, and the implicit figure of similitude or *homoeosis* in this question. Both topic and figure construct another basic figure, *hyperbole,* which has itself been implicit all along in Surrey's use of the Trojan myth for the lover's personal dilemma. Comparison and similarity/dissimilarity were traditional topics of invention for Renaissance love poems; *hyperbole* was, of course, an almost standard feature of such poetry. Using the mythic contexts, however, to provide a structure for such *hyperbole* or logical topics of comparison, as in Surrey's poem, was a new and original use of humanist erudition, which gave a brilliant technical effect. In a further structural sophistication, the disposition of the first eighteen lines—which develop the implicit *hyperbole* on

all levels—has now served as an introduction to the last twelve lines of the final two stanzas.

Furthermore, the final shape of the last twelve lines (arising out of the first eighteen) is built on the arrangement and disposition of what has been implicit from the first lines of the poem: the logical development of a syllogism. Simply seen as "condition, analogy, conclusion,"[43] this structure recapitulates a more complex strategy. Its first premise is in the first Ciceronian *hirmus,* which involves the initial announcement of the condition that must be analyzed in order to be understood and confronted and lead to the lover's liberation. After this announcement, the analogy is the first step in the analysis. It fuels the argument for action and liberation: the long bloody war at Troy was for a woman Helen. This historical fact completes the major premise, out of which the poet, following Aristotelian rhetoric, will construct an enthymeme. Surrey's enthymeme will not be, in this context, a truncated syllogism but rather, a false syllogism with a faulty or unexamined premise, usually a minor premise, as here: his love is "worthier." This type of enthymeme, a specific mode of argument called "urbanely fallacious" by the Metaphysical poet Tesauro in the seventeenth century, was allowed by Aristotle for certain occasions, especially oratorical ones in which persuasion was necessary for good effect.[44]

Thus, in the final stanzas of "When ragying love," the extended syllogism of the whole poem might read: *If* Helen were the cause of the effect of so much death, *and* the speaker's beloved, the cause of his "death," is "worthier" than Helen, *then* he can "still endure" the extreme pain of love because (implied) knights and a king's innocent daughter have died for lesser cause. What a critic like Tillyard misses when he admires the structure of this poem but thinks it fails because it lacks drama is precisely the humanist background that provides this drama.[45] He fails to see that the structure, with its mythical premises and logical development, *is* the drama; such logical form can lead to action as completely as in any drama or epic. Therefore the lover as true hero—the stance at the end of the poem that Surrey has been developing—can do nothing less, given the structured mythic contexts of reality that so logically compel him, than "endure" (in the larger Vergilian use of this motif) and renew his life.[46]

This logical conclusion of renewal and transformation is the burden of the final stanza. It is the definition of heroic action within

the terms of the dramatized moral stance of the voice in the lyric. It is typical of Surrey that he uses here a figure of similitude drawn from nature. Such a natural phenomenon as winter into spring gives a final definition by metaphor for the new resolution. The seasonal change dramatizes the lover's own heroic attitude toward his existential dilemma. But it is more than a figure of speech. The lover, the isolated voice in the poem, however oppressed by his dilemma, now finds at last an integration with the forces of nature. It is an integration not always found in Surrey and radically different from solutions usually found in both Petrarch and Wyatt. For this lover is also integrated with the larger forces of human history, equally a product of nature as understood by the medieval and Renaissance mind.

The lover, the voice that has spoken (or, more probably as Surrey intended, sung) the poem, has followed a line of heroes by successfully confronting the rages and ravages of time and love. Because after "rough winter" there comes "straight" into use "pleasant spring" (Chaucerian phrasing recurring throughout Surrey's work), so, by the logic of comparison, "after ragyng stormes of care"—the "ragyng" that precipitated the initial action of the poem—the lover reasons: "Joyful at length may be my fare." In this final epigram the rhymes of "care" and "fare" show the distance the poem has traveled. Echoes in "endure" and "ure" also show the progression of the lover's hope and his new stance. As an integrated human being, he is now at peace and resolute. In fact, the entire rhyme scheme of the final stanza recapitulates this evolution of moving from rage and near death to renewed life: "repent" is "spent"; "endure" is now "in ure"; and "care" becomes "fare."

The pilgrimage of the lover is therefore heroic. To use Surrey's own residual myths, it is an Aeneas-progression toward the lover's own destiny with a possible ("may be") happy ending, a personal destiny· mirroring the larger Rome of human community, which itself recapitulated and transformed the losses of Troy, the oldest subtext in Surrey's mythologizing. Such a possibility of happiness and such an end for the lover's own destiny gives direction to the destruction endemic in his alienation and that of the human condition, whether the condition be lover's or brave knight's. The moment is still one of dialectic, however, and the figure of *chiasmus* that describes the seasons ("rough . . . spent"; "pleasant . . .

straight draweth in ure") describes the final attitude of this Petrarchan lover.

The language describes a lover recognizing no certainty of happiness or of always being loved and useful, and no escape from time, the stretch of seasons. In the closure of the text there is only the lyric voice waiting at the end in hope. In the context of the evolving drama of the poem, this speaking voice has moved, nevertheless, from imprisonment in dead language—clichés of his own making or of his generation—to language that freshly and originally reflects universal emblems of human nature. The solid structure of Surrey's poem has dramatized, through its progressing form, the process by which the lover has learned to live at least in hope. Integrated itself, the voice in the text can now trust its own integrity. In terms of the poetic argument, the lover has learned to endure the ambiguity of history, united at last with the possibilities of his own powers of loving and hoping to love. If this closure expresses an heroic moral stance, it has been a revelation from the integrity of lyric structure, whose harmonious form developed as a song.

Chapter Three
The Sonnet

From the beginning Surrey probably did not see the new invention of the sonnet, even in its Continental forms by contemporaries and immediate predecessors like Seraphino and Saint-Gelais, as a necessarily foreign form impinging on native experience. In fact, Chaucer had translated a Petrarchan sonnet into English in the 1370's. In book 1 of *Troilus and Criseyde* (11. 400–20), in the crucially placed "Canticus Troili," Chaucer weds the love complaint of Troilus, with the first despairing notes in the narrative, to the antithetical, oxymoronic syntax of the Petrarchan lover debating himself. This is Chaucer's own translation of Sonnet 88, *In vita* ("S'amor non e"), where Petrarch's speaker details the contrary effects of his love for Laura. In three stanzas of rhyme royal Chaucer attempted to imitate Petrarch's sonnet of fourteen hendecasyllabic lines generally rhyming *a b b a a b b a c d e c d e*. This was the first time in English such a structure of language and experience appeared. There had been nothing like it before. Having visited Italy in the early 1370s when Petrarch's *rime* were first appearing, Chaucer obviously understood at once the revolutionary nature of this art. He perceived that it transformed the modes of courtly love then dominating lyric verse in Europe. Whatever his immediate source,[1] Chaucer brought this new development of the sonnet to England.

For Surrey, the literary heir of Chaucer, the sonnet must have appeared indigenous or at the least a continuous form in which he could compete and to which he could add. With the powerful translations and adaptations of his contemporary Wyatt, the sonnet in Tudor England must have offered opportunities as challenging as the epic or any other Mediterranean form. There was nothing extraneous or "foreign" in using it or any of these forms. Indeed it is altogether likely that in Henry's court Chaucer was still Roman Chaucer in a continuation of Latin culture. It is even likely that reading *Troilus* was, for Surrey and his generation, not unlike the experience of reading the *Aeneid* and entering an authentically clas-

sical world. That the Troilus figure who spoke the contradictions of this first English translation of a sonnet was given such an heroic cast would certainly help to explain how, in Surrey's generation, Troilus became a central literary voice and "*the* figure of the courtly lover."[2] What we separate so easily in later centuries, epic hero and lover, romance and epic, was not so dichotomous in generations who probably viewed the *Aeneid* as contemporaneous.

There were therefore, from the beginning, resources in Surrey's own English subtexts that allowed him to invent not only the best English form for his own lyric statements and outbursts like those that Troilus spoke but also to invent the best English rhythms for a perennial epic hero who spoke his own stories of loss and love. A process of intertexuality led to Surrey's own special translation or "bringing over." His revolutionary forms thus sprang from his perception of continuity. In fact, in the composition of his fifteen sonnets, Surrey was probably more aware of this transference or continuity, of his own "competition" with his masters and their subtexts, than of accomplishing any revolutionary or original act. Indeed it is likely that his particular moment of revolution sprang from accidental events: the fifteen-year-old Surrey's discovery in 1532–33 of the original Petrarchan sonnets at the French court, a discovery subsequently enhanced by rereading Chaucer's *Troilus* in a splendid new edition, and then by Wyatt's own simultaneous composition of sonnets.

Later in the sixteenth century the importation of the sonnet into English was to be viewed differently. In 1557 Tottel himself formulated in his preface to the first edition of the *Miscellany* what he viewed as the essential difference between the medieval and this new style of verse: its power of concentration. Because for Tottel the lyrics by Surrey and Wyatt were direct translations from the Mediterranean, Tottel remarks in the very first sentence of his "The Printer to the Reader": "THat to haue wel written in verse, yea & in small parcelles, deserueth great praise, the workes of diuers Latines, Italians, and other doe proue sufficiently."[3] This economy was, in fact, the really revolutionary dimension of these 1557 texts although the sources had not all been short-circuited through Italy. By 1589, however, what had been viewed as technical originality was characterized by Puttenham as a virtual revolution. It was another positive reformation:

In the latter end of the same kings raigne sprong vp a new company of
courtly makers, of whom Sir *Thomas Wyat* th'elder & *Henry* Earle of Surrey
were the two cheiftaines, who hauing trauailed into Italie, and there tasted
the sweete and stately measures and stile of the Italian Poesie as nouices
newly crept out of the schooles of *Dante Arioste* and *Petrarch,* they greatly
pollished our rude & homely maner of vulgar Poesie, from that it had
bene before, and for that cause may iustly be sayd the first reformers of
our English meetre and stile.

Giving his own erroneous historical account of this revolution (Surrey
never traveled beyond France, for example), Puttenham then focused
his revisionism on the new and original styles of these two progenitors of English verse, who were one to him, especially in their
humanist imitations of Petrarch: *"Henry* Earle of Surrey and Sir
Thomas Wyat, betweene whom I finde very litle difference, I repute
them (as before) for the two chief lanternes of light to all others
that haue since employed their pennes vpon English Poesie, their
conceits were loftie, their stiles stately, their conueyance cleanely,
their termes proper, their meetre sweete and well proportioned, in
all imitating very naturally and studiously their Maister Francis
Petrarcha."[4]
It was, of course, a question of just how "naturally" or "studiously" either Wyatt or Surrey imitated the original texts of Petrarch. Certainly, besides English subtexts, they both knew of
Petrarch's imitators in the fifteenth and early sixteenth century,
especially in Italy.[5] Obviously Surrey had read the Petrarchan originals, but in neither him nor Wyatt is there any loving lingering
over the physical attributes of the beloved, any idealizing of woman,
or any of Petrarch's introspective and metaphysical elaboration. Both
poets resort more frequently to the simpler strategies of *petrarchismo*
in their use of Petrarchan material. Although Surrey's art is more
pictorial, both "courtly makers" resort to the emotion of personal
response, even to the satiric wit of the Continent, or to the involved
demands of argument rather than to an adoring contemplation of
the beloved, a set icon. If there is transcendence in the Petrarchan
sense in Surrey's verse, it is found, by and large, in his emphasis
on fidelity in friendship, marriage, and love, as in the resolution
of "When ragyng love" (J1). Although Surrey's lover, like Petrarch's, is fully involved with nature, symbolic landscape is used
in Surrey only to depict the actual nature of the lover in the poem,

whose voice sounds, more often than not, like Troilus's. Beyond this anguish, or the resolution to be faithful, Surrey's lyric simply does not go.

But, however Surrey uses these Petrarchan texts, he does in fact translate and adapt either whole poems from Petrarch or sections of his poems. There are nine such poems; three of Surrey's sonnets are direct translations (one of a *ballata* from Petrarch's sequence *In vita* instead of a sonnet) and two sonnets are adaptations. This number is small, of course, compared to the many English translations and adaptations Wyatt made of Petrarchan originals and of Continental Petrarchan imitations. It is even smaller compared to the canon of Petrarch himself, who wrote profusely and widely and who was, by any standard, one of the great literary figures in Western culture. Surrey and Wyatt simply do not compare to his stature, nor can Surrey's brief achievement of hardly more than ten years be meaningfully compared to Wyatt's, his master sixteen years older.

The tendency of twentieth-century criticism to denigrate Surrey in order to raise estimates of Wyatt is easy enough to understand, if often tasteless. Almost four centuries of earlier criticism obscured Wyatt's genius, not only the merit of his lyrics but also his prosodic and technical discoveries. From Tottel to the early twentieth-century literary historians, Wyatt was an incomplete Surrey or simply disparaged for his technical blundering and, in some cases, bad choice of models. The natural reaction to this depreciation has led to some of the best modern editions and critical studies in recent Renaissance scholarship, all of which cumulatively establish Wyatt as an important poet in his own right. What such scholarship has generally forgotten is that Surrey himself gave the first such praise and estimate of Wyatt. Indeed, not even the contemporary resuscitation of Wyatt is equal to the comprehensive depth of Surrey's own praise of Wyatt in his elegy, written almost immediately after Wyatt's death in 1542. Furthermore, Surrey did not develop the English sonnet form— his greatest lyric invention—in defiance of Wyatt. The more obvious facts of friendship and competition explain better the relationship of Wyatt and his art to Surrey's, and indeed Wyatt may have borrowed from Surrey, who was writing at the same time, possibly composing his first sonnet as early as 1537. The appearance of the English sonnet is less a lock-and-step development than a process of selection and adjustment from common Italian and English subtexts.

Within such an incremental process, Surrey invented the English sonnet, which reached its zenith in Shakespeare and influenced all other English literary forms. Of course, other poets like Grimald and the uncertain authors in *Tottel's Miscellany* also used this same invention, although by 1557 it is entirely possible that Surrey is himself being imitated.[6] The proof of a poem written in this form as early as 1537 suggests that Surrey may have been the actual fountainhead and not part of a larger scene. We do know for certain that Surrey wrote fifteen sonnets, all of them appearing in print for the first time in 1557. Ten of them are exactly in his new invention to be called the English or Shakespearean sonnet. One other sonnet has the same rhyme scheme as Wyatt's last double-sonnet (M175); three more have three rhymes only; and one has only two rhymes. Of these fifteen sonnets by Surrey, three are direct translations of Petrarch and two are adaptations.

If we look at the direct translations first, we may observe in them something of the incremental process by which an original text and even its earlier subtext is transformed into a new poem, in this case, Surrey's own sonnet text. This is a method we may use to examine all the sonnets in this chapter (sonnets in the elegaic mode will be discussed later). Surrey's sonnets range from the more obvious Petrarchan imitations and adaptations to the poems to Geraldine where he achieves mastery of his own sonnet form in the poem of social occasion. Ironically it is in these sonnets to Geraldine that Surrey follows, for once, the Petrarchan idealization of a beautiful young woman, although his actual translations and adaptations of Petrarch are quite different.

Sonnets: Imitations of Petrarch

"Love that doth raine and live within my thought"(J4).   This sonnet is a direct translation from Petrarch. It is written in Surrey's rhyme scheme *a b a b c d c d e f e f g g* and is perhaps the most anthologized of all of Surrey's sonnets. It can be easily compared to the Petrarchan original, *rime* 140, and to Wyatt's "The longe love, that in my thought doeth harbar" (M4), which itself translated Petrarch's original. In fact the sonnet has been used by various critics to show, by comparison to Petrarch's and Wyatt's texts, the inferior nature of Surrey's poem and of his art in general.

In dealing with the Petrarchan original here, Surrey is on familiar ground. Like his fellow "courtly maker," Surrey understands the Petrarchan imagery of the warfare of love. The chivalric mode that still dominated the interplay of men and women in the palaces and halls, on the ramparts of a castle like Windsor, or in the drawing rooms of early Tudor court life, often resolved itself into such martial imagery. Thus, for the Petrarchan, the field of arms became another battleground where the prize was consummated desire and the honor of another kind of possession, and the failure, another kind of death in the name of Eros and his honor. Furthermore, this love-god was not a chubby little Cupid, but the terrible god of Ovid's driven lovers, the lovers in the *Romance of the Rose, Troilus,* and *The Knight's Tale* where Theseus, hearing the suffering stories of Palamon and Arcite, remarks: "The god of love, a, *benedicite!/* How myghty and how greet a lord is he!" (11. 1785–86).

For Surrey's sonnet, it is important to keep this figure of Love in mind because it is a personification that Surrey deftly weaves out of his two subtexts, an invented character not found in Petrarch and Wyatt. In Surrey, the character is part of a drama, the center of which is the lover himself. The voice in the lyric is caught between the master of the first quatrain and the mistress of the second.[7] It is clear, as the drama of the sonnet progresses, that Surrey has appropriated the almost theatrical confrontations of his subtexts and their lines of dramatic action: Love appearing, Love repulsed by the beloved, Love fleeing, then lover making a moral stance in the face of his dilemma (the lover's resolution turned into an epigram in all three versions of the sonnet). What Surrey has done, for better or worse, is to tighten and objectify these lines and relationships. He has turned them into a narrative, weaving them, on a reduced scale, into a design like one of the tapestries hanging in such English Renaissance palaces as Surrey's at Norwich, his father's at Kenninghall, or Wolsey's at Hampton Court—a design that reflects in the sonnet something of the allegorical tensions of the tapestries on the walls of Spenser's fictional castles.

Thus, the special achievement of concentrated conceit that had made Petrarch's handling of the traditional courtly love idealization and imagery so special and so subtle is simply carried forward here in another mode. Surrey's concentration builds on the dramatic concrete elements of the conceit. This is also characteristic of Wyatt, who, by such use of drama, with Surrey opened up the English lyric

toward Donne and the Metaphysicals. Wyatt concentrates, however, the psychological symbolism of an individual's "longe love" carried through an almost dreamlike story resembling a Freudian (or Jungian) case study. He absorbs what is probably Petrarch's own subtext, medieval allegory, and turns it into his own powerful self-drama. On the other hand, Surrey takes the same allegorical configuration, especially that of the love-god, and turns it into a bristling drama of three persons.

Surrey develops this drama through logic. He utilizes the Petrarchan division of octet and sestet, with its central aspects of "Amor . . . regna" and "Amor paventoso," (in Surrey's precise translation "Love that doth raine" and "cowarde love") to form a distended syllogistic argument. In the first quatrain of Surrey's sonnet the major premise is the main action of the story, what starts everything: Love shows his colors, his banner of desire, in the face of the lover. This action results in consequent actions that set a kind of double minor premise: the beloved is angry at such a display of desire, and Love flees, hiding his face, which he had shown so boldly. The conclusion of the argument is not, however, the conclusion of the sonnet but the beginning of the final tercet: "For my lordes gylt thus fawtless byde I payine." The lover is innocent of what his master has done but still, without justice, he must suffer.

Such suffering is the nature of love in this mutable existence, and it is precisely this kind of love that leads Surrey to the conclusion of the poem and his epigram. Mutability and death are sweet when taken for the cause of love, says Surrey, echoing Petrarch and his probable Ovidian source.[8] This acceptance leads the lover to the real conclusion of the sonnet, not the last line but the penultimate: he will not desert his master Love, says the lover in his resolution of the dilemma, restating a passage from book 2 of the *Aeneid*.[9] Thus, within his logical frame, Surrey also weaves a structure of psychological encounters. These encounters develop the characters of a ménage à trois. Here Surrey approaches some of the implicit mock heroic tone in the Petrarchan subtext. As a result, Surrey has condensed into his narrative a whole history in which the first quatrain reveals the dominance of the figure Love; the second, the dominance of the imperious and possessive beloved (and significantly, neither interferes in the other's quatrain); and the sestet, the dilemma of the lover, dramatized in its first tercet and resolved in the second, the last unit of the sonnet.

In the third level of psychological encounter, the lover with himself, the sonnet comes closest to its two subtexts. The lover must take a moral stance, an action that is finally a truer act of love than either Love or the beloved is capable of. He will die and, true to the military metaphor, will sacrifice himself in the absolutely faithful service of a squire to his master in the chivalric code. The lover is willing to face his own annihilation "all for love." The ultimate romantic gesture is finally in Surrey's epigram: "Sweet is the death that taketh end by love." In this pattern of monosyllables moving, like most of the rhythm of the poem through powerful phrasal units, there is none of the questioning found in Petrarch or Wyatt. There is only the moment of recognition of pain and its inevitability and then, before self-pity can begin, the resolution to serve a master who hurts but can alone offer meaning to the lover's existence.

This resolution is emphasized by a technical device Frederick Morgan Padelford noted[10]: initial trochees that had dominated three lines of the first quatrain and had given the poem its bold martial opening appear again in the final tercet. There they give the same bold strength, but newly defined, they emphasize the crucial twelfth line, the completion of the logical argument, and then the final line with its stress on "sweet," one of Surrey's most repeated words. Thus, once more, in the closure of a poem, in the moral stance that resolves the action, Surrey's lover affirms his faith in love. Surrey is closer in this affirmation to Petrarch than to Wyatt, but his objective narrative frame, which smoothes out surfaces in order to focus plot and characterization, is Surrey's own invention. This sonnet is lyric, but its structure, in order to arrive at that moment of lyric closure, is posited on a narrative form.

"Set me wheras the sonne dothe perche the grene" (J3). This sonnet, also in Surrey's invention of *a b a b c d c d e f e f g g,* is a direct translation of Petrarch's sonnet *rime* 145, "Pommi ove 'l sole occide i fiori e l'erba." There was no subtext by Wyatt for Surrey to consider in his translation, but there was an original Latin text for Petrarch that Surrey would have known, perhaps better than the Italian: the famous ode by Horace (1.22) that begins "Integer vitae scelerisque purus." As Warton noted in the eighteenth century, Surrey's Latin, the Latin of the humanists, was his first language after English, which allowed him to read the Latin classics much more easily than contemporary works in the modern European lan-

gauges. Surrey recognized no doubt the syntactical relationships between Petrarch's sonnet and the Horatian ode and could have placed the ode beside Petrarch as he began writing his own poem.

Surrey made these syntactical connections the basis of the structure of his own poem. In the Latin text, in the Italian text, and in the Surrey poem the overriding pattern is a contrast between extremes in the natural landscape and the fidelity of the lover to the beloved. This pattern is sustained particularly in Petrarch by a catalogue of antitheses that Surrey directly translates. The result is that Surrey's "Set me" is one of his most symmetrical poems. Each quatrain beginning with the imperative "Set me" is obviously directed toward a beloved for whom all the contrasting antitheses of the first twelve lines unite in the final couplet in an act of faith. "Yours will I be, and with that onely thought" the lover will be comforted even when his existence has become nothing. This final couplet, logically the result of the series of contraries, is strengthened in its nature as a generalizing epigram by the use of emphatic initial trochees. These trochees can be found earlier with the imperatives "Set me" (for the Petrarchan *pommi*), repeated three times to begin each four-line unit, and within the last unit, with the initial "Sike" that starts the last tercet. Also these trochees, starting the last two lines of the couplet, balance the rest of its smooth iambic pentameter to make "thought" a complement to "yours" and "comfort" to "nowght."

The result is that out of his own symmetry, his own syntax of contraries, Surrey achieves the same powerful closure as Horace's evocation of Lalaga and Petrarch's of his faithful lonely lover. This strategy was built, like the structures of Petrarch and Horace, on the figure of *anaphora* in a kind of implicit ritual leading to the powerful last lines (exactly as Surrey's invention will be used by Shakespeare in his sonnet 73, "That time of year thou mayst in me behold"). What balances this steady insistent progression is a set of antitheses in a counterrhythm to the central drive of logic dramatized by the *anaphora*. What is ironic in this structure is that the strong dynamic logical classification reverses itself in a surrender. It sinks into the generalization of the last couplet—"Yours will I be"—with Surrey's typical chivalric theme of honor and "all for love." In both the Horatian and Petrarchan subtexts, this final reversal is the point of the lyric. Integrity of the lover is the moral stance in all three of the texts. Surrey is faithful in his translation, rendering a very consciously crafted placement of language and idea.

One special instrument of this craft is what Thomson calls Surrey's "props of phrasing."[11] Such phrasal units, suited to the inherited antitheses of his models, are remarkably set in Surrey's lines. These lines often hover between a fundamental ten-syllable line and the old Anglo-Saxon accentual meter, frequently with appropriate alliteration, as in line four, the ending of the first quatrain: "With prowde people, in presence sad and wyse" or line nine, the beginning of the sestet; "Set me in earthe, in heaven, or yet in hell." What gives these phrasal units in this sonnet an extra power are two other devices: Surrey's skillful use of monosyllables at crucial junctures such as in line twelve, "Sike, or in healthe, in yll fame or in good"; and his caesura after every fourth syllable (except possibly in the first line). These caesuras generally carry weight but, even when one of several in the same line, they still manage to keep the echo of the old medieval accentual rhythm as seen in *Piers Plowman.* Surrey's line also tends to be end-stopped, a general tendency of all his verse. All these devices emphasize the phrasal units, which in this sonnet contain the catalogue of the antitheses.

Surrey uses another generalizing device that helps to keep the structure of these antitheses and their meaning clear: he balances the lines between the landscapes of nature and those of human society. In the first quatrain three lines about nature are followed by the juxtaposition of proud people and the surprising "sad and wyse" presence of the humble; in the second, two human lines frame two natural; in the third, two natural lines followed by two human. The result of such a manipulation of this type of *amplificatio* is that the natural landscape has so melded into the social by the moment of closure that the resolved surrender of "Yours will I be" has unusual climatic force. Puttenham remarked on this manipulation when he used this sonnet in 1589 (which he attributed to Wyatt) as an example of the figure *merismus,* or *the distributer:* "Then haue ye a figure very meete for Orators or eloquent perswaders such as our maker or Poet must in some cases shew him selfe to be, and is when we may conueniently vtter a matter in one / entier speach or prosposition and will rather do it peecemeale and by distribution of euery part for amplication sake." Then having quoted Tottel's mangled version of the sonnet, Puttenham adds: "All which might haue bene said in these two verses. *Set me wheresoeuer ye will, / I am and wilbe yours still.*"[12]

Finally, another possible subtext for this sonnet is the marriage ceremony of the Catholic church whose vows at that time were pronounced in English in the midst of the Latin marriage liturgy (separate from the Mass at that time): "I N. take the N. to my weded wyfe to haue and to hold from this day forwarde for bettere for wers for richere for pouerer: in sykenesse and in hele tyl dethe vs departe. . . ."[13] Surrey defines another kind of integrity for his lover when he takes the antitheses of this familiar ceremony and incorporates it subtly into his own text. In his eleventh line, modulating the sharper antitheses of the lines before, Surrey begins to prepare for the familiar juxtapositions of this liturgy by focusing on the human conditions of being "thrawle" or free, "alive whersoo I dwell." Then he proceeds in the next line and a half to define a condition of thralldom that is actually freedom. The lover is alive wherever he and now she dwell, the condition of such life and freedom being their fidelity to each other within the terrible antithetical states of the human condition. Such liturgical echoes no doubt added to the popularity of this sonnet with Elizabethan readers (this poem was also turned into a ballad). Finally, these lines with liturgical echoes lead to the highest expression of human fidelity: "Yours will I be." In the phrase the resonant ambiguity of the genetive is the climax of Surrey's carefully orchestrated structure. Its syntax supports Richard S. Sylvester's perceptive judgment: "When Surrey does look in his heart and write, he seeks not so much to analyze himself as to portray relationships with others."[14]

"I never saw youe, madam, laye aparte" (J6). Sylvester's observation about Surrey's instinct in composition, to develop relationship, reminds us that Surrey often turns his initial text or subject matter into a social occasion, or at least a social response. What critics of Surrey often miss is the social occasion in his text, a subject natural enough for a Howard at the court of Henry VIII. The social occasion counted, of course, because it was dramatized within the text of the lyric, as language and image. Thus Surrey's instinct for defining relationships in his texts simply meant first, elaborating a rhetorical structure. This structure, whatever its formal development, had an oratorical base (at least as rhetoric was understood in ancient Greece and Rome), and that meant an assumed audience. The clear assumption of audience is a crucial difference in judging the texts of Surrey and his subtexts, whether of Wyatt, Petrarch, Horace, or Vergil. These are not those modern texts where

poets are their own audience. The index of audience assumption here and its very nature determine not only how a reader might view an objective structure like a Surrey lyric, but also how a writer handles his own expanding self-perception in the text.

Thus, if this third direct translation of Petrarch is presented as a poem addressed to a lady, we need to remember that such rhetorical address not only immediately sets up a dramatic situation but, by its terms of love-complaint, an implicit dramatic conflict suited to entertain and enlighten an audience. The poem therefore becomes another narrative situation and another dramatized social occasion. Unlike his Italian subtext, Surrey's sonnet is less a refinement of the persona's feelings through imagery and diction; it is more the urgent dramatic progression of the complaint whereby at the end of the poem the veil becomes a symbol for Surrey—a kind of cosmic statement. The loss rendered in this final tercet is focused on the mutability of nature that finally becomes an occasion in the poem of social and personal loss. Once more, in a pattern typical of Surrey, nature leads to the definition of the lover's human relationship. Here there is integration but only in the loss of the element vital to both lover and nature: light itself. Indeed, in the elaborated conceit of the sonnet, the lady's veil has become the instrument of cosmic darkness and a symbol of larger mutability and loss. It is probably this sense of loss that dictated Surrey's taking of Petrarch's original form, a *ballata* from *rime* 11, and turning it into the more reflective form of his sonnet with its plainer diction and more amplified lines. This quieter, more reflective, inward turn is shown in the very rhyme scheme Surrey chose for this translation *a b b a c d d c e f- f e g g.* This is his only use of this scheme, which interestingly was used just once by Wyatt in his final double-sonnet (M175) probably addressed from prison in 1541.

"In Cypres springes, wheras dame Venus dwelt" (J5).   This sonnet is an instance where Surrey develops a single figure of an unrequited lover, for once a character and subject strictly out of *petrarchismo*. Surrey probably used a contemporary source for his sonnet, likely a *strambotto* from Seraphino or Cariteo, for he transforms the landscape to the mythological Cyprus where "dame Venus dwelt." Although in this poem he translates Ariosto, who has behind him Boiardo and, behind both, probably a classical text in Cicero, [15] the effects of the Cyprian springs read like the exaggerated devices of *petrarchismo*. Only the final epigrammatic couplet catches some-

thing of Surrey's sense of absolute loss. Yet not even the typical Surrey narrative flow nor his standard rhyme scheme *a b a b c d c d e f e f g g* can keep this poem from being anything but an exercise in humanist translation. Surrey simply did not write such a love lyric well. Except for its highly ornate tapestrylike situations, the sonnet has no dramatic focus, certainly no fully developed interplay between lover and nature or social relationship.

   "Alas, so all thinges nowe doe holde their peace" (J7). Both this poem and the next "The soote season" are Surrey's adaptations of Petrarch's sonnets; they are not translations because each varies the original Petrarch text in a significant manner. Both sonnets are similar in that each, from different Petrarchan sources and with varying structure, has the same theme adapted from Petrarch and, more significantly, from Petrarch's own subtext in Vergil. This theme expresses the paradox that, while nature functions with its own integrating peace and regenerative power, the lover is outside the natural order of things. He (in Vergil, she) is suffering a cosmic dislocation. Both sonnets also have similar rhyme schemes, varying only in the couplet, a through-rhyme *a b a b a b a b a b a b c c* (or *-a a*), both reminiscent of medieval rhyme schemes, a rarity in Surrey. These are the only examples of such a rhyme scheme in Surrey; even the one example in Wyatt (M184) may be Surrey's poem.[16] Both also are outstanding illustrations of how Surrey can also be asymmetrical, letting the rhythm of ideas control the octet-sestet or three-quatrain pattern. In both the final couplet functions as an epigrammatic closure. This is a typical pattern in Surrey and, in the first of these two sonnets, the closure completes and focuses the human gesture of isolation and, in the other, it reverses the life-force of the first twelve lines.

   What all this suggests is that the two sonnets are exercises in Surrey's own mode of translation. It is entirely possible that the real root of these sonnets—from the poem that mesmerized the young Henry Howard in his late teens and early twenties—is the text behind all these texts themselves: Dido's nocturnal lament in book 4 of the *Aeneid* (ll. 522–53). For his own translation of the *Aeneid*, which he composed at the same time as these sonnets, Surrey takes the two-fold structure of the original Vergilian lament, the overture of the calm night and then the voice of the collapsing Dido, and turns it into one of his own bravura pieces:

It was then night; the sounde and quiet slepe
Had through the earth the weried bodyes caught;
The woodes, the ragyng seas were falne to rest;
When that the starres had halfe their course declined;
The feldes whist; beastes and fowles of divers hue,
And what so that in the brode lakes remainde
Or yet among the bushy thickes of bryar
Laide down to slepe by silence of the night,
Gan swage their cares, mindlesse of travels past.
Not so the spirite of this Phenician:
Unhappy she, that on no slepe could chance,
Nor yet nightes rest enter in eye or brest.

(J42,bk.4,ll. 702–13)

"Alas, so all thinges nowe doe holde their peace," an adaptation of Petrarch's sonnet *rime* 164, follows this same Vergilian structure. It juxtaposes two landscapes, outer and inner, within its asymmetrical handling of the sonnet's fourteen lines. Lines 1–5 describe the peace of nature that is so painful to the waking lover; lines 6–9 present the disharmony of the lover within such harmony; and the last section, lines 10–14 explore these contraries of *petrarchismo* until they lead to the final awareness of human isolation: "When that I thinke what grief it is againe / To live and lacke the thing should ridde my paine." In fact, one might say that in the sestet where it departs most obviously from its Petrarchan original, Surrey is using the Petrarchan clichés of opposites in order to render direct emotion, as in Vergil. Surrey's language is not so flat in these last sections of his sonnet, as some critics have thought, because it is deliberately imitating here two substructures of language expressing lament. Surrey's diction was strongly influenced by Chaucer's (particularly the use of abstract nouns like those in Troilus's song) and by Wyatt's own use of Chaucer's diction.[17] Thus words like "doubtfull" and "swete," especially in such a deliberately imitative structure, have more resonance than modern readers, expecting more concrete diction, might perceive.

A logical device establishes at once the structure of "Alas, so all thinges." Its divisions of argument mark an immediate difference from its subtexts: the speaker's "alas" in the first line, with its generalizing statement, acts as a topic of invention to be developed. Surrey's voice here makes an "entraunce," as the oratorical textbooks call such a beginning.[18] In such a rhetorical and dramatic stance,

the lyric thus begins by presupposing an inherent dichotomy between the first and last words in the opening sentence. The voice
proceeds to develop this division logically. Indeed the uses of *amplificatio,* which expand this last word "peace," form the first phase
of the sonnet. In this section Surrey must reduce the details of
Vergil's text into brief compass, and strict logical consistency, such
as deducing parts from a whole, is one way to work this concentration
into his text.

The first five lines particularly betray the Vergilian subtext. Classical verse techniques, typical of all of Surrey's work, abound in
these lines: ellipsis in the second line; inversions of syntax in lines
three, four, and five (with strange placement of adverbs and very
artificial effects like beasts and air singing); and mythological personification as in "the nightes chare." More frequent in his translation of the *Aeneid,* these classical techniques here cause Surrey's
verse to creak a bit. Yet the imitation can be brought into focus,
as in the fifth line, which Padelford found "noble" and "prophetic
of the Georgian poets."[19] Probably in deference to the Vergilian
subtext, Surrey adds this line to the original Petrarchan model,
making his sonnet asymmetrical. What the line gives the speaker
is his own moment of poise in the structure, his own peace set as
a kind of *onomatopoeia* with its own classical serenity: "Calme is the
sea, the waves worke lesse and lesse." *Chiasmus* and an exact placement of caesura have focused all the previous inversions and phrasal
units of description into this paradox in the line of working "lesse
and lesse."

In line six, against this backdrop of types and phenomena with
little concrete diction and little sensuous imagery, the lover enters
stage center. With his own assertion—and another "alas"—he recapitulates the structure: "So am not I, whom love alas doth wring."
This lover has a face and before it come all the contraries that once
came to Troilus, the quintessential English lover of the early Renaissance. In confronting what he sees, this arguing lover declares
his logical topic as comparison and contrast. His method of invention
clarifies the dichotomy in the initial statement of the sonnet by
showing the cause of such disharmony. He is wrung by love, a
process amplified in the next six lines (ll. 7–12) in the mode and
language of Chaucer's Troilus. The first three of these lines are
logically connected to the psychological process in the next three
(ll. 10–12). This precise foreshortening structure (sharply reducing

and concentrating its major subtexts) Surrey must now bring to a moment of closure, a final stance and action. His key word in the thirteenth line is "againe," syntactically out of place (really belonging at the first of the line). What Surrey has dramatized is the lover's awareness of his condition: "When that I thinke what griefe it is againe / To live and lacke the thing should ridde my paine."

This statement of the human condition is as far as the moral stance of the sonnet goes. Yet its abrupt epigrammatic form provides the reader with a statement of a mystery as old as its subtexts in Vergil and Saint Augustine: human isolation from love. Such dramatized isolation is credible, however, because, as Davis remarks, "Surrey was less interested in metaphor, in projecting the self onto nature, than in seeing the self in *relation* to nature."[20] The corollary to this final isolation Surrey implies by the protest implicit in the structure of the poem: such disharmony of landscapes, of the self and nature, should not be.

"**The soote season, that bud and blome furth bringes**" (J2). An implicit sense of protest also runs through the insistent rhymes of "The soote season." The problem here is that this marvelously objective structure, with its own interweaving of imitations, does not provide an overtly simple surface for easy interpretation. The art here is complex and understated and moves out of several texts at once. The irony is that this complex structure is also one of the most anthologized of all of Surrey's poems, a particular favorite of the Surreydolators from the sixteenth to the late nineteenth centuries.

As in the previous poem, the lyric strategy arises from the paradoxical contrast of vital nature, sure in its own processes, and the lover, isolated and despairing. Here the strategy involves an interlayering of textures precisely and concretely rendered. There is, for example, not a single metaphor in the entire sonnet unless we count the pun in the final word "springes." The poetic text itself becomes a landscape, as it were, of solid actuality. The result is that what seems immediately accessible is, like any actual landscape, difficult to generalize about. As Alastair Fowler comments: *"The soote season* exploits the resources of language and associative imagery so intensively, to produce so rich a yield of condensed meaning, that it is unexpectedly hard to interpret. Contrary to what one supposed, discriminating sensitivity is needed to tune even the poet's signals, let alone their overtones."[21]

Surrey's Petrarchan model is specifically about death; Surrey adapted the only poem he took from Petrarch's sequence *In morte di madonna Laura, rime 110.* In Petrarch there is no anticipation of death or contemplation of suicide as a way out of a terrible human dilemma, as in the Dido topos. Rather, Petrarch's lover moves through a natural landscape without the living presence of the beloved. It is an almost ceremonial dream landscape, however, for which concreteness of object was not necessary but rather mythological transformations of nature. Surrey varies all this intention in his poem. His landscape is actual and concrete. For his purpose, to the Petrarchan model he weds two sources indigenous and native: the medieval lyric and Chaucer. Padelford correctly notes the result of Surrey's strategy: "Surrey's sonnet is as typically English with its green-clad hills and dales, its blossoming hedgerows and shady streams. It is the spring of Chaucer's Prologue and of such lyrics as *Sumer is icumen in.*"[22] Petrarch has been turned upside down.

Furthermore, although the sonnet has the two-fold Vergilian structure of its companion piece "Alas, so all thinges," its asymmetrical shape is more striking: twelve lines about Chaucerian and English landscape reversed by two about the isolated lost lover. This is a structure Surrey bequeathed to Shakespeare, who added his variations, as in sonnet 66 "Tired with all these." Even if the cataloguing in the twelve lines reflects devices of *petrarchismo,* its simplicity, enhanced by the direct appeals to nature, is almost revolutionary in English (or European) poetry at this time and unlike devices of the earlier Chaucerians or the cataloguing of Skelton.[23] The effect is probably due less to Surrey's observations of nature, which, given his sportsmanship, were likely extensive, and more to his humanist schooling and the classifying "place-logic" of Agricola that influenced all scholastic curricula in Surrey's time. In such concentrated patterns of classification a general heading could be set, only to exclude a particular (such as the concluding image of the isolated lover) for a logical or rhetorical purpose.

This exclusion means that in the first twelve lines Surrey follows a deliberately understated strategy. First, he adapts the Chaucerian diction and images to his own reduced scale of the new sonnet form, for which he appropriates the older medieval technique of a through-rhyme *a b a b a b a b a b a a .* He also uses in every line examples of alliteration, medial caesura, and accentual rhythms, all of which suggest a series of native subtexts in addition to Chaucer's.

He further concentrates his effect by using the figure of *asyndeton,* allowing few connectives once he has set his generalizing premise in the first two lines. This premise states that the sweet season that brings out the buds and blooms (Chaucerian doublet) has turned all the landscape (hill and vale—another doublet) to green. These deliberately archaizing techniques distance, reminding the reader of an imitative structure. The strategy is nostalgic from the start, and the nightingale, with its familiar classical sexual legend, and the actual dove singing its own story to its mate, foreshadow the effect of the closure of the sonnet where the Petrarchan lover is brought stage center. Ironically the theme of the Petrarchan original has been imitated but, with a Chaucerian frame, in a completely original way.

Given the Petrarchan closure, the *amplificatio,* which distinguishes the strategy of pairing in the first twelve lines, is also ironic. It is this pairing that the lover at the end lacks. The catalogue begins and ends with birds or flying insects: nightingale, dove; swallow, bee. At the center of the list two creatures of the same species, hart and buck, meld into two larger kinds, fish and serpent, all observed in vivid kinesthetic imagery. This list evokes a deliberate turn toward memory, for in the second of two pauses (the first at the beginning of the second quatrain simply and categorically generalizes that summer or spring is here), the voice at the end of the third quatrain remarks that winter, which destroyed flowers, is itself worn out, a reversal of emphasis. The reversal prepares us for the ironic reversal in the next lines of the closing couplet. In this closure steady rhymes change the previous easy alternation of sounds: "And thus I see among these pleasant thinges / Eche care decayes, and yet my sorow springes." The Petrarchan lover's flower, the lover's bud, does not spring, the final verb merely completing a whole system of implicit erotic images, especially echoed in the alternating odd-line rhyming verbs. These verbs themselves interweave a pattern with alternating rhyming -ale nouns (except the Chaucerian adjective "smale"). Only with the surprise of the couplet rhyme at the end does the alternation stop in a verb and pun that unites the whole structure of the lyric, "springes." Furthermore, as though to emphasize these verbs, word order in each verb line is inverted, with object before verb; the even lines have normal word order. Similarly the verbs in the six odd lines and in the couplet are in the present tense, and the first four of the even lines are in the past tense. What

all this careful handling of language accomplishes is to represent and render alive the landscape that the isolated lover watches with despairing irony.

It is these carefully rendered details that make the final stance possible. Their concentrated precision and the knowledge of natural and literary scenes they evince may be open to all kinds of emblematic possibilities, as Fowler suggests, but essentially they dramatize the central thematic core of the sonnet: the fleeting nature of time. Thus, the bee "minges" or remembers what she is to do; the swallow—the harbinger of time in Keats's "To Autumn" and Dylan Thomas's "Fern Hill"—begins its cycle of destruction; the fish either are fleet or float, in verbal ambiguity that simply highlights latent wordplay throughout the text; and finally the snake "slinges" her skin away in an action suggesting both the eternal cycle of time and human original sin. The syntactic key to this structure of loss is relationship, of part to whole and then part to part, leading to the ironic pun that ends the poem. This pun points both toward the season of love and erotic new growth and toward the lover's lack of relationship and alienation, his isolation from life.

If Lewis is right when he says that Surrey's "love poetry is best when it is least about love,"[24] this love sonnet may be such an example. The lyric does not mention love. Its theme is death; it includes the same ghostly wandering through a landscape as Petrarch's but with the music of mutability of the English native lyric.[25] The virtuoso nature of this sonnet lies in its Renaissance character, however: it is a concentrated objective ritualizing of a moment of recognition, in this case, of utter loss. "The soote season" is the last of Surrey's sonnet imitations of Petrarch; in a later poem, in Poulter's measure, he turns to another adaptation of Petrarch with something of the same intention of using that text to dramatize an experience of human mutability, another instance of the failure of love.

Sonnets: Social Occasions

"The fansy which that I have served long" (J10).   In this sonnet, probably written late, Surrey demonstrates another use of the sonnet form: to make a clearly public statement. In only one sonnet, his elegy on the death of Thomas Cromwell, "The piller pearisht is whearto I lent" (M173), did Wyatt use the new Italian

form for a public subject. Otherwise, it is Surrey who introduces this use of the sonnet form, which Milton and Wordsworth, among others, would make famous.[26] In fact, the topical sonnet responding to some event in court, society, or public life was a form Surrey used in the remaining nine sonnets we shall examine, both those in this chapter and those that are more properly called elegies. Surrey's topicality builds on the nature of the sonnet as epigram and, when the brief impression or social gesture is expanded into a carefully articulated fourteen-line structure, we have not only the first examples in English of the poetry of the social occasion, but also at least three of the very best examples of such poetry in English.

The public sonnet "The fansy which that I have served long" has a direct reference in line twelve to the time between September 1545 and March 1546 when Surrey was commander at Boulogne, living in his headquarters in the Lower Town where he was Lieutenant-General of the king's army on the Continent, Surrey's highest public honor. Except for this allusion, the whole sonnet is generally obscure. As in "Love that doth raine," Surrey's narrative uses medieval allegorical personifications. The voice in the poem has served a "fansy" long but always finding such service to be inimical to his "ease" and lately positively dangerous, he flees when this "fansy" bids him to "prease out" of some mysterious "throng." In the second quatrain, in taking an action of retreat that he thinks will please his "painfull hart," the narrating voice sees a figure of "faith more strong." At this point the octet ends, and the sestet shows the resolve of the narrator who speaks to himself directly, if obscurely: " 'Alas, those dayes / In vayn were spent, to runne the race so long.' " At that moment, "with that thought," the narrator meets a third figure, "my guyde," identified by most commentators as Reason, who leads him, as Vergil does Dante, from wrong wandering to his present paradoxical situation, the dilemma with which the poem closes in its triple rhyme: "Brought me amiddes the hylles in base Bullayn; / Where I am now, as restlesse to remayn, / Against my will, full pleased with my payn." The rhyme scheme here is completely original, *a b a b a b a b a c a c c c*, another variation on medieval through-rhyme.

More general interpretation is not easy for such an incompletely structured poem. The sonnet appears hastily written, as though a combination of a verse-letter justifying a position and an epigram the poet felt he needed to write in order to focus his mind. There

is also basic ambiguity in the subject matter itself. The key, if one can be found, lies in the operative term "fansy." It is likely that Surrey is simply alluding to his own political situation at court and to an image of himself that, as a good courtier, he had to reshape.

"Th'Assyryans king, in peas with fowle desyre" (J32).   The sonnet "Th'Assyryans king" lacks any topicality or obscurity on the surface. It appears the straightforward emblem of the Eastern king Sardanapalus, whose unknightly behavior betrayed the highest ideals of honor, an *exemplum* of the degenerate prince used by Gower and Lydgate. Its antithetical structure produces, however, a sustained invective and reduces syntactical units, especially phrases, into violent juxtaposition. The emotional pitch of this structure has led readers to attempt biographical solutions for the object of such rage and dispraise, an obvious answer being Henry VIII. Thus in this poem topicality rises from obscurity, as in the previous sonnet obscurity arose from clear topicality. Both methods remain conjectural, however, and like all such biographical readings of topical allusions, they are never very good unless they embody clear signs from the text itself.

The structural success of "Th'Assyryans king" has led readers to wish to expand the context of the poem, even to invent their own legends about it. Surrey's initial figure of *antonomasia* encourages this sense of cryptic identity. This violent satire on the court of an ancient king (although Eastern, still associated no doubt in Surrey's audience with ancient Roman decadence) is almost too powerful for a literary text and therefore invites readers to conjecture beyond the text. Why Surrey chose, for his only sonnet of utter dispraise, the figure of Sardanapalus may be simpler than biography, however, and another matter of intertextuality. Precedents include not only medieval subtexts in English but also Juvenal's Latin texts whose strategy also distanced Juvenal from the court of his time, setting his satire in the past.

What is not conjecture about the text of Surrey's poem as we have it is its basic dichotomy: the roles of war and peace in a drama of the disintegrating self. Through logic (the topic of comparison and contrast under *inventio*) the event buried in time—the legend of Sardanapalus—becomes quite alive, and the moral stance of repulsion with resultant verbal invective arises from the logical definition of the present text in its response to the past. Whatever Surrey's original emotion may or may not have been, the poem

renders its own interpretation of the mythic event of the Assyrian king.

The sonnet is thus another virtuoso performance in rhetorical strategy because of this careful focusing of intrinsic dichotomy. Surrey's own invented English rhyme scheme *a b a b c d c d e f e f g g* is especially right for the alternation of his antitheses in this sonnet. The ironic reversal of the final couplet, its epigrammatic twist to the previous catalogue of phases in the self's degeneration, turns the suicide, the overt act that completes the death that has been looming all through the sonnet, into Sardanapalus's one manly act. Through irony this act fulfills both sides of the dialectic. On the one hand, it finishes the inner process of self-indulgence and self-consumption; on the other, it preserves the ideal of the knight's honor. Surrey has carefully prepared for the final effect from his sestet on. In the sestet he begins with his one reference back to the opening figure; with that relative pronoun we can generalize once more on this figure "who scace the name of manhode dyd retayne." With vivid trochees Surrey begins his next two lines (ll. 10–11) of description. The king is "Drenched in slouthe and womanishe delight" and "Feble of sprete, unpacyent of payne." This latter vice, its phrasing couched in Stoic terms, is the last of the insults paid to this degenerate knight.

It is natural therefore that, in the final line of the last quatrain, this king should lose "his honor and hys right." What is also logically and socially appropriate in these terrible times, which the king with his power has created, "Prowde tyme of welthe, in stormes appawld with drede" (1. 13), is that he should kill himself, the action of the last line of the sonnet. What is surprising is the other logic of the structure: that in death, in the boldness of self-destruction, he would gain the name of action, in this case, the name of manhood. Grammatically in this final line Surrey relates back to the initial "Who" of the sestet as subject for a second past-tense verb (the first in line nine): "Murdred hym selfe to shew some manfull dede." The initial trochee and the alliteration in this fourteenth line of the sonnet echo the earlier ninth line and focus on this final act of manhood, already prepared for in the octet by negative implication, through the figures of *chiasmus* and *zeugma*.

Because the sestet completes this picture by showing the false nobility of this king, the chiasmatic construction of the final couplet supports the dichotomy now brought to the end. In the thirteenth

line, a noun ("tyme") modified by two adjectives, each completed in prepositional phrases, is chiasmatically balanced, and in the last line, the infinitive acts as medial balance for the units, working backward, of "hym selfe" and "Murdred," on the one hand, and "manfull" and "dede," on the other. This final picture in the closure—graphically and precisely rendered by Surrey's language—represents options for a Renaissance courtier. At least for Surrey's world the language offers a definition of possibilities, as the courtier seeks a role in this world of power, seeks the name of action, as Hamlet calls it, for himself and others.

"From Tuscan cam my ladies worthi race" (J9).   In this sonnet and the next, "The golden gift," Surrey represents a fiction based on the fact of his relationship to the Lady Elizabeth Fitzgerald at the court of Henry VIII in the early 1540s. Along with his elegiac sonnets, these lyrics demonstrate the highest point to which Surrey will take his sonnet form. Using the new rhyme scheme he developed for the English sonnet, *a b a b c d c d e f e f g g,* a form suited to fluctuating conversational idiom and polite verse mode, and translating the courtly love motifs from Petrarch, these poems demonstrate completely new achievements in English poetry. In these sonnets Surrey dramatizes the idealization of a young woman, neither with the metaphysical raptures of Petrarch nor with the bitter astringency of Wyatt but simply in terms of social occasion. The drama takes place within the place and history of the young woman herself, her narrative dramatized by the textures of the life of the court and its human society.

Once more, it is humanist training that gave Surrey directions for the making of his poetic structure. The first of these sonnets, directly naming the Lady Elizabeth as Geraldine, follows, according to Douglas L. Peterson, "rhetorical instructions to the letter."[27] Specifically, Surrey is following here the rhetorical and oratorical tradition of Aphthonian "places" including the facts of lineage and of upbringing and education. Based upon certain facts, the fiction is so arranged and structured as to provide a perspective in these poems totally Surrey's own. Their effect is not derived from just topicality or fiction but from the structure of text and various subtexts. This kind of intertextual reading was impossible, however, for Surrey's audiences through the centuries deeply moved by the powerful aesthetic structure of these poems to Geraldine. Such readers in the sixteenth century had to have actual social occasion trans-

formed into greater fiction, preferably that which would conform to their fantasies, and so in the early 1590s shortly after the death of the real Elizabeth Fitzgerald, the Earl of Surrey became the hero of a romance based on the reading of this sonnet and little else. Fiction begat fiction that through revisionism entered history as actual fact. The legend of Surrey and his Geraldine, the new English Petrarch and his Laura, was amplified for three centuries, barely dying out in the late nineteenth century.[28]

Ironically the real facts of the story are far more interesting than the fiction. As Hughey has concluded,[29] the sonnet was likely written in 1541 during Surrey's visit to Windsor in May for the Feast of the Garter—hence his allusion to Windsor in line 12 of the sonnet—right after the highest occasion of his life as a courtier, his election as a Knight of the Garter on the preceding Saint George's day, 23 April, during the reign of his cousin Catherine as queen. The Lady Elizabeth was thirteen or fourteen (not younger as some modern debunking critics have asserted), a perfectly proper age not only for attracting a young courtier like Surrey but, more important for the intentions of Surrey in his text, for offers of marriage. Surrey's sonnet builds on this actual social status, the place of the Lady Elizabeth at this time in the English court. She was in reality a refugee, her father condemned and beheaded as an Irish traitor and her mother allowed at court only because she was a near cousin of Henry himself. As poor relatives, their position at court was tenuous; above all, the Lady Elizabeth had to find an economically advantageous marriage.

It was against this background, then, that Surrey began to construct the fiction of his sonnet, assuming, as he had in "When ragyng love," the convenience and the clichés of the Petrarchan admirer in order to give a frame for his real intention in the sonnet. It is probable that this real purpose, if we judge by the text of the sonnet itself, is to respond to the Lady Elizabeth's social situation by making the lyric itself a social event: an advertisement at court for the eligibility of the young Irish refugee. In order to accomplish this end, Surrey had to elaborate a fiction that would play up his role as Petrarchan lover and play down her family's recent bloody history. This muting and underlining of roles demanded a skillful strategy, which meant among other things reducing the Aphthonian "places" of praise to the size and concentration of the sonnet. The rhetorical "places" gave Surrey, in fact, the means by which to

distance these bloody facts of the recent past and build a romantic history not only for her traitorous family but for himself as isolated melancholy lover.

Thus the sonnet begins with that most romantic of all facts, the medieval (and questionable) origins of the Fitzgerald family in Italy and Florence. The periphrastic constructions are so delicate that the notorious Ireland is not even named in the beginning except only as a "westorne ile" that faces "Wylde Chambares cliffes," a Latinizing phrase that portrays Wales, and not Ireland, as wild. In this whole first quatrain the young girl is not mentioned, only her family (the "her" in lines two and four are archaic forms of "their"), and they too are not named. In the second quatrain, when Ireland is named, it is as unessential fact: she was "Fostred," as were all children of the upper classes at this time, by an Irish nurse. Then Surrey quickly reminds his audience that her real sire was nothing less than an earl and her dame-mother of royal blood. Furthermore the Lady Elizabeth had early come to "Britaine" where she stayed in the residence of a princess and either took the English Holy Communion or was educated in Britain (the phrasing is ambiguous). Britain as a term for England, as the OED shows, was new and already by Surrey's time had become part of the new English nationalism. Thus this new chauvinistic and propagandistic term, with its call to the future, serves the same purpose as the vaguely ceremonial diction such as "worthi" and "auncient seate," reminiscent of fifteenth-century aureate terms, and the archaic usages like "sire" and "dame." These terms and diction thus ironically distance a present object at the same moment the language lets us see it. These names of places, part of the epideictic strategy, quickly become a device to set the figure of the young girl in her true place in society. The names both distance her from, and pull her into, the present and even future of that society of which the court is the center and where the young woman must find a husband. The ending of the octave has led Surrey's audience, therefore, to a superb integration of origin and lineage and education. In short, it has demonstrated in a public forum Geraldine's nature as a gifted human being.

With the sestet (marked here, even though the rhyme scheme is not Petrarchan) the speaker himself enters the poem. He gives his praise, its highest form being the playful Neoplatonic charade that her beauty automatically taught him love. Their first moment of meeting, the holy moment in Petrarch and Dante when the eyes of

the lover and the beloved seek each other's, is given an almost parodic lightness here. The emphasis is really on the place, as the initial trochee suggests, and on the narrative he is telling of which they are a part. Even the speaker's description of the young woman is generalized, "Bryght ys her hew," echoing the "lyvely heate" of the family. When her name is finally given, it is simply a rather formal way of stating not the infamous name of Kildare but the child of Gerald, "Geraldine." Only in the eleventh line does the speaker dramatize his mask of unhappy Petrarchan lover by telling of his attraction to the girl when they met at Hampton, but immediately he narrates how at Windsor he just did not get to see her enough.

Nowhere is there any bold statement of love. Surrey's objective structure in the sonnet has been so controlled that muted love complaint is given its place and nothing more. The progression of his argument can move on to its epigrammatic and summarizing conclusion, building from *hyperbole* to the wry *litotes* of the last line of the text, a statement clearly designed for public consumption: "Happy ys he that may obtaine her love."

"The golden gift that Nature did thee geve" (J8). The only proof we have that this sonnet is addressed to Surrey's Geraldine, the Lady Elizabeth, is textual. In the second July 1557 edition of *Tottel's Miscellany,* the beginning of the octet is not the standard reading "Now certesse, Ladie" but "Now certesse Garret," the latter word a common corruption of Gerald and a spelling used in the records of the Earl of Kildare's family and even by the aged Lady Elizabeth herself when she designates her own sister as "Garret" in her final will.[30] No mere textual crux directs us to this identity of Geraldine or the Lady Elizabeth, however, but the language of the text and its structure. With philosophical and, what has been little noticed, theological subtexts, the lyric gently mocks with parody and even double meanings. Its tone is kept in balance by a firm syllogistic argument set up in two declarative and one imperative sentences. Within the grammatical frame of the syllogism, the poem has an octave with major and minor premises and a sestet with a conclusion extended into the coda of a couplet that, in fact, explains the intention of the sonnet.

If restated to show the structure of this syllogism, the argument of the sonnet might read: (1) *if* the "golden gift" of Nature to the young girl—that is, of making friends easily and bringing them

delight, whenever she wants, by means of her sheer beauty and her attention—has taught the speaker that she was made to show Nature's greatest skill," herself (first quatrain); *and* (2) since such beauty will be known by the other graces that will necessarily follow it (second quatrain); *then* (3) in conclusion, "Now certesse, Ladie," do not "deface" these "elect" gifts "wyth fansies newe" nor allow "chaunge of mindes" to "infect" her "minde" (third quatrain). In fact, she should "mercy" her friend who serves her and who is himself always trying to preserve her honor (the couplet). The echo of the sexual pun here, like the amatory diction throughout, dramatizes, as in the previous poem about Geraldine, Surrey's deliberate pose as Petrarchan lover. Like the very different Calvinist theological diction of "elect" and "infect," such language sets up a tone whose resonances weave in and out of the continuous argument of the poem. These resonances keep both their total meaning and the logical structure in ironic balance.

The point of such balance is the social moment, the occasion of friendship between the two young people. It is in the talk itself, turned so carefully and formally that Surrey seems to have learned his greatest lesson from Chaucer, how to take simple words, without any mythological adornment, and control them through a complex syntax, without loss of coherence or direction. Only Surrey's insistent musical form, however conversational it may appear, acts as a tiny metronome, an accent just enough inside the ear of the reader to remind him or her that this conversation, like one whispered in an ear during a dance (like Romeo's to Juliet at their first meeting), is after all a carefully crafted lyric. In fact, like Romeo's at that first moment, it too is a sonnet.

Chapter Four
The Songs

In twentieth-century debunking of courtly love, most readers have forgotten what Shakespeare shows us through superb shorthand when he depicts the first meeting of Romeo and Juliet: the very long tradition of courtly love with its motifs and songs. This tradition shaped the social fabric of Europe at the end of the Middle Ages and the early Renaissance. As Johannes Huizinga notes about French court life (where Surrey and his grandfather Howard spent crucial years of their youth): "In no other epoch did the ideal of civilization amalgamate to such a degree with that of love."[1] Courtly love embraced all the activities of the noble life, and even if one were not a lover, it was necessary, at least in mixed company, to play that role. Most of Surrey's songs reflect such role playing, from simple lyric forms to oratorical verse letters; even where his songs are translation or fulminating satire, they generally build on lyric song forms. Although clearly at the end of the chivalric world that produced the phenomenon of courtly love, Surrey nevertheless gave new vitality to this type of lyric. As we saw from the courtly love motifs in his sonnet "Love that doth raine," the influence was as ubiquitous in his work as the figure of Troilus, with whom courtly love motifs were often associated. In fact, the very first poem in *Tottel* in 1557 is an elaborate song, and one can argue that Surrey's basic lyric paradigm is that of the song, a text designed actually to be performed. When we remember all the musical activity at the court of Henry VIII and the intimate circle of Howards and their friends who treasured such collections as witnessed in the Devonshire manuscript, we can understand the place of songs, and not just those with love motifs, in Surrey's Tudor world and courtly aristocratic audience. In fact, many of them like "When ragying love" call for the kind of performance which Lewis describes in a comment on a ballad of Wyatt's: "It has little meaning until it is sung in a room with many ladies present. . . . We are having a little music after supper."[2]

Songs as Love Motifs

"Geve place, ye lovers, here before" (J12).   Surrey's text here builds on the *frottola* song form and fits just such a social occasion as Lewis describes. Possibly about Surrey's own wife, if the allusion to Penelope (l. 8) can be read as such, the poem has an iambic tetrameter rhythm stressing each syllable in a manner typical of the new Renaissance music from Italy. That is, it was melismatic, but it accented syllables[3] and appeared to call for some instrumental accompaniment like that of a lute or spinet. With two alternating rhymes and a couplet, the poem is a formal mate to "When ragyng love." In this form the voice boldly addresses rival lovers. He argues the excellence of his beloved through ingenious logical and rhetorical patterns that finally become a commentary on the nature of love poetry.

With his usual dexterity of grammar and syntax, Surrey sets up separate sentences for each stanza in this song. They mark, like musical pauses, the stages in the speaking lover's thesis that the rival lovers must give place to his beloved as the most beautiful. The dramatic situation of a direct challenge to rivals echoes many chivalric codes; it is one of many adaptations of the codes of chivalry into the love lyric Surrey inherited. Yet what transforms Surrey's dramatic situation and its grammar of expression into objective aesthetic structure designed for an audience is its progressive argument cast in the form of a classical oration.[4]

The *exordium* gives the bold entrance of the challenge, and lines 3–6 announce the *propositio* with its double analogy, the consequence of which is the heightened figure of *hyperbole* that carries its tenor into the remaining four stanzas. Thus, in the first stanza, Surrey concentrates into the dimensions of his song the first stage of his oratorical argument:

> Geve place, ye lovers, here before
> That spent your bostes and bragges in vain:
> My ladies beawtie passeth more
> The best of yours, I dare well sayen,
> Than doth the sonne the candle light
> Or brightest day the darkest night.

In "Of Ornament" in his *Arte of English Poesie,* Puttenham uses this stanza as an example of "Hiperbole."[5] In the second stanza the

narratio begins with an elaboration of the beloved as truthful as Penelope herself; what she says is like true writing "sealed." She has more virtues, in fact, than his own writing has skill to show. Indeed in the third stanza the lover "coulde rehearse," if he just would, how Nature herself complains. Here Surrey artfully reverts to the figure of *occupatio,* in which an orator or poet emphasizes something although appearing to pass over it. Not only does the lover not pass over this ancient topos of the medieval *planctus naturae* but he skillfully turns the complaint into the centerpiece of his *narratio* and the climax of his hyperbolic structuring of the topic of praise. Surrey accomplishes this turn by transforming the complaint into an allegorical narrative, a favorite Surrey device and the "simplest medieval structural formula."[6] Thus in this stanza and in the fourth, as support for his case, the lover relates how Nature lamented, "with wringing handes," that she lost her perfect mold with the creation of his beloved and swore "with ragyng mind" that no loss ever went "so nere her hart" because she could not make the like again.

After the rapid movement of the narrative, the final stanza of the song recapitulates in its six lines the *confirmatio* of the oration (the premise being that Nature herself "gave her the prayse / To be the chiefest worke she wrought"); the *refutatio* (there must therefore be "better waies" for rival lovers to make comparisons); and the *peroratio* (the epigrammatic couplet uses its proverb not only to show the superiority of the beloved but the inferiority of the language of the rival lovers: "Then to compare, as ye have done, / To matche the candle with the sonne"). This final act of the logical and oratorical structure completes Surrey's ironic distancing of his own topos of praise. In effect, the couplet makes the praise more objective by dealing with the very nature of the means of rendering any praise in song, the language of metaphor itself. The metaphors of the rival poets are poor, says the speaker, and by implication, his, in the very poem unfolding, are not. The proof that has led to this final assertion is not only the text of the poem itself, but the narrative of the lover and his language, which has been unfolding since his own double analogy in the first stanza. In the second and third stanzas the lover points out the limitation and at the same time the possibilities of his handling of language ("Than I with pen have skill to show"; "I coulde rehearse, if that I wolde"), climaxing his narrative with the narrative of Nature's complaint. Only he knows

how to interpret Nature: "And what she said, I know it, I." He
even begins the very next stanza, the penultimate, with the bold
"I know." The "better waies" of the last stanza thus have a model
for the true language of praise and love. This is a rhetorical strategy
by which the very language of the poem is made a context for the
speaker's topos of praise.

"Syns fortunes wrath envieth the welth" (J20).   This song is
Surrey's only other *frottola* in iambic tetrameter stanzas of six lines
each, but with only four stanzas this time. Tottel's title catches the
essential stance of this dramatic monologue with its clear address:
"The constant louer lamenteth."[7] Conceived obviously in the clichés
of *petrarchismo*, the song states its initial situation in those terms in
the first stanza. Fortune (with all its medieval overtones) has taken
away the sight of the beloved whom the lover saw "by stelth," a
vision that "fed" him the usual Petrarchan contraries of sweet and
sour, dread and delight. But, sings the lover in the two main clauses
of the stanza: "Let not my griefe move you to mone, / For I will
wepe and wayle alone." The progression of the poem follows from
this thesis: the lonely Troilus-lover moves through a series of harsh
natural landscapes but, in spite of nature, he is utterly faithful to
his beloved. The first of these landscapes in the second stanza, praised
by critics for its precise descriptive detail, may be Scotland where
Surrey went in 1542 on a military expedition, and the second landscape in the third stanza, the Provence visited in July 1533 with
Francis I. In such vivid and exact observation of nature as contrasted
to the lover, even the Petrarchan clichés of hot and cold take on
new life so that the figure of *hyperbole,* matching the lover's energy
of constancy with that of nature itself, seems only part of an unfolding *amplificatio* used to prove the lover's fidelity. This latter
declaration comes out of the third landscape in the last stanza of
the song, reduced to a vivid *periphrasis* "the waves of the salt floode"
that cannot quench the love her beauty set on fire. In language as
impossible to scan as Donne's, his final couplet allows only the
sincere idiom of the lover's plaintive declaration of fidelity: "Such
as I was such will I be, / Youre owne: what would ye more of me?"

"Yf he that erst the fourme so livelye drewe" (J14).   The song
is a witty epigram in the form of a *strambotto,* one of two Surrey
wrote. It reveals Surrey at his most playful. It also demonstrates
the sexual maneuvering implicit in any declaration of love and
constancy, and although Surrey may have known lines about Apelles

from Skelton's "Crown of Laurel" (a poem likely about Surrey's own mother), the real subtexts are continental.[8] In the brevity of the single stanza of *ottava rima (a b a b a b c c),* where witty logic must speed along, Surrey's initial teasing figure of *antonomasia* for Apelles, the famous classical painter of Venus, builds, through careful alliteration, to the father in the fourth line "By whose pencell a goddesse made thow arte!" At this midbreak in the structure the singing lover turns to the imagery of fire that has come from the figure of a new goddess and "surprysed manye a hart." Surrey has prepared for the witty thrust and unexpected point of the ending couplet, where the male's sexual performance is evoked: "There lackt yet that should cure their hoot desyer: / Thow canst enflame and quenche the kyndled fyre." This lyric is the only secular poem of Surrey's that Tottel did not publish from the manuscripts he had at hand, possibly because he considered it prurient.

   "O lothsome place, where I" (J19).   Retrospective is a major device of Surrey's poetic art. This song offers a good example, in a minor mode, of Surrey's technique of distancing a situation or event through inventing a retrospective of time or place. In such technique, a conventional lover's complaint becomes dramatic with a voice trying to resolve or understand his dilemma, his present conflict with a person (or persons) or with his own feelings. At the same time, at its best, as in this song, this complaint becomes universal in its definitions. In this text the conflict leads to the moment of resolution or moral stance that ends the lyric.

   To develop this retrospective, "O lothsome place" uses the figure of *apostrophe* formalized with a speaker or singer and, as in a dramatic monologue, an addressee: in this case, a place, not a person. The model for such address to a place is found in a scene from *Troilus and Criseyde.* When Troilus enters the palace of his lost Criseyde and gazes at the places that marked their acts of love, he begins his lament : "O! paleys desolat" (bk. 5,ll. 540 ff.). For Surrey, in the first of the five eight-line trimeter stanzas rhyming *a b a b c d c d,* the loathesome place, never named, is immediately seen in a retrospective of time. The beloved was once in this place, where her eyes sent such "grace" into his heart, but now he has been taken away by fortune envious of this "grace." Here, as in the whole lyric, the exigencies of Surrey's trimeter lines and his more than usual imitation of classical inversion, while tightening the music, blur the connections of syntax.

As one might expect, Surrey introduces into his lyric of nostalgia the narrative frame suited to the retrospective. Thus in the second stanza the lover tells how fortune furthered his desire only to throw "all ammiddes the myre" and what he has merited "with true and faithful hart" is given into the hands of a lover "that never felt the smart." This echo of the Troilus story is not developed, however, for the mode in the third stanza is Horatian and Roman, even alluding to Wyatt's translation of Plutarch:

> But happy is that man
> That scaped hath the griefe
> That love well teache him can,
> By wanting his reliefe.
> A scourge to quiet mindes
> It is, who taketh hede,
> A comon plage that bindes,
> A travell without mede.

In fact, sings the lover in the fourth stanza, this "gift" is such that whoever enjoys it will then have "A thousand troubles grow" and that "last it may not long" is "The truest thing of all, / And sure the greatest wrong / That is within this thrall." Surrey here returns to the plaintive theme of mutability in the medieval lyric. Thus, in the last stanza, the lover argues that "sins thou, desert place," cannot bring back "my desired grace," he has learned in this desolate place that he is not the first that love lifted, only to throw down again (the latter epigram a motto Donne and Herbert would transform for their own uses).

"Though I regarded not" (P17). There are five short love poems that may best be understood as songs. "Though I regarded not" is another lyric of constancy with the same iambic trimeter lines as "O lothsome place" and the same eight line stanza form *a b a b c d c d*. This speaker begins with a direct admission of unfaithfulness and then, in a bird metaphor, shifts to an immediate assurance that he knows too well his real situation.

> Though I regarded not
> The promise made to me,
> Or passed not to spot
> My faith and honeste,
> Yet were my fancie strange

> And wilfull will to wite,
> If I sought now to change
> A falkon for a kite.

The next three stanzas vary the metaphor for this admission and awareness, but still use metaphor as a logical base for a variation that marks the progressing argument: a pea for a pearl; an owl for a sparrow hawk; a ship into too shallow a port for a "hauen sure"; hunting a fox ("the ganders fo") for a deer. All these rather homely metaphors climax in the direct assurance at the end of the fourth stanza and the beginning of the fifth: "No, no! I haue no minde / To make exchanges so, / Nor yet to change at all / . . . Or new change to begin." Having stated his premises and given his illustrations, the lover takes his argument further by examining the very basis of his initial assertion (illustrated by the running metaphors): "How may all this be so?" The last stanza answers the implicit question in the addressee's mind by using the Petrarchan cliché of fire and showing from Scholastic logic and science that its "kind" does not allow it to freeze. Thus the central premise behind his assertion of faith appears: "Nor true loue cannot lese / The constance of the minde." In fact, ends the song, when fire lacks heat "to blaze and burn," only then will the lover "in such desire / Haue once a thought to turne."

"**Although I had a check**" (P12).   This love lyric is a second iambic trimeter poem, this time in four stanzas of *a b a b c d c d*. Its central metaphor is modeled on a chess game like that in Chaucer's *Book of the Duchesse* (ll.617–86) but the lover here is aggressive, starting out with a check in the love relationship and knowing "To geue the mate is hard" in his circumstances. He is fully insulted that the unknown person addressed in the song has given such a "great assay / Vnto a man of warre." The subject possibly alludes to Surrey's social encounter with the Countess of Hertford, the subject of a bitter satire in Poulter's measure. He will get her "ferse," Chaucer's word for queen, and if he wins her person in the field, it will be too late to yield herself; then the lover, "As captain full of might," will devour all those who have shown him spite, especially her who gave him check in such a degree. She had better defend herself if she can. The lover's final words are a full sexual warning: "Stand stiffe in thine estate; / For sure I will assay, / If I can giue the mate."

"As oft as I behold and see" (P14). In iambic tetrameter
stanzas of four lines rhyming *a b a b,* this poem and the next are
modeled on the musical *frottola* and show the formal influence of
Wyatt more obviously than almost any other Surrey poem. Despite
their logical bases, both beginning with an appropriate generalization (not found in the Wyatt originals they imitate), these poems
appear as blueprints of Petrarchan clichés and not as finished structures. The only apparent structure is a generalized logical premise
running through a kaleidoscope of uncoordinated images, resembling at best a humanist exercise from subtexts. Thus in a marvelously controlled first stanza the main clause and its paradox set the
mode of the poem ("the fressher" is the lover's wound, the "ner"
his "comfort" and "soveraigne bewtie"). In the next stanza Surrey
reverses himself with images of fire quenching flames and rain con-
suming "roounyng streames," saying her sight does appease the pain
of the wound. Like the flea in the fire, an image containing the
paradoxes of both the first two stanzas, his desire in third stanza
grows by its grief. Then setting up a little narrative, as in his Wyatt
subtext, the speaker shows how crystal tears lead to beams with "so
sweete a venvme" to which he adds, with associative imagery, such
venom holds a "crewell bytt" and "spoore" to run a race against his
inclination. Actually, continues the lover, "wilful will did prick
me forth" and blind Cupid whipped and guided him so that his
heart bounced against his "brest full bitterly" as "cruell waues"
against rocks. When he falls in the penultimate stanza, seeing "my
none decaye," he forgets like someone with "flame in his brest" to
take away the cause of "his vnrest." The last stanza is almost identical
to Wyatt's "Lyke as the wynde" (M245) but less coherent: as the
spider draws her line so "with labour lost" he has framed his suit
and the fault is hers: "Of yll sown seed such ys the frewte."

   "When youthe had ledd me half the race" (P15). As the title
of this companion *frottola* suggests, its tone is retrospective. Again
it is a place that generalizes this narrative of how "Cupides scourge"
made the lover follow this chase. The frame is undeveloped, however, in this history of too obvious desire. With greedy eyes, sighs
of "boyling smoke" that betray "fervent rage of hidden flame," "salt
teares" leading to fruit and bloom, cheeks from "dedlye pale to
flaming redd," this Petrarchan lover moves to the resolution that
he will hide his love in his breast. Despite the meretricious and
apprentice nature of these two *frottole,* they do show the groundwork

from which Surrey's best lyrics emerge. The fact that "When youthe" had a popular Renaissance musical setting[9] proves the success of such a presumably early song experiment.

"I that Vlysses yeres haue spent" (P20).　Retrospective is also the frame of this playful and less chaotic lyric. William Ringler has noted that the stanza form of this poem, six lines of iambic tetrameter alternating with iambic trimeter in *a b a c b c,* is one of four in Surrey that appear nowhere else in early Tudor poetry.[10] The alternation suits the fluency of the argument that progresses from disillusionment to constancy: "Such anker hold I haue." In the narrative that moves the progression to the final resolution, the lover learns that his Penelope whom he had spent Ulysses' years to seek has turned out to be a "Cressed." Those years spent as Ulysses involved for him, says the lover in a kind of mock-heroic, "seas and stormy skies / Of wanton will and raging youth," tossing him like the Greek epic hero "From Cillas seas to Carribes clives / Vpon the drowning shore." What he thought was a harbor was a "death," much like the mouse treading the trap (in another mock-heroic image) who "bites the bread that stops her breath." Now "repentance" has brought the lover back and where he first sank, he now swims. He now has, like the hero of the classical epic, the stream and wind and "lucke as good, if it may last, / As any man may finde." The song has ended, if less completely than in other Surrey lyrics, in a familiar moral stance: the "stedy stone" and "anker" of his resolved fidelity after the pain of the past. The device of a classical allusion to develop the familiar Petrarchan conceit was as atypical of Wyatt as was Surrey's conclusion of fidelity. As Berdan has remarked, the ease with which the allusion is used, the lack of distinction between the stories of Troilus and Ulysses, is a medieval characteristic, and "such stanzas as these might well have been written in the fifteenth century before the introduction of Greek."[11]

The Ulysses poem is one of several with nautical motifs in Surrey, and the sole manuscript source for this poem is a miscellany now in the British Museum (Harleian MS 78, first part), which belonged to Charles Blount, fifth Lord Mountjoy, and which contains the more famous nautical song "O happy dames." Lord Mountjoy, to whom Erasmus dedicated an edition of his *Adagia* and of his *Livy,* was a humanist whose house Ascham called "the home of the Muses"[12]; he fought in the vanguard of the English army Surrey led against France in 1544. The manuscript probably dates from April

1544, just before Blount and Surrey left for France, a date that gives a special context to all the poems in this manuscript.

Songs as Translations

"Of thy lyfe, Thomas, this compasse well mark" (J39). Among these poems in the Blount manuscript is a lyric of twenty lines likely written to Surrey's elder son Thomas, born in 1536. More reflective than Surrey's lighter *frottole*, this lyric is structured on a series of commonplaces, the advice-book frame that reached its zenith in *Il cortegiano*, the greatest of all such Renaissance texts and a text we know Surrey read. Perhaps it was the opening nautical imagery of Horace's famous admonitory tenth ode, with its theme of the golden mean, that prompted Surrey to turn to it as a model for his verse letter to his eight-year-old son:

> Of thy lyfe, Thomas, this compasse well mark:
> Not aye with full sayles the hye seas to beat,
> Ne by coward dred, in shonning stormes dark,
> On shalow shores thy keel in perill freat.
> Who so gladly halseth the golden meane
> Voyde of dangers advisdly hath his home: . . .

Surrey's reductive structure in his translation, with its phrasal units and erratic use of the caesura, indicates that he is probably thinking of a song model, although he generally does not succeed in translating Horace's lighter sapphics into his five quatrains of iambic pentameter that rhyme *a b a b*. In fact, only in the two places where Surrey uses enjambment, both in lines alluding to Apollo (a climactic passage in the Horatian subtext), does the verse settle into the controlled ten-syllable line Surrey was to demonstrate in the *Aeneid*. Classical inversion of syntax works against Surrey here, so much that, with the exception of the Apollo passage, the last five lines of the poem are difficult to understand without the original Latin subtext. Only in the one clear classical allusion and the violent descriptions of nature does Surrey seem to find his own mean.

"Marshall, the thinges for to attayne" (J40).   Like the former poem to his son, Surrey's brief translation of the Roman poet Martial has as its central theme Martial's phrase "mens quieta" (the quiet mind) from his epigram on the golden mean (10.47), the subtext that Surrey translates. Stoic in origin, the theme expresses the safer

realism for the Tudor courtier of the creaturely life as opposed to mental speculations and enthusiasms of the will—a favorite idea of Wyatt's. Thus this poem, like the previous lyric, begins with a directive for a good life. Here also there is little literary fiction; the structure is virtually a series of phrases, whose close translation of the Latin reveals Surrey's own control of Latinate iterative structure. Elaborating the thirteen lines of Martial into sixteen lines rhyming *a b a b* of iambic tetrameter quatrains,[13] Surrey accomplishes a bravura performance of brevity by a powerful use of medial caesura (typically after the fourth syllable). This use preserves Martial's own subtle manipulation of the figure of *asyndeton.* Furthermore, Surrey also translates as his own Martial's figures of *chiasmus,* (ll. 2, 3, 7, 8,); of *periphrasis* (ll. 8, 11, 12); of *litotes* (l. 7); and of *anaphora* and *alliteration* throughout. All of these devices work to keep Surrey's disjunction of *asyndeton* from breaking the idiomatic progression of the poem in English, as it does in the original Latin. Surrey combines all these devices to make not only the English phrase more flowing but to adapt its conception for an English audience, as in line 13, with its chiastic adjectival formula learned from the Italians (which Milton was to use so often) but Chaucerian in theme: "The chast wife wyse, without debate." The result of such antithetical handling of phrase in a unified structure is the gesture of the moral stance at the end. "Contented," the person addressed should neither wish nor fear death.

In this lyric, as in most Surrey's poems, a particular person is addressed, although here the identity is not clear.[14] Significantly, with the name "my friends" Surrey's translation appears as a song in a keyboard version in *The Mulliner Book,* one of the best known and earliest collection-manuscripts of music from the Tudor period, dated 1547–70, and containing 120 compositions for the organ and virginals.[15]

Songs as Verse-Letters

"O happy dames" (J23).   This poem was also a popular song in Tudor musical collections.[16] The language of this *frottola* lends itself to musical iteration because it renders so theatrically the tones and emotional shifts of a single voice under psychological stress. Surrey's lady speaking (or singing) this lyric has a lightness and poise that ironically define a terrible moment. The fluency of her

voice has, however, a bittersweet elegaic note that must have lent itself to a popular musical transcription just suited for the kind of musical evenings familiar in early Tudor courtly circles. The voice of the woman in the song, so different from those in Italian or Ovidian subtexts, follows the variations of Surrey's most intricate rhyme scheme *a b a b c c c*. The first four lines alternate iambic tetrameter and trimeter, forming a ballad stanza, and the last three solid rhymes are a final unit with two lines of tetrameter and a last of pentameter that anticipates, as a method of closure, Spenser's alexandrine. Although these seven lines are obviously Surrey's adaptation of *Troilus*'s rhyme royal, the whole prosodic effect is startlingly original. In fact, the six stanzas with the invented line of vocal flexibility combine to make one of the most remarkable love lyrics in English.

Of all his underestimated achievements, Surrey's special narrative invention in this poem is perhaps the most neglected. The dramatic unity that gives this song the cohesion that doubtless made it so popular arises from the unity of voice in the lover's complaint. It is, remarkably, the voice of a woman. Likely written by Surrey while he was at the warfront in France in 1544 and 1545, as English general protecting the fortress of Boulogne, the poem is a verse-letter in reverse. The epistolary form had been very popular at the French court during Surrey's sojourn there, both with the old rhetoricians and the *Marotiques* who were imitating Ovid's epistles, many with women speakers. Surrey writes another epistle with the same dramatic situation as though the theme needed greater artistic definition. Both are love complaints of a woman whose husband is overseas, but in the latter, this time in the more leisurely form of Poulter's measure, the woman is more clearly his wife. Both poems dramatize Surrey's theme, seemingly unique in the court of Henry VIII, of fidelity and constancy in love.

Establishing an objectifying dramatic context is the intrinsic formal premise of most of Surrey's lyrics and songs. Thus speakers, voices of dramatis personae, distinguish Surrey's texts, and although biographical facts, as in these two poems sung in the voice of his wife, are often relevant, the texts themselves determine the efficacy of any artistic device. Surrey structures this first lyric in the form of an oration—a speaking voice that here attempts by demonstrative form to convince an audience of its truth by giving a panegyric of the love relationship itself. The love lament at the heart of this

structure is the central means of its oratorical demonstration and exemplifies *ethopoeia,* "a certaine Oracion made by voice, and lamentable imitacion, vpon the state of any one."[17] Thus this lyric begins with the divisions of an oration as a frame.[18] The *exordium* invites (in a sexual image) the happy women who are embracing "The frute" of their "delight" to join in and fill out—as befits a Tudor part-song—her "moorning voyce." With an insistence like the Ancient Mariner's, the speaker will "bewail the wofull case" of her love, and in the second stanza, having established rapport with the audience of other women directly addressed, the speaker turns to a *narratio.* It will be the story of her love rendered in nautical terms made Petrarchan and easily accessible for Surrey's audience. His eyes that in Petrarchan cliché were her food appear to her in dreams but when she wakes up, "Lord how I mourne!"

With the motifs of dreams and absence of the lover, the real subtext for this poem emerges: Vergil's Dido. When in the fourth and fifth stanzas, Surrey's lady stands in her window surveying the sea below, watching through tears, as other lovers holding each other "Rejoyce their chief delight," Surrey repeats another familiar topos from book 4 of the *Aeneid* where Dido wakes to see the Trojan fleet departing. Observing the fleeing clouds and the green waves and the "rage of wind," Surrey's lady herself now enters into the nature of her lover, transforming herself, as she says at the conclusion of the fourth stanza: "Lo, what a mariner love hath made of me!" This is the landscape of love, the inner landscape, that contrasts with the actual. Like Dido, Surrey's lady now has "A thousand fansies," especially that her "swete fo," (the *oxymoron* by which Troilus also describes Criseyde in book 5, line 228), will be drowned. She ends her fifth stanza with an emotional outburst in a final pentameter line. This long line acts as a chorus or refrain from the third stanza on, and in this penultimate stanza she asks directly: alas, why did he leave her? The last stanzas integrate the two landscapes, the natural and the internal, so that the very sight of sea, even calm, brings "dreade," paradoxically her "wealth mingled with wo," and a pathos like Andromache's in the last line of the song: "Now he comes, will he come? alas, no, no!"

"Good ladies, you that have your pleasure in exyle" (J24). In the second of the two poems possibly in the voice of Surrey's wife, the social occasion of invitation that initiates the structure of the first is repeated. In Poulter's measure, this song, also an oration,

begins with the *exordium* inviting women whose husbands are away to join her song with a refrain: "Stepp in your foote, come take a place, and mourne with me awhyle." Here is not only a clear directive toward a part-song but toward a dance, which the lilting rhythm of alternating six's and seven's of Poulter's measure sets up. As before, the speaker not only makes a complaint but asks for help, using the figure of *mempsis.* In the next line, unlike the first orator-lady in "O happy dames," this speaker incorporates, into her building of a pathetic *ethos,* the figure of *sarcasmus.* For ladies who do not honor their absent lords, "Lett them sitt still" but to those "whome love hath bound, by order of desyre" the lady will tell her sad story. Thus in her *narratio* the lady tells of her lord's crossing of the seas, he whom she was "wontt for to embrace" so that they held, in what was the best description of their happy marriage, "contentyd myndes."

When Surrey depicts the dream sequences of this lady, his Poulter's measure allows him more idiomatic freedom. Thus, after the "fearefull dreames" of "roring seas" that "grow so hye, / That my sweete lorde in daunger greate, alas, doth often lye," Surrey invents a domestic dream with actual conversation. In it the lady finds her lord at home playing "with T. his lytle sonne" and kissing him, she says: " 'Now well come home, my knight; / Welcome, my sweete, alas, the staye of my welfare; / Thye presence bringeth forthe a truce betwixt me and my care.' " The husband, who looks so alive in the landscape of her dream, has a simple poignant reply: " 'My deare, how is it now that you have all this payne?' " At this the woman breaks down in a passage echoing Troilus (bk. 4, ll. 232 ff.). Then she wakes up with such anguish and torment that "unneth"[19] can she find a place to relieve her "unquyet mynd." And so, in the logical conclusion to her narration, Surrey's lady has become a lover like Troilus and Dido: "Thus everye waye you see with absence how I burne. . . ." Her final stance contains the same sense of paradox as the lady's in "O happy dames" except that, in the expanded lines of the second poem, she has a conversation with herself. She tells herself that later the husband and wife will find, in their joy at reunion, how little pain this separation will seem. Her *peroratio* is an *apostrophe* to the winds to ask them to protect her husband and "Do your good will to cure a wight that lyveth in distresse."

"The sonne hath twyse brought forthe the tender grene"
(J11).   This dramatic monologue is also in the epistolary tradition,
addressed rather generally in most of its fifty-five lines of iambic
pentameter to the beloved who is causing the speaker such anguish
(in the last seven lines, the address is more direct). The poem is in
the form of a *capitolo,* a sequence of *terza rima* hallowed in Italian
by Dante's use in his *Commedia* and then by Petrarch's in his *Trionfi*
and Chaucer's in "A Complaint to His Lady." The *capitolo* was, like
the verse-epistle, a more aristocratic form than the *frottola* and had
the same seriousness as the sonnet. On the Continent the form, as
Surrey inherited it, expressed true Petrarchan pathos but with ec-
logue additions and pastoral overtones, such as Surrey uses here and
in his longer complaints in Poulter's measure. Surrey also adapts
the *capitolo* and its *terza rima* into the satire of his next poem, but
for entirely different purposes. In many ways "The sonne hath twyse"
is a meditation by an isolated individual on his suffering, a familiar
Surrey theme, especially as placed in juxtaposition to nature with
its order and cycles of life. Once more Surrey uses the Petrarchan
frame as a means to get to his real subject: the utter mutability of
all existence, the dissolution of all things in time. Although an
audience is clearly implied, and the beloved directly addressed at
the end of the poem, the real dialogue in most of the poem is that
of the lover with himself. It is small wonder that this poem was
the first in *Tottel's Miscellany.* In its musical distillation of forms,
themes, and motifs, the poem presented a powerful model of love
poetry for the English Renaissance.

The lover begins his complaint with a formal painting of the
cylical natural landscape. In it Surrey probably translates lines on
the return of spring from Boccaccio's verse-epistle "Ad Pinum."[20]
Whatever Surrey's subtext, he uses the lines to begin his development of the figures of *merismus* and *amplificatio.* Here he shows by
analogy the contrast to his real subject as given in lines five and
six. That subject is his desperate almost narcissistic concern over
his split condition, his dichotomous existence, "Sins I have hidd
under my brest the harme / That never shall recover helthfulnes."
Expanding the Dido topos that contrasts lover and nature, the lover
quickly turns the petrarchan base of his elaborate images into profound statements about mutability: "What colde agayne is hable to
restore / My freshe grene yeres that wither thus and faade?" This
latter image expresses the lyric's real theme: the anguish of living

in time and yet not using time. Mutability for the lover means being lost in time, not living integrated with the forces of time as they renew nature's life. His own life is bound to the stasis of unnatural love—love that cannot express itself or find any response to its own life-force. The lover cannot enter any cycle outside himself, especially nature's. Such disharmony between the moving cycles of the outer landscape and inner stagnation leads to the lover's ironic meditations in lines 4–16 on the negative effects of time on him. The meditation leads to the climax of the first section of the *capitolo:* "Straunge kynd of death, in lief that I doo trye: / At hand to melt, farr of in flame to bourne. . . ." Using Petrarchan contraries, the lover describes his inner wasteland as a death-in-life.

In the next section, in line twenty, the lover argues that, if time gives disharmony, "So doth eche place my comfort cleane refuse." In nature all the creatures can rest at night, "Save I, alas," says the lover, specifically alluding to the Dido passage in the *Aeneid.* Yet if he curses his stars at night as the cause of his fate, by day he is like the melancholy Romeo and would hide from all others, longing for the night. In retrospective "with my mynd I measure paas by paas / To seke that place where I my self hadd lost," the very place, "That daye," where he was caught in ropes that seemed to slacken but now tighten ever more. But even if (like Troilus), he seeks the former place of love, such therapy will not help: "But never yet the trayvaile of my thought / Of better state could catche a cawse to bost."

In the third section of the poem, Surrey reverts, first, to the standard Petrarchan image of the lover as ship at sea, here unable to sail. The result of such stasis, continues the lover, is that his "sprites do all resort / To stand atgaas" either sinking or sucking in more of her harm.[21] Thus, the lover declaims his paradox in the next line, 46, "Loo, yf I seke, how I do fynd my sore!" The real climax to this section follows from this imagery: "And yf I flye, I carrey with me still / The venymd shaft which dothe his force restore / By hast of flight." Once more, Surrey employs a topos from the Dido story, as translated by Surrey: "Unhappy Dido burns, and in her rage / Throughout the town she wandreth up and down, / Like to the striken hinde with shaft . . ." (bk.4 ll. 86–93). This image transferred from Vergil, famous in the English Renaissance after Surrey and even used by Hamlet, is the climax of the soliloquy. Now self-conscious of his complaint, the lover in his *peroratio* turns

directly to the beloved, summing up, as in an oration, all the strategies, motifs and images of his lyric:

> And I maye playne my fill
> Unto my self, oneles this carefull song
> Prynt in your hert some percell of my will.
> For I, alas, in sylence all to long
> Of myne old hurt yet fele the wound but grene.
> Rue on my lief, or elles your crewel wrong
> Shall well appeare, and by my deth be sene.

What the speaker of this demonstrative oration has argued is that the language of self is not enough. In Surrey, nature is no chimera but a distinct reality that calls for an integrated identity of all living forms of life. Furthermore, typical of the medieval and classical world picture, nature is, for human beings, a social relationship. To be natural, to be human, is to be part of a living community. What Surrey is saying is that the isolation of the Petrarchan lover, or any other isolation in time and place, is finally broken by the language of the very plaint that speaks to another and hopes for the life-giving response of love from the other addressed. In the very telling, in the language, there is freedom. Language itself is not private but social and public. True language for this speaker, true poetry, is a matter of community; it effects his freedom from isolation.

Song as Satire: "London, hast thow accused me" (J33)

Surrey's conception of freedom and his perception of the failure of social community frames his next *terza rima* poem. The voice in this lyric text, which expresses his special intention and perception, determines the thematic and formal structure of a satire so sweeping that Surrey is likely drawing on his reading of the Roman texts of Juvenal. Composed as an oration and a verse-letter (with the addressee nothing less than the community of London), Surrey's minatory satire has none of the meditative pentameter structure of "The sonne" but the quick music of iambic tetrameter. This satire lacks the frequent enjambment of his other poem in *terza rima* where fluidity suited the meditative mode of Surrey's love complaint; here the almost universally end-stopped lines fit the structure of the poem, which was probably written from Fleet prison in 1543. Cast

as a judicial oration,[22] the poem argues its defense of what was clearly outrageous behavior by the young Howard aristocrat and his close companions, including Thomas Wyatt the Younger and Thomas Clere. The satire has been variously interpreted, because the poem is very topical with a structure that once more invites biographical considerations. In fact, the satire is another example of the poem of social occasion in which Surrey invents a superb fiction from his own autobiography. Here Surrey does not lie (although his defense of his own outrageous behavior is questionable) because in inventing a fiction, and making that inventing his chief concern, he "nothing affirmeth," as Sidney says. His truth is the truth of invention, nothing more and nothing less. In order for Surrey to interpret the first event he had to invent another event, his own poem.

Recovering from a military campaign in Scotland (and no doubt also from the sudden death the previous October of the elder Wyatt whose elegy he may also have been composing at this time), the Earl of Surrey in the Lenten season of 1543, likely early February ("About Candelmas last"), with his friends had a late dinner at the house of one Mistress Arundell in St. Lawrence Lane in the city. He had dined there before and was treated like royalty (a fact that would be used against Surrey at his last trial), and after the meal with meat, forbidden in Lent, and doubtless a great deal to drink, the hell-raisers headed for the banks of the Thames and the streets of the city. There, armed with crossbows and stones, they skirmished with apprentices, shouted teasing remarks at whores, and then turned on the houses of burghers and aldermen like Sir Richard Gresham, one of the Tudor new men who had made a fortune in Henry's destruction of the monasteries. They smashed Gresham's ostentatious new windows and those of other honorable citizens.[23]

The fiction that Surrey invented from this event was centered on his own bold act of warning London, through his attacks by night, of its wickedness: "Oh membre of false Babylon! / The shopp of craft! the denne of ire! / Thy dredfull dome drawes fast uppon." Surrey transforms himself in his own poem. His voice in the text becomes that of an Old Testament prophet who asserted the authority of God over human corruption. This was so clearly his intention that, as Hughey has shown, Surrey translates almost directly from the Bible in constructing his fictional persona of the just man attacking a wicked city in the name of greater freedom.[24] Constructing his fictional character or *ethos* of the brave warrior who

intends by his action to bring greater freedom remained a formidable artistic problem, however, no mattter how exalted Surrey's subtext. Whatever the truth or relevance of the biographical facts or subtexts, the poet had to start with language and its strategies, which included, as we have seen, the enthymeme or "argument urbanely fallacious" and other rhetorical forms. All such strategies Surrey worked into a judicial courtroom oration which, given as mock-heroic, was his defense—a defense that, as the record shows, he never made in actuality (if indeed he could!).

Thus, the vehement *exordium,* with its heavy trochaic opening and striking accent on "me," immediately makes the place of London a villain, itself breaching laws and a "roote of stryfe." In this Surrey reverts to the use of the figure of *exuscitatio,* necessary here because the speaker of the satire is himself on trial. Furthermore, the key word in line 5, "synnes," is a genus and a cause, the general effects of which the whole poem will show and the specific effects in the catalogue of the seven deadly sins forming the *confirmatio* of the oration and its self-defense.

In the *narratio* Surrey establishes the persona of his orator. Faced with "So fervent hotte thy dissolute lief" this prophet simply could not, so the speaker argues, keep his rage from expressing itself. Such outrage in Surrey's strategy was another form of the humility topos needed to establish an impressive *ethos.* Preachers had already used words to no avail and so he had to seek "unknowne meanes . . . / My hydden burden to expresse," says the speaker in lines 11 and 12. He had to act because in the eyes of God "no fault is free," and especially of those who "wourke unright / In most quyet" (here the speaker equates the burgher sleep with *accedia,* the sleep of the soul). Thus, in the narrative and fictional structure of the poem, a prophet is born:

> In secret sylence of the night
> This made me, with a reckles brest,
> To wake thy sluggardes with my bowe:
> A fygure of the Lordes behest,
> Whose scourge for synn the Screptures shew.

As in nature thunder tells us lightning is "at hand," so "the sowndless rapp" of his pebble stones might make London see the "dredfull plage" of God's wrath that is surrounding the city.

Having implied his *propositio,* the orator then proceeds to list the seven deadly sins and their effects. If the prophetic figure appears a contemporary Protestant configuration, the *amplificatio* of the seven deadly sins is medieval. In neat units of two lines for each sin (the second line showing the effect of the prophet's good action of chastisement), the passage recalls *Piers Plowman* in its tendency toward *personification.* The shift in *terza rima* here to *sixaines,* which allows less interlocking and creates more of an inset effect to paint each sin and its result, emphasizes this medieval device. From the final sin, gluttony, the speaker moves to the drunk whom with remarkable temerity (considering Surrey's own situation) the speaker also intends "To styrr to Godd, this was my mynd." So zealous and intense is the language by line 44 when the orator launches into his *refutatio* that the effect is almost comical: the windows themselves "had don me no spight" but "prowd people that drede no fall, / Clothed with falshed and unright / Bred in the closures of thy wall." These have heard presumably from the stones on windows[25] his "secret call" described by this defending orator with utter self-justification, as "wrested to wrathe in fervent zeale," recalling Jeremiah (20:7–9). In their hard hearts, of course, the wicked citizens of London hear nothing, "no warning feale."

Having proven that London, which has dared to imprison him, is the real criminal, the orator launches in his *peroratio* into a tirade against London, the new Babylon. Using all the prophetic sources for a curse, from Ezekiel to the Christian Book of Revelation, Surrey manages a fictional metamorphosis. The London of Henry VIII is now given universal dimensions: "Thy martyres blood, by swoord and fyre, / In Heaven and earth for justice call." Thus the initial act of insolence that provoked the satire has now become, in this final vision of doomed city, only a triviality. It can be easily justified, for it is nothing before the fictional enormity of evil that is London dramatized through rhetorical figures like *ominatio.* Because of this very fiction, mock-heroic has now become heroic. This kind of surprising transformation of genre, like the change in the figure of Folly in Erasmus's *Praise of Folly,* allows genuine prophecy to emerge here in the fictional structure. The text's eschatological terror is like that of Pope's *Dunciad.* London is a place where there is no meaning, except in this very satire directed toward it, Surrey's own strategies of language in his attack. Only this language is giving the damned world life. The prophet by his very voice and language is the one

just man who keeps society alive in a city that has become the true dwelling-place for Sardanapalus and his court.

All of this transformation has been possible because of Surrey's manipulation of the various levels of irony implicit in the fictional structure. Such multi-leveled structure led to the final ironies that reverberate at the end like the crescendo of a Renaissance opera. In utter fictional metamorphosis, hell-raising has become heroic; the orator (like the character David in *Absalom and Achitophel*) has taken on the rhetoric of his opponent; and irony of ironies, the method of outraged self-justification that started off as *hyperbole* becomes genuine prophecy with final fictional images of a collapsing city. In the doomed city there are flames; famine and pestilence with stricken lechers; towers and turrets beaten down "stone from stone" with "idolles burnt"; and, worst of all, no one pitying this fall. In contrast, the elect are rendering "unto the right wise Lord," who judges all Babylons, "Imortall praise with one accord."

Thus Surrey ends his satire with true musical bravado, the rhetorical equivalent of an aria he might have heard in one of the bolder Italian musical dramas performed at Fontainebleau or elsewhere in the court of Francis I. This final oracular invective completes the tetrameter structure of "O London" with a public stance that differs from the more intimate musicality of his love motifs. It is music nevertheless, and within the song the voice of prophecy.

Chapter Five

Minor Forms

Poulter's Measure

Although Surrey has eighteen poems in this meter, these poems have suffered from general neglect since the Renaissance because Poulter's measure is itself probably the most maligned of all meters in English. Poulter's measure is composed of rhyming couplets, the first line twelve syllables and the second fourteen, or a line of iambic hexameter, an alexandrine, followed by a line of iambic heptameter. Most critics since the edition by George Frederick Nott at the beginning of the nineteenth century have universally condemned Surrey's use, even blaming him for its influence on the English Renaissance. It was certainly popular in the sixteenth century, as Gascoigne, himself greatly influenced by Surrey, noted about thirty years after Surrey's beheading when he gave the meter its name: "And the commonest sort of verse which we use now adayes (VIZ. the long verse of twelve and fourtene sillables) I know not certainly howe to name it, unlesse I should say that it doth consist of Poulters measure, which giveth xii. [eggs] for one dozen and xiiii. for another."[1] The problem with modern negative analysis is that it does not take into consideration what Surrey thought he was doing with a meter into which he put some of his most interesting experiments. These include more love complaints, his only other example of satire, and his biblical translations or paraphrases of the Psalms and Ecclesiastes. The longer line must have appealed to Surrey; he certainly aspired to a more expansive lyric form like the *capitolo,* and the blank verse experiments in epic form were obvious attempts at a long line. Surrey also seems to have been fascinated by Chaucer's handling of a long narrative like *Troilus.* Indeed, the best uses in Surrey of this controversial meter occur where the speaker is more the narrator and less the actor. Finally it is probable that Surrey viewed his use of this meter as providing another kind of music.[2]

"Suche waiwarde waies hath love that moste parte in discorde" (J13).   As an exercise in translation, this poem represents

the third direct adaptation of Petrarch. Its opening also translates the first stanza of the second canto of Ariosto's *Orlando Furioso*. Surrey adapts lines 151–90 of the third section of Petrarch's long *capitolo Trionfo d'amore*, turning the original *terza rima* stanza into couplets of the longer Poulter's measure. Once more Surrey uses an original Petrarchan text, which he translates very carefully and whose structural dimensions he uses as a device for his own text and representation. In his translation Surrey presents nothing less than a microcosm of the human condition: the contraries of lovers reflect the essential nature of a broken universe. Almost unrelieved sorrow is accented because, as throughout his work, Surrey avoids two Petrarchan methods of giving breadth to the lover's lament: the dream-vision (both erotic and allegorical dreams) and classical mythology. The direct voice of Surrey's lover telling "be roote, the tale that I wold tell" (l. 25) evolves therefore into a realistic lyric of human mortality amid mutability, not unlike the lyric of the English medieval world. In fact, the opening may derive from Ariosto's declamation on the discords of love, but it is love in a very Anglo-Saxon setting.

Surrey accomplishes this realism and consistency of voice through careful control of a logical and oratorical structure that counters the naturally amorphous and discursive meter. The first line sets the cause for all the effects of the poem and is the *propositio* for the actions that will be so plentifully catalogued in the forty-nine lines to follow. Love has "waiwarde waies" and lovers part and go their ways. The second line takes this cause, however, a step back before proceeding, by explaining the real subject: the human condition as flawed, split between intentions ("Our willes") and performance ("our hartes") or between desire and reality. The result, then, says the speaker in the next two lines, which complete his compressed *exordium* and *narratio* is that Love delights in "Disceyte . . . to begyle and mock / The symple hertes which he doth stryke with froward dyvers stroke." In line 5 the speaker shows the effects of this striking of hearts; he uses once more the familiar Petrarchan figure of *syncrisis* to show the crushing contraries. For the rest of this first section of the poem, until the shift in line 15, the figure of *amplificatio* is worked to enumerate the Petrarchan clichés familiar to the audience but also to list homely images like the contrast of wading across a ford and being driven "into the darke diep well."

This long monologue contains the general structure of a sonnet, albeit expanded. The equivalent of an octet section runs up to and climaxes in lines 14–15 when the lover is allowed "to pursue a conquest well nere woon" in order to follow where his "paynes were spilt" and his suit was begun.[3] From line 15 to the end of the poem, the equivalent of a sestet occurs when the response to this situation is given in a series of "rules" or recognitions rendered by more *amplificatio* and *syncrisis*. These "rules" are expressed in neat units of experience, marked by Surrey's precise translation of Petrarch's *anaphora*, in English a series of independent clauses beginning "I know."

These units effectively form epigrams based on vignettes of the social occasion of the encounter of the sexes. The series of epigrams extend to personal generalizations in the closure whose effect suggests the implicit substructure of the sonnet form. All the situations in the epigrams—from naturalistic face-changes, hearty sighs and laughters of the spleen, the lover's inadequate words, to the symbolic lurking green snake and "hamer of the restles forge"—turn to the lover's most profound encounter: "but chefelye this I know, / That lovers must transforme into the thing beloved, / And live (alas, who colde beleve?) with spryte from lief removed." The demands of love finally transcend all other forms of existence, and in that condition— so truly imitative of Petrarch—where a "seldome tasted swete" or "glyns of grace" may prove a bliss, this lover concludes on the bitterness and agony of human experience. In the two lines of the closure the speaker bemoans "that slipper state" of human love and, in the last line, the mutability of life itself.

"Laid in my quyett bedd, in study as I weare" (J25). This lyric also springs from translation, in this case from two passages in Horace. Surrey adapts the opening of Horace's first satire in which, praising Maecenas, Horace notes how human beings are never satisfied with their situation in the order of life. Then in the general structure of the poem, Surrey adapts Horace's ages of man from his epistle to the Pisos, better known as the *Ars poetica.* Tottel caught the generalizing, even proverbial nature of the poem when he gave it his title in 1557: *"How No Age Is Content with His Own Estate, & How the Age of Children Is the Happiest, If They Had the Skill to Understand It."* Such reflection on the nature and mutability of human life is immediately set in a place and a dramatic situation: in his bed the speaker contemplates the human comedy that makes

him sigh and smile ("now I sight, and then I smylde"). This lyric in the long lines of Poulter's measure is another instance of Surrey's careful establishment of a place for retrospective reflection on the nature of existence, a mode further developed in the poetry of the eighteenth and nineteenth centuries.

The first four lines logically set the generalized cause from which the poem will deduce the effects through Surrey's method of illustration and *amplificatio*. The speaker (no lover this time) narrates how "laid" in his bed he "saw within my troubled hed a heape of thoughtes appeare." The situation is typical of Surrey in that the interior landscape is the central one. Typical also, however, is the setting of an external place—"laid in my quyett bedd"—that has provided the occasion for this soliloquy. In a complete restaging of the Horatian strategy, the young man in his bed has a vision of himself as a death's head, himself as another text, a momento mori, and from its "tothelesse chapps" the future self speaks directly to the young man. The monologue becomes dialogue. This full reversal of structure onto the speaker himself now gives a fuller irony to the "quyett bedd" in which the young man is "laid." It is an emblem of his tomb.

"If care do cause men cry, why do I not complaine?" (J17). The popularity of this lyric and "Laid in my quyett bed" reveals not only the substructure of musical form in Surrey's texts but, if we can judge from the evidence, the Renaissance view of Poulter's measure as producing an effect very much like a line-variation of the English ballad.[4] The variation in this poem is significant, however, and keeps the base of Chaucerian narrative within long lyric lines. But this text in its meaning, unlike Chaucerian subtexts, is a resounding paean to fidelity and reciprocal love. Indeed, the very answer to the opening questions, where once more the topic of invention cause and effect is used to structure the poem, is that the lover does not complain. He does not show his pain because his beloved is faithful in his absence and "So doth good hope clene put away dispayre out of my minde, / And biddes me for to serve and suffer pacientlie." The lady here is more graphically portrayed than in previous poems, one result of the discursive nature of the innovative meter. It is natural to surmise therefore how this poem may be another verse-letter written from France by Surrey to his wife. The description in the poem of early courtship and of mutual tran-

scendent love is elaborated in the rather diffuse manner of a verse-letter, one perhaps from the trenches and fortifications of Boulogne.

In any case, Surrey's line and thematic structure make these graphic moments possible. That control of scene and social relationships is especially evident in the building up of the speaker's *ethos* and believability through the figure of *occupatio*. The figure in turn works to establish a character of *pathos* through the figure of *mempsis*. Thus, the lover says that he could complain, if he wanted to, because he certainly has good reason, launching into an *amplificatio* that builds on the Dido topos of the sleepless lover and ending in a figure of *graditio* that vividly demonstrates the lover's real suffering: "and thus my life it wears." By line 21, with just cause for sorrow, Surrey's speaker withdraws into "some secrete place" to wail his fate in an image of "the striken dere." In secret the lover acts out the Petrarchan extremes, ending in "a ferther fere." Using the figure of *anastrophe*, Surrey reverses the normal pattern by not telling what the fear is but rather the effect that he fears he will lose—namely, the woman herself, "Lest absence cause forgetfulness to sink within her brest." But he has no reason to "mistrust / So swete a wight, so sad and wise, that is so true and just." Indeed, in line 44, he can answer his fear prefiguring Donne's "Valediction: forbidding mourning": "The farther off, the more desirde; thus lovers tie their knot." After a familiar Petrarchan image, the lover as a ship at sea, the closure of the poem builds on a stance of faith. He will serve her until his last breath and at the end, like Troilus and Arcite, he will "bequeth my weried ghost to serve her afterwarde."

"When sommer toke in hand the winter to assail" (J15). This poem and the next, "In winters just returne," appear on the surface to be paired in a familiar Renaissance patterning. In actuality they are not, except insofar as they show that at any season or time the lover with his complaints remains the same melancholy image of mutability. Although both poems take their origin from Chaucerian narrative, borrowing major structural designs from Chaucer, their uses do not reflect any significant contrasts with the originals or with each other. The essential model in both is still the lamenting Troilus-figure. Both make use of the figure of *chronographia,* which implies Ruskin's "pathetic fallacy," that is, natural landscape responding to character's "inscape," to use Hopkins's term.

In "When sommer toke" the essential premise is, however, the disharmony between the two landscapes. The bright Chaucerian

world when summer "clothed faire the earth about with grene" does nothing for the lover who remains by the lyric's end, "undone for ever more." It is the same lack of integration found in other Surrey poems. The difference is that, in the more leisurely development of the Poulter's measure, the familiar contrast between the isolated single consciousness of the lover and the order of nature (the Dido topos) is more dramatic. Thus Surrey's narrative, immediately after the introductory contrast, turns to a typical Surrey device: the introspective as drama. The speaker has a dialogue with his own desire in a figure of *personification,* a desire whose configuration may be allegorical in form but whose speech is realistic and colloquial English, with strong Anglo-Saxon accents and alliteration.

In the next stage of the narrative the lover ventures out into the spring world, with its conventional motifs of joy. Here the Chaucerian "Ver" is especially focused on the natural coupling of birds, "new betrothed" since Saint Valentine's Day, and their grateful songs. The narrative then turns to the allegorical relationship of the speaker with Cupid, the cruel god of love, but the whole of Cupid's appearance becomes only "mine empressed mynde." The isolated consciousness of the lover is confirmed once more. The lover in the closing couplet is "A miror" of mutability for all lovers: "Strive not with love; for if ye do, it will ye thus befall."

"In winters just returne, when Boreas gan his raigne" (J16). This lyric emphasizes the lover's isolation even more, ironically by enlarging the dramatic scene of the narrative and making it more objective because there are two characters in dialogue. The drama develops from a Renaissance winter landscape that envelops the actors so that the Chaucerian subtexts and early French pastoral subtexts (with their imitations of Vergil) complement, with melancholy backdrop, the tensions of Surrey's miniature drama and the center of its landscape: the dying lover and his complaint.[5] Thus a shepherd "In misty morning darke" goes out into the introductory winter landscape to "unfolde" his sheep. Under a willow tree, the traditional place for unhappy lovers, he hears the lament and cry of a lover soliloquizing, calling for his own death and then the cursing of the instruments by which that love was expressed: his feather pen and the bird, the man, and the knife that caused the pen to be; "the time and place where I could so endite"; finally the very hand of the lover. The artificial inset of the curse, equating the act of

writing poetry with the act of love, establishes the formal structure
of the whole poem, giving it the rigidity of a Senecan drama.

Hearing the curse, the shepherd is deeply moved. He rushes to
the speaker and holds him in his arms, a natural man against this
unnaturally broken lover. After sighs and shrieks, the lover, bracing
his back against a tree (in Chaucerian posture), tells his story. It is
nothing less than the Troilus story reduced to the microcosm of
Surrey's drama. Remarking that he has suffered "a greater losse than
Priam had of Troy," the lover tells the innocent shepherd: "Thou
hast seen dye the truest man that ever love did pain." Then, apos-
trophizing his death, the lover expires. Thereupon the shepherd in
his own melancholy "to see so piteous sight" has a breakdown that
only time will heal. In the closing action of Surrey's lyric, this
shepherd in a classical landscape (which the reader only learns about
at the end) must find a place to bury the lover. He remembers that
nearby is the tomb "Where Chreseids love, King Priams sonne, the
worthy Troilus lay" and so next to him he will bury the lover "in
token he was treew," and cover the tomb with blue. The wide
popularity of this lyric, both literary and musical, led to its being
made into a popular song and commented on by both Gascoigne
and Puttenham.[6]

"**To dearely had I bought my grene and youthfull yeres**"
(J18). This lyric, short for its meter, analyzes the courtly nuances
of the social occasions of love at court and dramatizes a special kind
of sophisticated violence. It is clearly a dramatic situation, an address
to a friend who needs advice from an older lover. In this form of
verse-letter, probably a response to an actual situation at court, the
poem is as close to an epigram as a single poem in Poulter's measure
can be. It bristles with satiric thrusts from the very beginning. The
older man had indeed bought his green years expensively if he does
not now know "when craft for love apperes" and, although he
distances himself from the social arena for love, "seldom though I
come in court among the rest," yet he can judge those "colours
dim," those rhetorical devices to make falsehood seem truth, "as
depe as can the best." The speaker then turns to his friend directly;
knowing how grief "tormentes the man that suffreth secret smart"
the older man announces his own sympathy: "This case is thine for
whom I fele such torment of my minde." Yet in a reversal of
expectation, the older man unburdens himself, using the figure of
anastrophe to make a delicate gesture of friendship. The young man

is not asked to unburden himself immediately but to bear with the older man as he does.

After the tenth line, the speaker turns directly to the condition of the young man. The structure of the poem in its first part has established the *ethos* and authority of the speaker and his open friendship for the troubled young man. Now, with wisdom, the older lover analyzes the melancholy of the lover whose "wittes" yield "to thy desire, and folowes the by fittes." The older man knows the words, the language of such social occasion, such seemingly polite society, in which the "fayned wordes" of the woman have been used "they fredom to devour." In fact, his wise old eyes have seen that "her pleasant chere" is for the "chiefest of thy suite," one of the young men's own servants. This lowering of social status is the ultimate crime of the woman: "wisedome would mistrust" no such woman's word "to endure."

"**Wrapt in my carelesse cloke, as I walke to and fro**" (J21). There is clear disdain toward women in the male speaker of this long lyric. His cloak is carelessly drawn because he is not in love; he does not have to worry about his dress or his appearance. In a logically structured monologue the speaker now sees "how love can shew what force there reigneth in his bow"; and, from that cause, how various the effects of love that one lover "may rage" and the other show nothing. The narrative then describes these effects on one male lover (not the speaker) who, like the young man in the previous poem, is "that wounded wight" who "is fed with yeas and nayes, and liveth all to long." These effects come from the woman's deceptive artifice that allows her "but to glory in her power, that over such can reign." Because she never stops her teasing, the speaker by line 25, in the last part of his proof, shows in one terrible effect the root cause of love's power:"Lorde, what abuse is this! who can such women praise / That for their glory do devise to use such crafty wayes!" In this woman there "is greater craft then is in twenty mo," a fact especially sad, says the speaker in his closure, because her "tender yeres, alas, with wyles so well are spedde." What will she do when white hairs "are powdred in her hedde"?

This satiric analysis of sexual behavior at court was a particular talent of Wyatt's, and Surrey's last line echoes Wyatt's famous "Ye old mule, that thinck yourself so fayre" (M35), a poem in which Wyatt, after remarking that no man would now ride in her saddle, says the woman is for market "syns gray heres ben powdered in

your sable." If Surrey's poem is addressed to the Lady Elizabeth Fitzgerald, as it might well be, it is in a very ironic mode. The satiric analysis of polite behavior at court is overshadowed by a general misogyny and, as always, the universal figure of the suffering Petrarchan lover. Irony helps to distance the frivolous moral action of the young woman, but the fact of the speaker's stinging attack remains.

"**Gyrtt in my giltlesse gowne, as I sytt heare and sowe**" (J22). Although there is debate as to whether this dramatic monologue in a woman's voice is Surrey's poem, it is a companion piece to the previous poem. If the first poem is addressed by Surrey to the Lady Elizabeth Fitzgerald and if this long lyric is indeed Surrey's, then the framing of this poem is another masterstroke of objectivity on Surrey's part. The persona Surrey invents provides an ironic displacement that puts the misogynous attack of the earlier poem in an entirely different perspective. It illustrates once more Surrey's adaptation of his courtly love subtexts to his new, more realistic *vers de societé*. The speaker is a woman most likely invented here, as in the Geraldine fiction of the sonnets, from the real Lady Elizabeth Fitzgerald.[7]

This fictional persona answers directly the insinuations of the first poem and calmly assaults that male speaker so that, once more, Surrey transforms himself into a woman. This transformation is not a wife, as in his other female persona poems, but a young woman who must preserve her honor at a ruthless court ruled by male passions, no matter how beleaguered, no matter how young, because she and her family must survive. In a dramatic situation, "as I sytt heare and sowe," the girl addresses, through a kind of verse-letter, the speaker of the earlier poem. Her gown is "giltlesse" and, sitting there, she sees "that thinges are not in dead as to the outward showe." Indeed, any one who looks closely enough at social occasions at court, that arena of avaricious and lusting aristocrats, will find that "playnesse" may be nothing but "craft." The cause for which she gives the effects is set in this first general introduction: the dichotomy of appearance and reality at court. Thus, with objective "indifferent eyes" she can note the different levels of actors at the court (a part of Surrey's poem that became a popular ballad).[8]

This focusing on the eyes of the young woman is a superb device of characterization. Through her introspective analysis, the reader can enter her scene, *her* social occasion, and find two types of hu-

manity: those who guiding a ship in a storm do not stick to the stern but lose control (although in calm they could guide a barge) and those who "can do ten tymes more than they that say they can do all," and for whom, "the more they understand, / The more they seeke to learne and know and take lesse chardge in hand." This latter type, an effect of her initial cause, leads her to the earlier poem whose charges she is refuting. This young woman of thirteen or fourteen announces that "the auctour" of that song, "cam, wrapt in a craftly cloke, / In will to force a flamyng fyre wheare he could rayse no smoke." The male speaker of "Wrapt in my carelesse cloke" is but another type at court, who, if his "powre and will had mett," then "truth nor right had tane no place, their vertues had bene vayne."

Having given the effects that logically proceed from the general cause of the court's deceptive appearances, the young woman proceeds to the greatest effect of all, that on herself. She structures her narrative by telling a story within a story, using as model for her own situation at court the biblical tale of Susanna and the Elders, one of the most popular in the Renaissance, appearing on English tapestries, in painting, as sculpture. For the young female speaker reading the Susanna story, it is God himself who always "dothe defend all those that in hym trust," who now "Did raise a Childe for her defence to shyeld her from th'unjust." Surrey has chosen a term from chivalric honor, a young noble waiting knighthood, to signify the Daniel who will now appear to defend this Susanna. Thus, in the closure God who has preserved her so far "and lett them of their lust" and has defended her "will do still I trust," the female speaker concludes.

"Eache beeste can chuse his feere according to his minde" (P34). Surrey's one satire in Poulter's measure also springs from a social occasion, but it is one whose biographical tensions threaten the structural invention of the poem and its fictional ironies. As in his other satire, "London hast thow," Surrey invents a structure that begins as a covert defense of his questionable behavior in a social situation. The satire continues in doubtful taste by extending this defense through the entire poem. Although the lady who refuses to dance with the speaker (thus provoking the outburst of the poem) is not identified, it seems to have been known from early time that the woman was Anne Seymour, Countess of Hertford. She was

twenty years Surrey's senior, and the second wife of his bitterest enemy Edward Seymour, now the Earl of Hertford.[9]

Surrey's strategy here is to invent a fiction whose distancing is immediately apparent in the opening generalization. Here the careful diction sets up the logical topic of the invention, a cause for which the satiric fiction in its two parts will show the effects. The generalization also reveals the voice of an outside third figure watching this social drama and narrating it to an unknown fourth person who is the audience. Thus the first lines are almost proverbial in their generalizing, typical of the beast fable. Each beast can choose his mate "according to his minde," a statement of male freedom, but also, in the second line, "to shew a frindlie cheare," to show the natural social grace, courtesy, and hospitality "lyke to their beastly kynd." Thus we are not dealing so much with any kind of passion or sexual attraction (other than admiration of mature beauty and a young hot-headed male response to rejection) as much as with the requirements of hospitality in the manners of a noble aristocrat. The real battle, therefore, is between claims to nobility, that of the Howards as against assertions of new Tudor men like the Seymours. It is a question of manners on which can turn the violent destinies of men and their families, and their civilizations.

Thus, the first part of this satire, lines 3–22, introduces the cast of characters in this beast fable and describes the encounter that leads to the refusal and harsh rebuke by the lady-wolf. Distant from the two actors, the narrator enjoys looking upon "this gentyll beast," the lion "as whyte as any snow, / Whiche seemyd well to leade the race" and "still me thought, it seemyd me, of noble blood to be." The double use of "seemyd" introduces the figure of *litotes,* an understatement necessary not only to establish the character of the third-person narrator but to deepen the fiction of the white lion, so easily identified with Surrey himself because of the immediate audience recognition of the heraldic Howard emblem of the rampant lion. The lady-wolf is also white, an allusion to the heraldic argent,[10] and, says the narrator, "A fayrer beast, a fressher hew, beheld I never none" except for her fierce looks "and froward eke her grace."

Surrey has chosen just the right genre—the beast fable—to shield the sting of the actual event behind a fictional event. The narrator can even imply the pretentiousness and arrogance of the lion himself (Surrey looking at Surrey), who in the story approaches the lady-wolf. Using the same term as Criseyde when she first contemplates

sexual love (bk 2, l. 896), the lady-wolf rejects the lion: "Do waye! I lett the weet, thow shalt not play with me." The lion should find some more suitable partner.

The second part of the satire opens with a violent description by the narrator of the rejected angered lion: "Forthwith he beatt his taile, his eyes begounne to flame; / I might perceave his noble hartt moche moved by the same." The latter comment by the narrator is another instance of *litotes,* a gentle ironic allusion to Surrey's reputed temper. The restraint that the fictional lion now shows, "and eke his rage asswage," suggests the distance of the poem from the actual Howard lion, Surrey himself. It is, in fact, the distance in which the text is born. The long monologue that follows to the end of the poem is a deeper movement not only into the introspection of the lion-lover but into the structure of the text; its problem is that it tends to displace rather than extend the objectifying irony of the beast fable. This is because of its outbursts and Surrey's references to himself and to his uncle Thomas Howard and the Lady Margaret Douglas, the daughter of the Queen of Scotland and the niece of Henry VIII (and grandmother of James I), the two the most famous "star-crossed" lovers in the Tudor court.[11]

Thus the lion contrasts his family or "kynd" to that of the lady-wolf. After specifying the difference between the families, by line 53, the lion utters that most serious of declamations for a knight, particularly for Surrey, a vow. The vow begins with a revealing slip in the fictional perspective: "I am no man that will be traynd nor tanglyd" by her "coy lookes," or bow as some beasts that run to fawn. No, says the lion, he "will observe the law that nature gave to me, / To conqueare such as will resist, and let the rest go free." It is his freedom that he defines by seeing himself as a "ffaulcon free, that soreth in the ayre" and has never been captured. This freedom will include revenge upon her and her kind, "A thowsand spoyles" he "never thought to do," and, as for her, if she should come within his beastly power, "I shall be glad to feede on that that wold have fed on me." The end of this monologue is the closure of the whole satire, and it is significantly a definition of proper social gestures. "And thus, farewell! unkynd," says the punning lion, "to whom I bent to low." Since a lion's heart is no prey for a wolf, let her bloody mouth find "symple sheepe" to slake her wrath. He will refrain, although restraint pains him, from expressing "more dispight and

ire" because, after all, "my self was awthour of this game," and "It bootes me not" that his own wrath now "should disturbb the same."

The closure is ironic. On the one hand, with sardonic humor, the lion says that he started the whole social occasion, "the game," knowing the tensions involved, and so will not lose his control of that structure of polite courtly discourse. On the other hand, the inventor of the "game," the social manners that comprise the structure of the poem, is trying to practice the courtesy of staying within the limits of that game. It is a question whether Surrey succeeds with either social occasion, the fictional strategy of the lion (is he simply rationalizing at the end?) or his whole poem. The figures of *litotes* that he has practiced at junctures in his text, even here at the end, demonstrate Surrey's awareness of the problems of poetic structure; yet the use of this figure simply does not brook the violence at the heart of this text, which will not turn into fiction.

Biblical Paraphrases

Surrey's biblical translations are meditations structured as poetic texts. Essentially they all focus on the nature of entrapment for a passionate human being faced with social and actual extinction. With the exception of Surrey's rendering of Psalm 8, the objective "Thou" of God hardly enters the text except as a vengeful power to defend the injustice done to his elect. Although repentance may be considered the ostensible subject of all these translations, its dramatization is far less important than the complaint of this isolated and threatened consciousness. Thus these meditations—most in the familiar prolix lines of Poulter's measure—turn original Latin texts into Surrey's English attempts to respond to what was for him the harshest human rejection, that of society, which he saw as not only an act of personal but cosmic injustice.

Surrey's subtexts are the ancient Jewish wisdom books of Ecclesiastes and Psalms as given in the Vulgate, the Latin of Saint Jerome, and in the new translations into Latin by Campensis, one of the new Renaissance Hebraists, and finally into English by Surrey's contemporaries Coverdale and Wyatt. It is Wyatt who doubtless provided Surrey with the best contemporary subtexts, especially his innovative Penitential Psalms, and a model for artistic integrity. When Surrey turned to his own translations of these ancient texts popularly conceived as written by Solomon and David, he desperately

needed such models. With one possible exception, Psalm 8, these meditations were all composed in the last year of Surrey's life, in periods of great crisis. Internal evidence shows the lines of these poems are, with Surrey's translation of the fourth book of the *Aeneid,* the most irregular and "reflect hasty composition rather than metrical uncertainty," as Charles W. Eckert notes, done with little if any revision.[12] If Nott is correct, the paraphrases of the first five chapters of Ecclesiastes were written after Surrey's return from France in early 1546, when he had been dismissed as Lieutenant-General of the king's army, effectively defeated at court by the forces of Seymour and the new Tudor men.[13] The Psalms and the poems connected with them (with the exception of Psalm 8) were likely written during Surrey's last days in the Tower during the weeks of his trial and before his beheading in January 1547. The artistic problem was therefore the same for Surrey as in his satires: can objective structure control the poet's subjective response to events and topical allusions within the poem?

"The great Macedon that out of Perse chasyd" (J31).   Wyatt offered Surrey an artistic model that may have provided him a solution to his dilemma in translating these biblical texts into English. Four years before his imprisonment, Surrey had responded (if dating is possible) to Wyatt's religious sequence by writing what is probably the first commendatory sonnet in English. In it Surrey begins with a classical topos found in Plutarch. Alexander (his name given here in a grand use of *antonomasia*) placed Homer's works above all his own "huge power" and the defeat of Darius—in Surrey's extreme classical inversion, "In the rich arke if Homers rymes he placyd." The speaker then asks in the second quatrain "What holly grave, what wourthy sepulture / To Wyates Psalmes shulde Christians then purchase?" From use of this figure of *erotesis* (clearly there are no Tudor arks or worthy "sepulture" for Wyatt's translations), Surrey moves in line 7 to direct praise of Wyatt's Psalms; with no *volta* or sestet in this sonnet, which uses the rhyme scheme *a b a b c d c d e f e f g g,* Surrey expands: "Wher he dothe paynte the lyvely faythe and pure, / The stedfast hope, the swete returne to grace / Of just Davyd by parfite penytence."

This statement is the core of Surrey's epideictic strategy in the sonnet. Its alliterative patterns stress the key influence of the literary devices Wyatt used in his translation of the Psalms. Utilizing as throughout his work that special Tudor meaning of "swete" that

implies natural harmony, Surrey underlines key religious acts that lead to this ultimate "returne." These strategies reflect the intellectually attractive Protestant teachings at the French and English courts at this time, especially significant for a strong Protestant like Wyatt. Thus, carefully positioned through *chiasmus,* the phrase— "the swete returne to grace"—is the center of a series of phrases marked by *asyndeton* moving from "faythe" and "hope" to "returne" / "grace" and then backwards, from "penytence" and "just" to "grace" / "returne." Surrey gives further emphasis to the real center of Wyatt's Psalms by using the device used by Dante and Petrarch, already noted in Surrey's poetry, of making a noun the center of two adjectives: "lvyely faythe and pure" (Milton used the same device in *Paradise Lost,* book 1, line 18: "Th'upright heart and pure").

Surrey now can turn to the real purpose of his artistic structure, the target of the last four lines of the sonnet: "Where Rewlers may se in a myrrour clere / The bitter frewte of false concupiscense." Coming from the purity and innocence of the dead Wyatt, Surrey must face his own living court of Sardanapalus. Surrey's closure echoes the jeremiad of "London hast thow" and the theme of the sleep of the morally dead, even using the same biblical prophetic stance: "In Prynces hartes Goddes scourge yprinted depe / Myght them awake out of their synfull slepe." The *exemplum* of Alexander at the opening of the sonnet has now served its simple rhetorical function: there is no one at the court of Henry VIII, certainly no Alexander, to put Wyatt's translations in a holy ark, although these Psalms are clearly mirrors for magistrates written by David, the holiest of all princes, and not the "fayned gestes of hethen prynces."

Paraphrases from Ecclesiastes

"I, Salamon, Davids sonne, King of Jerusalem" (J43). Ecclesiastes offered Surrey a special opportunity to dramatize his themes of innocence and repentance, and it should be stressed how very original Surrey's translation of its first five chapters was. There had been a number of Psalm translations in England but none of Ecclesiastes. The obvious appeal of Surrey's Ecclesiastes even in manuscript form can be traced in the decades immediately after his beheading, an appeal even for a Protestant martyr like Anne Askew. [14] Once more, true to his method of composition, Surrey dramatizes a voice within his text. To objectify his innocence, to make

the process of repentance believable, Surrey makes the implicit voice of his speaker identifiable with the biblical persona.

Thus in the first line of this translation of the first chapter of Ecclesiastes, Surrey expands the Vulgate, changing the name of the preacher with another use of *antonomasia*. In this line, which Puttenham particularly admired as "a very good Alexandrine,"[15] Surrey boldly asserts his identity with a famous king, an assertion that recalls the accusations against Surrey of plotting for royal position. The second line continues these emphases: "Chossen by God to teach the Jewes and in his lawes to leade them." Even as the wisest king in the world, the speaker in Surrey's text makes, however, a general confessional of the vanity of all things. In doing so, he states with *alliteration* and *asyndeton* the logical topic, the cause, for which the rest of the poem will show the effects: "The world is false, man he is fraile, and all his pleasures payne." In this *amplificatio,* even the Chaucerian Boreas and Zephirus act out contraries that only show the world's mutability: "What may be called new, but suche things in tymes past / As time buryed and dothe revive, and tyme agayne shall waste?" Every human effort is vain, even, says Surrey in completely original lines, man's attempts to restore "Defaults of nature" numberless "like the sandes uppon the salte floode shore." But vaunting his own wit, the speaker thinks of his "rewles of wysdom." When he tries them out by contrary method, against human follies, pride gives him his only delight (and echoing Marlowe's *Tamburlaine*): "Thyerby with more delight to knowledge for to clime." This too is a vanity, however; wisdom leads to doubts. In fact, says Surrey in his closure, "such as enterprice to put newe things in ure" (is Surrey thinking of his own inventions of language and Wyatt's?) should expect scorn.

"From pensif fanzies then, I gan my hart revoke" (J44). If Surrey's first paraphrase of Ecclesiastes is generally a rather close reading of his subtext, his second paraphrase is not. It is closer in form to what Robert Lowell called "imitations," that is, using the original text as a kind of spin-off for the poet's own structures. From such "pensif fanzies" as those in his first translation, in his second Surrey turns to "sporting plaies," although, with such, "a king did yll agre." Of these pleasures that bring "broken slepes" (an important leitmotif in these translations), the most revealing occur in a rather complex, possibly autobiographical passage in lines 11–24, developed from a simple section in the original Latin. It is

a reference to Surrey's elaborate residence, Surrey House, built on Saint Leonard's Hill (renamed Surrey Mount) above Norwich in East Anglia. An assertion in line 12, "By princely acts thus strave I still to make my fame indure," a line that has no source in any of the subtexts, becomes the logical base for this development. Not only this passage of description but the implicit contrast in the whole poem between noble man and cosmic injustice follows from this cause.

Thus, in the lines that follow, this lordly figure in the midst of his glory and power and "goodly witte that compast my desyer" also sees his folly—a recognition that comes from the action of "grace" in line 35, Surrey's more modish Calvinist translation for the Vulgate *sapientia*. Comparing even his folly to wisdom, however, the speaker realizes that both come to nothing. Thus, just as slander in folly's just reward is silenced in time and made small, "Evn so dothe tyme devoure the noble blast of fame / Which showld resounde their glories great that doo desarve the same." At this point in the monologue of the poem, the two forces of Renaissance fame and Calvinist negation meet in one of their first (of many) encounters in the English Renaissance. The "wise mans fattal thred" is just like everyone else's "in this wredtched vale"; "An heire unknowen" may inherit the fruits of his work that came from many effects, including in line 72 "The quiete nights, with broken slepes, to fead a resteles brayne." What hope is left us then? Only "Our quiet herts" accepting "the frute of our payne," the path of moderation, the classical golden mean already described in Surrey's translations of Horace and Martial. The moral stance of the closure provides this sense of controlled liberality.

"Like to the stereles boote that swerves with every wynde" (J45).   Surrey begins his third translation from Ecclesiastes with a familiar Petrarchan image. Here "by crewell prof" the boat represents "The slipper topp of worldley welthe." What follows from this generalization and logical cause are specific effects described in a series of antitheses, in the manner of Petrarchan contraries. They reflect every aspect of life from nature to a hint of contemporary English society and the dissolution of monasteries: "Auncient walles to race is our unstable guyse, / And of their wetherbeten stones to buylde some new devyse." This series is Surrey's version of the famous *epanados,* the "time" sequence in the original Hebrew, most famous for English-speaking audiences in its King James version.

Surrey prefers here the inherent bouncing structure of Poulter's measure to dramatize his contraries rather than reductive syntax. From this catalogue the speaker turns to "the proper tyme and place" of all things and "graunted eke to man, of all the worldes estate / . . . to argue and debate," a medieval and Renaissance commonplace. But here too "all is labor loste"; sadly "the wandering eyes, that longe for suertey sought," find that even pain is no guarantee of anything. The pessimism may be Hebraic in the subtext, but in 1546 it has Calvinist echoes.

Thus, in lines 35–40, Surrey's text reflects the English translations of Coverdale and his followers: "Fulfilled shall it be, what so the Lorde intende, / Which no device of mans witt may advaunce, nor yet defende; / Who made all thing of nought, that Adams chyldren might / Lerne how to dread the Lord, that wrought suche wonders in their sight." Because "renewed in our dayes" are these "gresly wonders," Surrey's next image builds on both medieval allegory and the imagery of the Book of Revelation popular with Protestants. This is the image of the "carfull skourge" of God stealing on us unaware. As in Surrey's jeremiad against London and its court of Sardanapalus, this text reveals "a roiall throne wheras that Justice should have sitt" but instead "with fyerce and crwell mode, / Wher Wrong was set, that blody beast, that drounke the giltles blode." The voice in the text becomes prophetic: "One day the Lord shall sitt in dome, / To vewe his flock and chose the pure: the spotted have no rome." In his long closure, Surrey makes the same free paraphrase of his Latin subtexts, evoking as a solution for the repentant sinner the classical Horatian golden mean of temperance, translated as "A meane convenient welth." This moderation is quite enough and no foreknowledge is needed, for, argues the speaker in a rather strained use of the figure of *hyperbaton,* "to foreknow who shall rejoyce their gotton good with stryef."

"When I be thought me well, under the restles soon" (J46). The structure of Surrey's fourth translation from Ecclesiastes follows the original closely for the first thirty-six lines, then dramatically swings into a free adaptation with Surrey's direct reference to his own imprisonment. The first line begins the soliloquy used in all these meditations. In the opening scenes of this text, the speaker meditates on innocent human beings who have had to suffer so terribly that for them the dead are happier "And happiest is the sede that never did conceve." The speaker then begins a dialogue

with himself and announces that the life "Of faythefull frends that spends their goods in commone, with out stryef" is the best solution to the harsh changeability in human society—an interesting solution since it is More's in *Utopia* and that of the monasteries Henry VIII had just destroyed. Surrey is probably thinking of his family here, certainly if, as the poem later suggests, he is in the windy cold Tower: "The frendly feares ly warme, in armes embraced faste; / Who sleapes aloone at every tourne dothe feale the winter blast." In the second part of the poem, the text contains a vignette about a fellow prisoner in the Tower "that never knewe what fredom ment, nor tasted of delyght" and in whose identity Surrey obviously saw his own plight, "unhoped happ in most dispaier," and one whose hands might "have a septre sett."[16]

"By" such "conjures the seade of kynges is thrust from staate," says the speaker in line 41, the result of "hidden haat." In a following scene the text describes this state and court: "a frend or foo, / With feat worne bare in tracing such whearas the honours groo" and especially, as in England of 1546, "at change of a prynce great rowtes revived strange." But the new king will be no better, says the speaker in his meditation: "I gan conclude eache gredy gayne hath his uncertayne end." Surrey's closure presents the only solution for survival in such a court: "In humble spritte is sett the temple of the Lorde," a paraphrase of I Corinthians 15:3. In such a temple "loke thy mouth and conscyence may accorde"; this church is "buylte of love, and decte with hoote desyre / And simple fayth." These are lines Surrey developed and expanded from the beginning of the fifth chapter of Ecclesiastes but which structurally he places here as a model, a moral stance, for the scene at court that has just preceded it. Unlike the king of that court, the host of such a temple "With gentill care" will hear the suit of the humble and furthermore grant the request. But "outwarde works" and "wast of wourds" give this king or host "no delight"; "suche sacryfice unsavereth in his sight."

"When that repentant teares hathe clensyd clere from ill" (P52). Surrey's last translation from Ecclesiastes continues with the theme of the contrite heart. Such repentance has been the goal in the process of self-discovery in all five meditations. Thus the tears of the penitent cleanse the heart where grace "hathe wrought" a new will. The individual simply makes the act of contrition manifested by tears and not formulaic words; then grace does the rest, the individual nothing. The penitent only offers sighs, and the

description of the process anticipates Milton's steps for repentance for Adam and Eve at the end of book 10 of *Paradise Lost*. At this point Surrey launches into an attack on perfunctory prayer such as Protestants of the day make on devotions like the rosary: such "chattering of vnholly lippis" is "As ferfull broken slepes spring from a restles hedde." Humble vowes, on the other hand, "by grace right swetly smoks"; it is better to confess one's "frayltye" and avoid "fayned words" and "craft" that "doth thy self defile," says this speaker to his silent interlocutor. In fact, "owtward works" are "all dampned" in the sight of God, and many words are like "sondry broken dreames." Rather, "with humble secret playnt, fewe words of hotte effect, / Honor thy Lord." The hand of justice will not be slow to follow "unrightius folke."

Having developed the correct moral stance of penitence in the language of Coverdale, so new in 1546, the speaker then turns in lines 29–30 to his main definition: "The cheif blisse that in earth the liuing man is lent, / Is moderat welth to nourishe lief, yf he can be content." This definition will act as the logical basis for a contrast drawn in lines 31–53 and in closure of the poem where it is repeated with more examples and effects. Of these effects or sins that temperance and moderation must control, those of prodigality and greed are catalogued next in the poem. One vignette may be autobiographical, a reference to Surrey's own estates and their seizure during the Christmas season 1546: "The plenteus howsses sackt, the owners end with shame; / Their sparkelid goods; their nedy heyres, that showld reioyce the same." The final attitude in this meditative text arises from an image of magnanimity. The result of moderation is true liberality. "For sure the liberall hand that hath no hart to spare," says the speaker in line 55, "This fading welthe, but powres it forthe, it is a uertu rare." This human being cannot be hurt: "No care may perce wher myrth hath tempred such a brest; / The bitter gaull, seasoned wih swet, suche wysdome may digest."

Paraphrases from the Psalms

"Thie name, O Lord, howe greate is fownd before our sight!" (J47). Surrey's translations of five Psalms appear less the single unit that the paraphrases from Ecclesiastes suggest and more a series of individual poems. Surrey's Psalms range from settled structures to almost incoherent outbursts in which language appears the only

resource left for the self to express its freedom. Surrey's first Psalm experiment, a translation of Psalm 8, is less individualistic and more communal in its intention, however, by virtue of Surrey's subtext. Surrey constructs a text more suited for liturgical needs, the kind of experiment in communal language and religious expression occurring on the Continent at this time.[17] Its public nature immediately distances it from the dramatized cries of the Ecclesiastes texts. In its structure the poem simply develops from the generalization and statement of cause, the logical topic in its first line— "Thie name"—into a series of effects, another use of *amplificatio*. The first sixteen lines sketch this naming or ordering, which become a praise, through all aspects of nature. With line 16 and until 36, Surrey turns his catalogue to human beings, particularly the worker: "What thing is man, / Whose tourne to serve in his poore neede this worke thow first began?" On the human head, says the speaker addressing the Creator in line 37, "thow hast sett a Crowne of Glorye to, / To whom also thow didest appoint that honour shuld be do." This assertion is the climax of the poem. Such honor means that the human being made by God as "Lord of all this worke of thyne" interacts in ordered hierarchical creation, described in a catalogue or *enumeratio* that follows the assertion. This honor paradoxically leads to an act of humility, to "know and playne confesse that marveilous is thie name." The Gloria ending the poem affirms God's marvelous act of creation then as "now, even heare within our tyme" or even "when we be filth and slyme."

"When recheles youthe in an unquiet brest" (J36).   Surrey's other Psalm translations reflect none of this optimism about the human place in the order of creation. On the contrary, their whole theme is the agony of the isolated human being in such a bitterly disordered scheme of things. The texts reflect Surrey's last days. At places in the text where the structure of the translations breaks down, it is easy to assume that Surrey's whole being was also breaking down, although not completely. To the bitter end, even on the scaffold, as the details of his biography affirm, Surrey continued to speak. More like dramatic monologues than religious songs, these last poems show us Psalms very different from conventional Renaissance translation. Two of them have prologues specifically addressed, which give the meditations of the Psalms a topicality. The first is a prologue to Surrey's translation of Psalm 88, addressed probably to Sir Antony Denny, who was a particular favorite of

Henry VIII empowered as one of three to affix the stamp with the king's sign on all warrants issued in his name. At the king's collapse, Surrey's fate thus depended heavily on Denny's help. In actuality, Denny signed Surrey's death warrant and was intimately involved with every stage of Surrey's trial. As Surrey must have known, the gift of a Psalm would appeal to Denny, who zealously promoted Protestant teaching and had amassed a considerable fortune as the recipient of many grants from the dissolved monasteries.

The poem is a *strambotto*, its rhyme scheme *a b a b a b c c*. In this one-sentence poem Surrey immediately begins his self-justification in a long subordinate clause. His negligent youth with "unquiet brest" (because of the attacks on him by anger, revenge, and sheer cruelty) has finally, "After long warr," been conquered by patience "And justice wrought by pryncelye equitie" (an ambiguous reference, probably one more of hope and request than fact). In the turn of the poem, addressing "My Deny," Surrey relates how his recognition of how "depe imprest" his "errour" was would have led him "to worke dispaire of libertye" (another ambiguity probably meant both literally and spiritually) "Had not David, the perfyt warriour," the noble knight who on the field and in the cave had fought his own wars, especially for internal patience, "tought / That of my fault thus pardon shold be sought." Thus, implies Surrey, the appended translation, an instrument of language that David's language had taught him, is intended as an act of humility and penitence.

"Oh Lorde, uppon whose will dependeth my welfare" (J48).   What Surrey appends to the Denny prologue is his translation of Psalm 88. It is a question if Surrey achieves in his actual text the intention stated in his prologue of Davidic and public penitence. He does ask the Lord—no longer the more Catholic "our Lord" of Psalm 8—to "Graunt that the just request of this repentaunt mynd / So perce thyne eares that in thy sight som favour it may find." If this request is fully stated, is in the form of the question, not appearing until lines 35–36, that summarizes the effects of suffering in the poem: "Within this carefull mynd, bourdnyd with care and greif, / Why dost thou not appere, Oh Lord, that sholdest be his relief?" It is significant here, as in all Surrey's work, that "this carefull mynd" is the center of all dramatic activity. This activity here makes the meditation threefold: lines 1–16 state the case; lines 17–34 show the suppliant calling for the means to

fulfill his elected role; and lines 35–44 present the request and the restatement of the suppliant's suffering.

The first section describes a soul "fraughted full with greif of follies past" and a "restles bodye" being consumed "and death approcheth fast," the original Psalm subtext obviously appropriate for Surrey's immediate personal situation. In the second part of his text, Surrey's speaker has "humble hart and stretched hands" and asks: "Wherfore dost thow forbeare, in the defence of thyne, / To shewe such tokens of thy power" so that the "hart with fayth" will be so fed "That in the mouthe of thy elect thy mercyes might be spredd?" The unelected, in whose "blind endured herts" the "light of thy lively name" cannot appear, cannot judge such brightness. In the next lines 27–30, as the voice of such elect, the poet and his vocation are directly evoked, climaxing in the Pauline trumpet image: "Nor blasted [blazoned] may thy name be by the mouth of those / Whome death hath shutt in sylence, so as they may not disclose, / The livelye voice of them that in this world delight / Must be the trumppe that must resound the glorye of thy might." The third section provides the closure in which the Lord is given the ultimate question and asked to behold "one from youth afflicted still, that never did but waile" surrounded by "Great heaps of care" as "the sunken shipp" by "roring waves." Even those who love him, "whome no myschaunce could from my love devyde / Ar forced, for my greater greif, from me their face to hyde." These last lines differ considerably from the Vulgate; for Surrey, it was not God who was keeping his true friends and loved ones from him.

"Thoughe, Lorde, to Israell thy graces plentuous be" (J49). This text translating Psalm 73 offers an even more prophetic and objective contrast between the wicked and the suffering elect, whose gifts of language could blazon forth "thy secret works" in public and social occasion, "in sight of Adams race." Thus the poem starts out with a generalization to be developed through two sections of negative examples before its positive affirmation can be exemplified. Declaring like a logical topic that the Lord gives "graces plentuous," the speaker immediately in the second line remarks but only to the chosen, "I meane to such with pure intent as fixe their trust in the."

In the first section of the poem, lines 2–28, Surrey shows the faith of the speaker fainting and his feet slipping as he sees the very rich and proud rejoicing in nothing less than the court of Sardan-

apalus. In such a wicked society, Surrey describes how "thy foes" who "tast no other foode, / But sucke the fleshe of thy elect and bath them in their bloode" begin to scoff like the enemies of Christ at the Crucifixion, saying: " 'Shold we beleve the Lorde doth know and suffer this? / Foled be he with fables vayne that so abused is.' " Surrey ends this section with a bold description of this court of Sardanapalus: "In terrour of the just thus raignes iniquitye, / Armed with power, laden with gold, and dred for crueltye."

In the second section, lines 29–53, the speaker contrasts his own struggle in such a world: "Then vayne the warr might seme that I by faythe mayntayne / Against the fleshe, whose false effects my pure hert wold distayne." In the face of such wicked men, he is unable to fathom God's justice, "no witt cold perce so farr, thy holly domes to knoo." Then the speaker comes "to the holly place, the mansion of the just" where he sees the purpose God's justice has "For such as buyld on worldly welth, and dye ther colours faire." The apocalyptic scene that follows is the revenge the speaker has longed for: the proud shall wake to destruction of their false buildings, the foundation of their pride collapsing. Until then, says Surrey, in an original line, "My eyes yeld teares, my yeres consume bitwne hope and dispayre." Worst of all, in this period before God's revenge, the speaker is humiliated before this society: "Alas, how oft my foes have framed my decaye," another interpolation not in Surrey's subtexts.

In the third and last section of the poem, lines 54–66, the speaker remembers, as he "stode in drede to drenche, thy hands still did me stay." Using familiar nautical imagery, Surrey's speaker remarks that the Lord was "my guyd" in every voyage "that I toke to conquer synne." Why should he trust in any other help but the Lord's? The wicked "shall perishe with their golden godds that did their harts seduce" whereas this speaker "that in thy worde have set my trust and joye, / The highe reward that longs therto shall quietlye enjoye." The reward will be that of enjoying the purest language— Surrey is here following Campensis rather than the Vulgate[18]—and "my unworthye lypps inspired with thy grace, / Shall thus forespeke thy secret works in sight of Adams race." This eloquent speaker will be elect; he will show the secrets of reality to a public, a society, a corrupt court that should recognize his natural election and inspired language.

"The soudden stormes that heave me to and froo" (J37). Surrey's text for Psalm 73 also has a prologue. Its form, as Ringler has noted, is nowhere else in Surrey or his contemporaries,[19] and is a stanza of twelve lines of iambic pentameter rhymed *a b a b a b a b a b c c*. Addressed to George Blage,[20] the poem centers around a persistent image in Surrey: the speaker as ship at sea. Terrible storms have almost "perced faith, my guyding saile," says the speaker, as he goes "on the noble voyage" like a true knight "To succhor treuthe and falshed to assaile." But he is constrained "to beare my sayles ful loo" and never can find "some pleasaunt gale" (these "prosperous winds" are given to those "As ronne from porte to porte to seke availe"). As the structure of Surrey's Psalm 73 shows the same contrast of the suffering faithful and the prosperous wicked, "This bred dispayre" and these doubts lead to a weakening, "and all my courage faile." Now, says the speaker to Blage, "myne errour well I see: / Such goodlye light King David giveth me." In both prologues, the ending allusion to David recalls Surrey's master Wyatt and his translation of the Penitential Psalms of David.

"Give eare to my suit, Lord, fromward hide not thy face" (J50).   Surrey's translation of Psalm 55 has a text so disjunctive that it is difficult to find a clear structure. The first forty-one lines of the poem follow rather closely the original subtexts. Then an original interpolation occurs before a final return to the Vulgate, a return that abandons English and uses a Latin line as closure. Surrey also abandons Poulter's measure in this text and gives what, in form at least, is his purest classical imitation: unrhymed alexandrines, a steady hexameter line (even the final Latin follows this) with six stresses, imitated by the humanist Cheke.

Almost immediately, by line 3, Surrey evokes in his text the image of a man being hunted and entrapped: "My fooes they bray so lowde, and eke threpe on fast, / Buckeled to do me scathe, so is their malice bent." Powerful verbs and abstract subjects with concrete modifiers portray the victim: "A tremblynge cold of dred clene overwhelmeth my hert." Surrey so develops his drama that the outburst in line 8, while closely following the Vulgate, seems personal, one more of Surrey's structural introspections: " 'O,' thinke I, 'hadd I wings like to the symple dove, / This peryll myght I flye, and seke some place of rest / In wylder woods, where I might dwell farr from these cares.' " The series of end-stopped lines in this text, recalling Surrey's translations of the *Aeneid* with their

unrhymed long lines, is momentarily broken by two uses of *apostrophe,* the emotion of which is not in the original: "Rayne those unbrydled tungs! breake that conjured league!" In the same emotional swing, Surrey in the next lines (14–17) depicts the familiar wickedness of his city. "For I decyphred have amydd our towne the stryfe," says the speaker in a classical inversion. "Gyle and wrong kept the walles, they ward both day and night" while "myscheif with care doth kepe the market stede" and "wickidnes with craft in heaps swarme through the strete."

At this point Surrey develops in his translation a linguistic structure as poignant and powerful as the original Latin of the Vulgate. It is built around the theme of betrayal. "Ne my declared foo wrought me all this reproche," the speaker declares; he "cold have hidd my face from venym of his eye." In what is likely a reference to his boyhood friend and cousin Sir Richard Southwell, the speaker announces in a bitter use of *oxymoron:* "It was a frendly foo, by shadow of good will, / Myne old fere and dere frende, my guyde, that trapped me." By line 26 the speaker's bitterness asserts itself fully, with the same sense of ultimate justice as before: "Such soden surprys quicke may them hell devoure," says the speaker in another awkward classical inversion, clearly unrevised, and continues: "Whilst I invoke the Lord, whose power shall me defend." The speaker will not cease praying and making humble suit to "perce thy pacyent eare."

Shifting, as Surrey frequently does in these translations from direct address to God to the third-person narrator, the speaker announces that "It was the Lord that brake the bloody compackts of those / That preloked on with yre to slaughter me and myne." In this last passage from the original Latin text, Surrey again prophesies God will strike "The conseyence unquiet" with heavy hand "And proves their force in fayth whome he sware to defend." Despite the betrayal described toward the end of the poem by a "Friowr," the speaker has the "ease" he finds "in the th'other Psalme of David." Then Surrey concludes his poem with the next Latin line in the Vulgate text. That Latin line number 23 is probably "th'other Psalme." In any case, Surrey ends his poem with the Latin line: "Iacta curam tuam super dominum et ipse te enutriet" (Throw your care upon the Lord and he himself will nourish you). This leap of faith is about as close as Surrey comes in these biblical paraphrases to the kind of reconciliation and resignation that classical sources such as Plutarch,

Seneca, and Boethius (not to mention the Christian texts) might have offered such a condemned man—sources which Surrey had already dramatized in his elegy on Wyatt. Otherwise, in these poems the fury is barely contained.

"**The stormes are past, these cloudes are overblowne**" **(J38).** Surrey's last Psalm paraphrase, if one can call it that, begins in its manuscript with a Latin title "Bonum mihi quia humiliasti me," (it is good for me that you have humiliated me). This title is the first part of line 71 of the Vulgate Psalm 118, the second part being "Ut discam justificationes tuas" (so that I may learn your justifications). The Latin title in the manuscript is the only clue to Surrey's formal conception of this text, which weaves a series of antitheses through disjunctive leaps (even a line is missing). This disjunctiveness also appears in almost relentlessly end-stopped lines. In another totally original stanza form, the poem seems modeled on a Petrarchan sonnet, seventeen lines of iambic pentameter (although with marked accentual rhythms) rhymed *a b a b a b a x c d c d c d c d e e*. Furthermore, this Psalm "imitation" is Surrey's last poem, according to his son, writing fifty years later in a dedicatory letter to his Howard cousin Queen Elizabeth.[21]

With a theme familiar from other Surrey poems, the initial nautical image recalls the image of self as ship. It is a common figure for the isolated consciousness amid the flux of time and mutability, related to the emblem figure of fortune. The speaker here seemingly accepts the closure of life itself. As revealed in familiar chiastic and antithetical structure (normal syntax, as in the first line, followed by the inversion of the second) the speaker describes self-control, the "paine foreknowne" (his beheading in a matter of days) joined to "pacience graft" through the devices of *alliteration* and parallel past participles. His "determed brest," an echo of the Roman "mens certa," was once a "hart where heapes of griefes were grown," but now is able to plant "mirth and rest" because, in Surrey's final use of a favorite word, he has been able to make his revenge "swete." He now has seemingly learned the lesson of Scipio, as Cicero had written, and of Boethius: "No company so pleasant as myne owne," so that, continuing over the missing line, "Thraldom at large hath made this prison fre." The elegantly set epigram in line 9—"Danger well past remembred workes delight"—builds on *litotes,* accentual rhythm and caesura, and *alliteration* to show the same control and derives probably from the *Aeneid.*[22]

With line 12 the poem disintegrates. This prison is far crueler than that first one at Windsor in 1537 when he remembered his dead friend the Duke of Richmond. Here the voice in the poem cannot sustain the formal antitheses of its own language. The poem breaks into a single outburst using that most frequent image for introspection in the English Renaissance, a mirror. Although, from earlier doubts, says the speaker, hope has sprung so that nothing is unpleasant in his sight, the speaker, nevertheless, like Shakespeare's Richard II almost fifty years later, has a glass brought to him. Now looking in it, he sees the ultimate horror, which is not his own death but that of his world. Surrey sees the terrible dishonor, "the curelesse wound that bledeth day and night," the defeat not only of his family and its blood but, in Surrey's eyes, the defeat of a whole civilization by the forces of Sardanapalus and his court. Thus, the allusion to "a wretch that hath no hart to fight" may recall Surrey's previous sonnet on the Assyrian king or it may refer to his bitterest betrayer, Southwell. Its ambiguity, like the lack of specific meaning in the "curelesse wound," has an obvious context, however. All these forces will now "spill that blood that hath so oft bene shed / For Britannes sake, alas, and now is ded." Given this context and concept of honor, the bitterness and lack of resignation at the end become in this sense affirmative. In Surrey's final lyric, which continues, as Peterson suggests,[23] the reflective and didactic strength of the medieval plain style, the voice demonstrates an essential fidelity to honor and the highest forms of human life, at least as this speaker has known them.

Chapter Six

The Elegy

Surrey's elegies are justly famous as highly crafted works of art. At least three are permanent members of any anthology of poetry in English. The early Tudor period saw the transformation of the elegy, largely under the influence of the humanists and in the example of the "courtly makers."[1] As a Renaissance legacy from the classics, elegy as a term had a variety of meanings, ranging from threnodies to didactic disquisitions, epigrams, epistolary love complaints, and Ovidian erotic lyrics like Donne's. But from the time of Wyatt's sonnet on Cromwell (M236) and Surrey's poem on the death of Wyatt, memorial verses on the death of outstanding English men and women became a poetic fashion and a cultural phenomenon in a quite new realistic manner, which has lasted into the twentieth century.

Poems on Wyatt

"W. resteth here, that quick could never rest" (J28).   Surrey's elegy of 1542 was an achievement for which he gained renown in his own lifetime.[2] When the elegy appeared again, as one of twenty such personal elegies in *Tottel's Miscellany* (in number surpassed only by love lyrics), it became the model in the Renaissance for all such elegies. Surrey's strategy in his elegy is that of a public gesture. The event the poem was written to commemorate (the recent death of his deeply admired friend) is a social occasion. Its structure as "enduring monument" develops from the devices of the epideictic oration.[3] It also reveals a substructure of blame that will become sharper satiric invective in the two sonnet-elegies Surrey also wrote on the occasion of Wyatt's death. Such dispraise of Wyatt's enemies in the structure of this poem merely confirms in the text the social and even political context of Surrey's Tudor audience. Of course, in themselves, the subjects of grief and loss, mutability and nostalgia, were natural ones for Surrey, but the implied context here of public audience demanded a didactic mode of which, for any poet

trained by humanists, praise and blame would be instruments. Thus, in this poem Surrey dramatizes an antithesis to the speaker's grief at the loss and vilification of so splendid a human being. This antithesis is expressed in the theme of Wyatt's labor, Wyatt as worker. There emerges in the text therefore a dialectical structure of action. Themes of grief and loss appear at the beginning and end of the poem, but progressing through the middle of the text is the definition of Wyatt as a human being not only active but dramatized as actually working within the very progression of the poem. In this definition, personifying Castiglione's courtier for whom virtue is action,[4] Wyatt is directly posited against the figure in the sonnet Surrey likely wrote about the same time (and which appears immediately after the Wyatt elegy in *Tottel*), the idle Sardanapalus. This theme of labor and activity especially suited the Tudor figure of Wyatt, for it was beloved to the humanists in their attacks on medieval forms of contemplation and so integral to later Protestant conceptions of social anthropology.

Surrey begins with two figures and a parody: *paradox* and *polyptoton* and a special use of the familiar *hic requiescit* formula. The initial dramatic situation is also implied in this formula; the poem is a formal *epicedium* in which the mourner stands over the corpse of a beloved. In this first line the ironic structure by which the poem will progress becomes focused. Wyatt is resting "here" yet alive he could never rest. Although not confronted until the end of the poem where the terms become heaven and earth, this initial antithesis between death and life is reflected in the alternating syntax of Surrey's *a b a b* stanza form and continues throughout the nine stanzas and final couplet. Lines 1 and 3 have independent clauses, for example, and subordination at the end of line 1 leads into the subordination of all of line 2; and line 4, although independent, is heavily inverted like subordination. This kind of alternation of syntax and diction reflects the larger ironies shaping Surrey's tribute and praise. Furthermore, their ironic alternation serves the purpose of objectifying the text by setting up a kind of dialectical reader-response, reflecting the strategy of the poem: to embody the dead Wyatt, by direct metaphors of language and not by similes of description. Thus in the first stanza Surrey sets up his initial conflict between the virtuous Wyatt who had on earth "heavenly giftes" that the disdain of the court did not destroy but, on the contrary, increased in his body, sinking virtue (meaning both goodness and

manhood) "deper in his brest." This labor of transforming the court's scorn was Wyatt's. It was achieved by his own ironic displacement and control of reality, which yielded its own special reward, says Surrey in an epigrammatic paradox that ends the stanza: "Such profit he by envy could obtain."

With stanza 2, Surrey's own strategies of ironic displacement evolve into a method of distancing that gives his subject even greater objectivity. Surrey makes the poem into a body that itself incarnates the nature of Wyatt, giving the life of poetry to the dead body before the fictional persona of the *epicedium*. Surrey's method is to take Wyatt's "heavenly giftes" and show how, as "quick," they never did rest. He catalogues various parts of Wyatt's literal body in the first of the Renaissance literary anatomies. His form here is the heroic quatrain, which he invents. Inverting the Petrarchan method of the blazon for his own new purposes, Surrey makes a parody of erotic technique by naming the beauties of this beloved body. This catalogue evolves into a series of phrasal units, divided further into appositive phrases and subordinate clauses. This is the syntax that dominates the inset of the seven central stanzas of the elegy. Although the inset uses the figure of *isocolon*, the larger method is, of course, but another example of Surrey's favorite figure of *amplificatio* and, as such, gives density and objectivity to the poetic structure. Because of its elliptical form, the catalogue probably appeared in 1542 as revolutionary syntax. Furthermore, each of the seven stanzas centers on a simple substantive, the name of the gift itself, with modifying clauses and phrases, but with no verb. Surrey's language moves fast with these Seurat-like phrasal units but only because of the first and ninth stanzas and final couplet that frame them and help to give the fullest ironic perspective on the function and meaning of the catalogue.

If there is Petrarchan parody operating here in the naming of head, face, hand, tongue, eye, heart, and then body "where force and beawty met," there is also a substructure of theology.[5] As a customary resource for the early Renaissance, theological language points specifically to the seven gifts of the Holy Spirit epitomized in the virtues of each of these parts of Wyatt's body. Such theological language operates antithetically in a text of "places," a method rhetoricians prescribed for epideictic strategy. According to Peterson, Surrey here follows such "rhetorical instructions to a letter."[6] Thus in the *partitio*, the logical topic that directs this middle struc-

ture of this elegy, Surrey starts with the head as prudence, one of the cardinal virtues of the church and a gift of the Holy Spirit. This is a place "where wisdom misteries did frame." The word "misteries" still carried its old meaning of the sacraments of the Catholic church and possibly the classical religious rites behind the Christian. At the same time it is *ministerium* with its overtones of work and activity, leading to the next line: "Whose hammers bet styll in that lively brayn / As on a stithe." In a line anticipating Ben Jonson's praise of Shakespeare and his "living line" that comes from striking "the second heat / Upon the muses' anvil," Surrey states that on Wyatt's smithy, "some work of fame / Was dayly wrought to turne to Brit-aines gayn." This is the humanist conception of labor at its best, service to the state. Thus prudence, translated and parodied from theology, represents the highest wisdom for Surrey's public audience.

Justice appears in Wyatt's "visage stern and myld" that can condemn vice and rejoice in virtue. This kind of justice as Calvinist justification provides a "grace," furthermore, that can defeat the trials of fortune "Amid great stormes." Wyatt is not fortune's fool but is as Horatio to Hamlet, one who can keep his Stoic composure and in the last line of the stanza "lyve upright and smile at fortunes choyce." This kind of control exhibits the greatest temperance and fortitude as well. Thus the Wyatt that emerges in this portrait is not the ironic introspective Wyatt of popular twentieth-century criticism; he is magisterial in every sense. Again the practical effect of such temperance and courage leads to work. Wyatt's "hand that taught" expresses a gesture recalling the academic lectures of Surrey's day. Its double effect is to point toward Wyatt's poetry: Wyatt taught the possibilities of language in the new English of the Tudors, "what might be sayd in ryme," and did it so well by example that the hand "reft Chaucer" of "the glory of his wit" and made, says Surrey in an original realistic image from archery, such a "mark" on his time. This achievement, "though unparfited," later generations "may approche, but never none shall hit."

The "toung" that follows in Surrey's blazon logically goes with such a hand. It too performed the highest functions of humanist teaching: Wyatt's tongue or language "served in forein realmes his king." Furthermore, its "courteous talke to vertue did enflame / Eche noble hart" and like Castiglione's ideal courtier, Wyatt was "a worthy guide to bring / Our English youth by travail unto fame," a reference perhaps to Surrey's own relationship to Wyatt. "Travail"

has at least two purposes in the text: first, to support the ubiquitous work theme and, second, to show the effects on English intellectual and artistic life of Wyatt's travels in Europe as a diplomat. Wyatt's temperance and fortitude demonstrate themselves also in his use of his eye. Its power of judgment cannot be blinded by any effect but it can "allure" friends and, significantly, reconcile foes. Furthermore, the focus of his eyes, his "persing loke," represent the quiet mind, an allusion in Surrey to Wyatt's translation of Plutarch and the balance of the contemplative life Wyatt had praised in his satire "Myne owne John Poyntz" (M105).

At the end of the sixth stanza, line 24 focuses, with a tightening of the figure of *asyndeton* that has dominated the syntax of the whole poem, on the inner human being. Wyatt's "loke did represent a mynde / With vertue fraught, reposed, voyd of gyle." This innocence so plaintively announced is continued in the next stanza describing Wyatt's heart where its control is stated negatively, in an elaborate figure of *litotes*. The figure balances, as in some Stoic doctrines the various temptations to power. The key word here is "dred" with its Tudor meaning of fear associated with tyranny, which, in this case, would extend to thought-control. Wyatt never had such fear or dread but he boldly expressed "the thought that might the trouth avance." Again deliberately inverting his structure to give syntactic and intentional balance, Surrey shows us a Wyatt who can smile at fortune's vagaries, whether "loft" or "represt," neither swelling "in wealth or" yielding "unto mischance." In language and figure, Surrey's Wyatt is the complete opposite of Surrey's Sardanapalus.

In the final stanza of his blazon, the whole body subsumes all these "heavenly giftes" on earth: "A valiant corps, where force and beawty met." The verb here marks the transition in the progression of the poem: the direct preterite form, which has virtually disappeared since the first stanza, now hits home. The "corps" in front of the speaker of this elegy is, in both meanings of "corps" in Surrey's time, a body whose parts have just been praised and a corpse. In the very syntax of the poem Wyatt is now dead, as the verbs show. He was "Happy, alas, to happy, but for foes; / Lived and ran the race that nature set; / Of manhodes shape, where she the molde did lose." *Hyperbole* in this passage, one of the few instances in the structure of the poem, parodies Petrarchan devices; it also directly imitates Dido's final speech just before she kills herself for love,

beginning, in Surrey's translation, "Happy, alas to happy, if these costes" (book 4, 1. 876.) Indeed, before these lines in the *Aeneid*, Dido also speaks a passage that significantly Surrey rewrote for the Wyatt elegy, lines Surrey translated in his *Aeneid* as: "I lived and ranne the course fortune did graunt / And under earth my great gost now shall wende" (ll. 873–74). Fortune overcame this lover; but Wyatt has followed nature, his own, as well as that of the universe. Surrey extends this athletic metaphor from Vergil into the Christian context as found in Ephesians and Corinthians, favorite Protestant texts: Wyatt "lived and ran the race that nature set."

From this theme of the mold of nature, the speaker closes with the theme of the Christian reward of "heavenly giftes" announced in the first stanzas. From the beginning Surrey has carefully interwoven alternate structures of mutability and eternity, yet the progression to the last stanza is quite literally a leap. "But to the heavens that simple soul is fled," says this speaker, lifting himself from his formal posture of the classical *epicedium* and fully addressing his public national audience. Wyatt has "left with such as covet Christ to know / Witnesse of faith that never shall be ded." The phrasing is decidedly Protestant, and its linguistic phrasing is faithful to Wyatt's own nature and belief, making Surrey's own poetic structure "Witnesse of faith."

The poem is, in fact, one more example of Surrey's dramatization of fidelity. Its method is to build an objectivity of form that as a blazon is as iterative in its structure as a litany. Because of the poem's carefully articulated strategies, the final moral stance exhibits faith as a structure as well as content and meaning. Thus from the beginning of his faithful portrait Surrey has contrasted the innocence of Wyatt with the "disdayn" and "envy" of those foes, blaming those who would not let his "happy" body alone. In this contrast, Surrey fulfilled the threefold need of an elegy by developing, within its antitheses, both public praise and sorrow and, in the last stanza and couplet, public consolation. It is a consolation that is Christian in naming, but has been earned through the progressing structure of the poem.

The poem ends, as in Surrey's satire on London and in certain of his biblical paraphrases, on a note of prophecy and blame. Echoing Isaiah, Surrey completes his stanza with an image of a cosmic human failure. As with Wyatt, so with Christ's own body: "Sent for our helth, but not received so." Wyatt's language might have redeemed

his time, Surrey suggests, but his body was destroyed. Yet the structure of the poem has resurrected that body, even to the point of having thirty-nine lines (if we count the original "AMEN" published at the end of all the early editions) for Wyatt's thirty-nine years, and recalled Wyatt's "helth" of language. The speaker thus finishes his demonstrative panegyric oration over the dead body in his couplet. Paraphrasing a line from Ecclesiastes (12:7), he turns the blame on society: "Thus, for our gilte, this jewel have we lost. / The earth his bones, the heavens possesse his gost."

"**My Ratclif, when thy rechlesse youth offendes**" (J34).   Although not an elegy, this extended epigram by Surrey, a single stanza *a b a b c c,* demonstrates how deeply the model of Wyatt determined Surrey's moral perspective. Probably addressed to Thomas Ratcliffe, third Earl of Sussex, almost ten years younger than Surrey, who had served with Surrey in France in 1544, the poem may have been written hastily at the war front, in the manner of a verse-letter. Its theme is typical of the philosophical lyrics Surrey had already incorporated into two songs: the need for self-control. Here too Surrey had Roman subtexts, such as a paraphrase of Tibullus in "Receve thy scourge by others chastisement."[7] Whatever social offense the young aristocrat had committed, Surrey's advice, in the spirit of the Wyatt of stanza 5 of his elegy, gently admonishes the youth. If he does not take the lesson of learning by watching others, he will learn the violence at the heart of Tudor society: "Then plages are sent without advertisement." The final couplet contrasts the wisdom of Solomon (actually a passage from Ecclesiasticus 27:21) that wrongs may be righted (except for the betrayal of secrets) with "But Wiat said true, the skarre doth aye endure." This is an allusion probably to Wyatt's verse-letter that describes his imprisonment (M 244). Surrey's point to the younger man is that it is better to avoid any occasion of violence because, however it turns out, one will never forget it.

"**Dyvers thy death doo dyverslye bemone**" (J29).   Surrey wrote two other elegies for Wyatt, both of them sonnets. "Dyvers thy death" begins with a generalization, the cause that becomes the topic or invention for the structure of the poem. In this poem the *partitio* is threefold, the octet naming two effects or kinds of lament, one for each quatrain, and the sestet a third, that of the speaker himself. The Petrarchan *volta* is deftly handled here to mark not just a division between octet and sestet but a major shift in the

development of the argument. The first line with its *alliteration* and *polyptoton* and its heavy trochees slows down not only for a proposition to be established linguistically but for a scene to be dramatized. The scene is the same frame of the classical *epicedium:* a corpse is spread out before mourners, and one, the speaker of this sonnet like a solitary lover bereft but faithful, is bending over the body but also watching the social gestures of other mourners. In the poem an elaborate parody of erotic subtext moves from linguistic play to the outburst of the final personal image.[8]

The poem thus progresses from the place of personal address, "thy death" in the first line, to "thy guyltless blood" in the second quatrain, to "thy fame" at the turn of the octet, to "thy coorse" at the end of last quatrain. The personal voice narrating the event is subordinated to the objective dramatic actions being narrated. These actions are themselves within a movement that runs from the dramatized allusion to Caesar's false tears over Pompey in the first quatrain (from subtexts in Wyatt and Petrarch) to the dramatized allusion to Pyramus and Thisbe in the final couplet. This final allusion is misread, perhaps deliberately; the lovers are reversed in roles. Yet both classical allusions transform the personal grief into a universal truth accessible to a public audience. The concentration involved in such a progressing strategy demanded, of course, the control Surrey had over the sonnet by this period, which enabled him to tighten the highly stylized *epicedium* and make the *hyperbole* and grand gestures in its closure appear both simple and sincere.

"In the rude age when science was not so rife" (J30). Surrey's second sonnet-elegy on Wyatt develops the satire and blame implicit in the praise motifs in his other poems on Wyatt. Here Surrey makes a bitter personal attack in his final couplet. The attack is held back until the syllogistic form of the argument addressed to this person has been carried through, at least in the fiction of the structure. The person attacked is not named although it is probably Edmund Bonner who had accused Wyatt of complicity with Cardinal Pole, Henry's cousin held responsible for the pope's excommunication of the English monarch. Bonner was a bishop who had also accused Wyatt of loose living and of speaking contemptuously of the king, charges that after Cromwell's death led to Wyatt's imprisonment. Yet the poem has textual problems; lines have been variously interpreted because of the heavily inverted syntax.[9] Only the structure is clear. After a decided Petrarchan break, as in "Dyvers thy death,"

the *volta* here has the purpose of introducing the innocence of Wyatt although only as a brief contrast before the completion of the argument and the final invective and blame.

The syllogistic structure of the sonnet rises essentially from the three "If" clauses and is built on the logical topics of comparison and contrast. Positing the figure of *chronographia* the major premise states how in pagan times Jove (and specifically in Crete, an association with euhemeristic overtones) and others taught "Artes" that gave human life "profyte." The minor premise, beginning "If vertue yet in no unthankfull tyme," shows how virtue still fails to blazon fame, a blazoning that could prevent "cryme" and encourage youth. The syllogistic conclusion begins the sestet. Now, therefore, "In days of treuthe," if "Wyattes frendes" praise him, do they deserve blame? In the closure, outside the argumentative and discursive frame, the attack is bitter on the addressee. In the final couplet Wyatt's "livelie face" (though dead, alive in fame) agitates the breast of an addressed fellow mourner shedding his false tears at Wyatt's funeral. In a violent ironic reversal in the last line, the "cynders" or ashes of the dead corpse, alive through fame and the mourner's envy, eat the mourner up, killing him in a special revenge.

Elegy as Epitaph: "Norfolk sprang thee, Lambeth holds thee dead" (J35)

Surrey's elegy on the death of his squire Thomas Clere is the most public of Surrey's sonnet-elegies and was literally an epitaph, its verses, according to Nott, "engraved on a tablet, suspended on the wall near to the tomb, upon which was the following simple inscription."[10] Whatever Nott is referring to, it is clear that Surrey's poem had some public function or occasional use. Another literal epitaph was certainly a subtext for Surrey. This was the epitaph for Vergil as reported in the first commentary of Donatus, "Mantua me genuit, Calabri rapuere, tenet nunc / Parthenope; cecini pascua rura duces" (Mantua bore me, Calabria took me, now Parthenope / holds me; I sang of pastures, fields, and leaders). Surrey reveals his subtext in his very first line, translating Vergil's "tenet" in "holds thee dead." Like the Vergilian text and all epitaphs, Surrey's poem builds on a structuring of names. The names here, even the personal references, also function as figures of *metonymy,* concentrating in their sounds whole histories, public and private. Further, the pro-

sody and music of the poem reflect methods of concentration Surrey was employing, probably at the very same time, in his translation of the *Aeneid*. Thus each line with its names is end-stopped, almost like a roll call, each quatrain and the final couplet acting as a complete sentence. As in his Vergil translations, there are strong pauses after the first two feet, echoing like a drum beat, with heavy accents also at the beginning of the lines.[11] Although the precision of the sonnet calls for Horace's "multum in parvo," it is Vergil's heroic stance that is evoked to praise Surrey's young squire.

Because the elegy was indeed social and occasional, its public nature made a special demand on the obviously grief-stricken Surrey. The problem again of objectifying poetic structure inevitably involved translating a source like Vergil's epitaph with its figures of *asyndeton* and *zeugma* into the immediate demands of explaining, as Surrey must do in his first quatrain, why, for example, Clere is buried in the Howard chapel at Saint Mary's church in Lambeth at all. In other words, as with his Geraldine sonnet, a whole social and political experience must enter the concentrated structure of Surrey's poem. The result is a restrained literalness in this narrative of names, so different from the common hyperbole of late medieval elegies. It thus demonstrates the humanist emphasis on experience and turns the poem into one of the first examples of near novelistic realism in English, producing an authentic, particular biography, built with Aphthonian places, in a solidly rendered landscape. The biographical element shows Surrey's concise version of a knight's tale and indicates that there may have been a chivalric sacrifice by Clere to save Surrey's life before the Abbeville gate at Montreuil, although this episode is likely as fictional as any of the other extratextual myths that emerge from Surrey's work.[12] Whatever the cause, however, in France, under Surrey's command, Clere himself received a wound or suffered an illness, in either case with lingering effects, from which, after seven months of suffering, he died in England in April 1545.

Surrey's method of concentrating this drama is to establish his own drama. Once more it is the formal *epicedium*, his poem spoken in the fiction over the corpse of the dead subject, and the voice in the poem addressing it, as though in a classical pastoral elegy, but now set as if in a public Tudor engraving. Figures of concentration naturally carry such drama, and through them Surrey ironically detaches his emotion in order to free the structure toward greater

objectivity. At the same time, with greater irony of structure, Surrey
enters the poem at the closure with full emotion, but only as a part
of his structure, a dramatized character, not its intruding and possessive inventor. The first line, therefore, through *litotes, asyndeton,*
and *zeugma* gives the whole cycle of the dead figure. It also give
the effect, as J. W. Lever remarks, of "opening like the military
clang of steel."[13] The social relationships that follow in this English
sonnet form *a b a b c d c d e f e f g g* are designed in the first quatrain to show the Howard connection. This includes a reference to
Anne Boleyn, the common cousin of both Clere and Surrey, and
although unnamed, a queen. In these four lines Surrey also fulfills
the rhetorical instructions for any epideictic oration: he "places" the
subject physically and lineally.

The fifth line repeats the *litotes, asyndeton,* and *zeugma* of the first
line, adding an alliterative pattern continuing through the next
line, the end of the second unit in the poem. In this unit, Surrey
shows Clere as an individual who may have sprung from a noble
race but who also chose ("chase" as past tense for "choose") his
destiny: "Shelton for love, Surrey for Lord thou chase: / Ay me,
while life did last that league was tender." The tenderness of these
leagues that defined by choice the life of the young Clere is significantly revealed in names, Mary Shelton, a close friend of the Howards at court and engaged to marry Clere, and Surrey himself (with
its punning emphasis on "Ay me").

It is precisely this last choice of "league" that determines, as
though a general cause, the structure of the rest of the lyric until
the couplet. From this cause Surrey turns to amplified effects in a
favorite mode: a general narrative. The narrative also serves here,
through its historicizing, to distance and establish tactfully Surrey
as the inventor of the lyric. Thus "tracing whose steps," the speaker
then catalogues a series of names for battles in which the two men
fought, Kelsall in Scotland, Landrecy and Boulogne in France, each
using again the figures of *asyndeton, alliteration,* and *zeugma.* Finally,
at the beginning of the sestet, but only as a development of the
discursive flow and not as emphatic Petrarchan *volta,* Surrey comes
to the event at "Muttrell gates" that became "hopeles of all recure,"
the event in France that finally precipitated the death of Clere.

In this event Surrey himself was either wounded or gravely ill,
and at some point gave his will to Clere. The ambiguous "Which
cause" that follows probably refers to either the earl's own grave

situation or to the action and encampment outside the gates and walls of the French city. In any case this ambiguous "cause" led to Clere's "pining death." The poem reverses roles here and the irony is that "Thine Earle" is "halfe dead."[14] Both now and, by implication, for all time, the speaker of the poem who is fully identified by virtue of the epitaph with the Earl of Surrey will be "hopeles of all recure." The naming of himself also allows Surrey to acknowledge his much higher social status than his subject (not to acknowledge this would be insulting to his friend and his subject); at the same time the naming is given a context of weakness and of humility.

Surrey's dramatic progression in this poem thus recapitulates the formal gestures of the objective *epicedium*. This dramatized structure functions so that, by the end of the brief sonnet-elegy, Surrey introduces his own full lament, but no longer as his. He is a character in a fiction who almost died in France and may (or may not) have been saved by a friend who himself died. To all his powerful figures of concentration, Surrey now adds the figure of *apostrophe*, directly addressing the dead body with special verb patterns and all-encompassing nouns, making the epitaph no longer a simple series of names: "Ah Clere, if love had booted, care, or cost, / Heaven had not wonn, nor Earth so timely lost." This final aphorism for his sonnet plays on schemes of *antithesis* that ironically transvalue and decenter through anticlimax, making earth and loss paradoxically the real focus of the text instead of heaven. This universal focus succeeds in its nostalgic paradox by turning Surrey's personal outburst into objective lament, which itself becomes universal.

Windsor Elegies

"When Windesor walles sustained my wearied arme" (J26). Surrey's two elegies placed at Windsor castle also dramatize loss through realized structures of experience. They too are products of the new realism (encouraged by northern humanists like Erasmus, More, and Luther) not only in their detailed description of an actual English landscape but also in the psychological rendering of isolated suffering in that landscape. The first of these elegies is one of Surrey's best examples of the English sonnet and is possibly his first. The probably later texts of Surrey's love sonnets provide a structure of experience that helps the reader understand this poem. The lyric design of this sonnet is essentially the familiar contrast between an

integrated natural landscape, another spring as in "The soote season," and the disharmony of the isolated figure in its midst, as in
"Alas, so all thinges nowe." Once more Surrey uses the Dido topos
that furnishes the structural basis for his *capitolo* "The sonne hath
twyse" and various love-complaints in Poulter's measure. If 1537
is accurate for Surrey's Windsor imprisonment, he was in those
summer months still suffering from the shock of the death of his
beloved friend the Duke of Richmond only the year before. [15] Windsor Castle had been the place where the two boys had spent the first
idyllic years of their life together, and ironically there they had both
read, no doubt together, in the elegant new editions of the early
1530s, the very Chaucerian subtexts for these two elegies: Palamon's
lament in *The Knight's Tale* and Troilus's at the palace of the lost
Criseyde. What had been fiction for Surrey here became realistic
experience, and the edge of actual loss marks the nostalgic fictional
structures Surrey constructs in his text.

The sonnet-elegy thus begins with the speaker in a famous melancholy posture, consciously or unconsciously a variation of the
formal gesture of the *epicedium*. He is leaning over a wall or parapet
of Windsor castle, his chin in his hand "to ease my restles hedd."
As elsewhere in Surrey, the head represents the isolated consciousness
and is another name for the mind, which Surrey makes the focus
for the many lamenting, introspective personae speaking in his
poems. The head is not randomly placed; it is not only in a specific
location but leaning over a specific part of that place, a parapet.
Surrey's graphic use of place in his elegies was strikingly original
in English literature at this time, and represented a bold step beyond
the Chaucerian context into the concentrated realism of the
Renaissance.

The syntax of the lyric is concentrated. Not until line 6 does the
subject and verb of the independent clause of this elaborately inverted *hirmus* appear. Before that syntactic hinge the speaker has
described a spring landscape in language alternating from Latin
neologism ("revested") to Chaucerian archaism ("lustie veare yspred").
The "weddyd birds" (a Surrey motif) and renewed green and "flowred
meades" are examples of natural harmony and integration. All these
"myne eyes discovered." The caesura in line 6 is strong; indeed,
rarely is a caesura so marked in Surrey's generally end-stopped lines.
A decided shift in consciousness occurs in the text: "Than did to
mynd resort" the happy spring of an earlier time, presumably that

of Surrey's life with Richmond. The remembrance of things past appears in a Petrarchan and Chaucerian *oxymoron* "joily woes," a phrase expressing bittersweet nostalgia over a past that included sports, "hateles shorte debate," and an easygoing life, "the rakhell life that longes to loves disporte."

But if the speaker is faithful in memory and nostalgia to his beloved friend, he is equally faithful in the sonnet to his own feelings. Thus, with the *volta* in line 9, the speaker begins to speak in the present tense, the result of his previous narration. The relationship turns on the logical "Wherwith." At the same time an outburst, "alas," begins a gesture of grief: "myne hevy charge of care / Heapt in my brest brake forth against my will." Echoing Troilus (bk. 4, ll. 236–37), the speaker releases his sorrow in transferred Petrarchan gesture and language: "vapored eyes" or tears fall from the walls to the ground to "quicken" the "tender spring." The pathetic fallacy at the logical basis of this image—another use of the Dido topos and the comparison of nature and isolated lover— here dramatizes a familiar Surrey situation: the lack of integration between the lover and the universe. In this case reversing *petrarchismo,* the split between self and nature springs not from the beloved's disdain but from his untimely death. Yet the interior restlessness here has ironically served nature; his tears have given life, although the speaker, leaning, comes close to his own annihilation. The formal gesture of the *epicedium,* the bending over, here becomes nearly, but just nearly, suicidal: "And I half bent to throwe me down withall."[16]

In this closure Surrey completes the ironic distancing of his deeply felt personal subject with the gesture of leaning. It is a last parody of *petrarchismo,* like the suicidal gesture, or near gesture, of many such lovers. Yet the erotic cliché is given new meaning in Surrey's transformation of it. In the dramatic structure of his text, the gesture becomes a device to metamorphosize private loss into universal fiction and symbol. Indeed what the erotic mode dramatizes in the text is the speaker's depth of feeling; at least that fiction of feelings is what is dramatized for us. The general interpretation of the sonnet as alluding to Richmond and Surrey's Windsor experience with him, although there is no overt evidence for this subject in the text, is one more proof of the power and success of such fictionalizing.

"So crewell prison howe could betyde, alas" (J27).   Fiction operates also in Surrey's longer elegy rising from his experience at

Windsor. Called the "most pathetic personal elegy in English poetry" by a Victorian critic,[17] this lyric has an objective, carefully
crafted structure built on a variety of subtexts, classical, medieval,
and Renaissance, each transformed into the other in the Surrey text.
In this sense, the *ubi sunt* motif, which had been the quintessential
medieval mediation on mutability, functions here as a Petrarchan
motif. The beloved is gone, and, like Troilus bewailing in the palace
of Criseyde, Windsor as place assumes almost human dimension.
Twice Windsor castle is directly addressed in figures of *apostrophe;*
the castle is in fact the silent interlocutor of this dramatic monologue, its "voyd walles" echoing Surrey's love complaint throughout
the poem. Only in the end, when the isolated consciousness has
withdrawn from its own mind to the real walls with which the
poem began, does the speaker recognize the emptiness of the response: "Eache stone, alas, that dothe my sorowe rewe, / Retournes
therto a hollowe sound of playnt." The prison by then has become
double, and the irony of the first term for Windsor, "So crewell
prison," is such that by the end of the elegy, in a figure of *peripeteia,*
the prison contains a deeper prison, that within the speaker himself.
   The poem traces this logical reversal through quatrains. They are
generally iambic pentameter (although heavily accentual as well)
rhymed simply *a b a b,* the same stanzaic form Surrey invented for
his long elegy on Wyatt, and later appropriated into English literature as in Gray's eighteenth-century elegy. Each stanza is a kind
of syntactical unit. The first is an introduction to the whole poem:
"prowde Wyndsour" is a prison for the speaker where before "in
lust and joye" he had passed "my childishe yeres" with the son of
a king, a social superior, an honor in itself. Against these overtly
biographical statements, Surrey immediately plays a classical allusion that transforms, through ironic juxtaposition, the personal relationship. These boys passed their years "In greater feast then
Priams sonnes of Troye." The allusion is epic, adding a new perspective on Surrey's choice of genre, and recalls at once both Troilus
and the story of the fall of Troy, as narrated by Aeneas to Dido in
Vergil's book 2. The immediate effect of the allusion is to continue
the chivalric image: both boys were like knights at the first court
of Western history; they were brave warriors in the primal conflict
of Western culture, the Trojan war. The local has become universal,
and Windsor and the boys are integrated through language and
myth into the greater fiction of history. The effect, as the poem

progresses and finally concludes, is that both boys are as true sons of Priam as Polites, who was himself murdered before his father by Pyrrhus, and for whom the Trojan "courtes" are also "voyd," to use Surrey's translation of this scene (bk. 2, 1. 685). These Tudor "sons" have also, one might add, just as violent an end, Surrey beheaded and Richmond possibly poisoned.

Unlike many Romantic or modern poems, Surrey does not rest his nostalgic structure on the contrast of symbols or resonant description. He uses logical topics of rhetoric learned from the humanists. Thus at the beginning of the second quatrain, syntactically related by place to the first stanza, the speaker sets up a generalization, a cause that itself contains a dialectic: "Where eche swete place retournes a tast full sowre." The ensuing catalogue builds on *enumeratio,* developing only one side of the antithesis and naming only the sweet "places" of his memory, although the "tast full sowre" of mutability is always in the background. Surrey's catalogue in these next thirty-four lines structures itself through the method of phrasal units, set here in figures of *partitio* and *parison,* the latter also a form of *isocolon,* where the simple naming of place or event is amplified by other phrases and subordinate clauses.

The scenes that follow, whether actual or idealized, represent, at least in literary structure, that grasping at the chivalric world that marked one of the most compelling illusions of the Tudor court, Henry's or Elizabeth's. These spaces in memory are large and "grene," the springtime of human life; in them the boys cast their eyes "unto the maydens towre," with its social and even sexual overtones, in a time of "easye syghes." Lines 9 and 10 sketch the earlier scenes at Windsor in figures of *chiasmus:* dances were short but the reading of long romances (no doubt like Chaucer's newly printed *Troilus*) brought "great delight" and enlivened traditional court pastime.[18] The major motif that determines this progression of memory is the game, and its freedom of play. The *amour courtois* is innocent here of such ferocity as that in Surrey's satire "Eache beeste can chuse," and the pretense of "wordes and lookes that tygers could but rewe" is but another game, although the mutual love that ends the stanza, "eche of us did plead the others right," is not. The athletic events that follow are among the most graphic of all descriptions of Tudor court life and, as Lewis notes, for once a happy view of court activity.[19] The game of love intermingles with that of sports, as the speaker's memory slowly progresses from inside the castle walls to

outside in the "palme playe" and the tournaments with their love motifs on "the graveld ground," then beyond the battlements themselves to an idealized pastoral love scene with music. Here the speaker hopes, in a figure of *symploce,* for good luck and dreads "long delayes." Finally there is a hunt scene with the two boys in "the wyld forest," or on (in another of Surrey's favorite figures, *hyperbaton*) "the clothed holtes with grene," another Chaucerian evocation.

With line 33 the speaker returns inside to "The voyd walles" of the present, walls probably stripped in the summer of 1537 of tapestries and hangings that would keep heat in winter and were always hung when the court was present. Even these walls can be turned by Surrey's memory into the vision of two boys sleeping together each night, walls "that harbourd us eche night." Now in the text's own tapestry of effects, in his amplified description of the lives of the two young aristocrats, the speaker of the lyric turns to his most intimate memory. Diction here reveals the Vergilian subtext, the familiar Dido topos: "voyd walles" that themselves echo Dido's "palace voide" in Surrey's translation (bk. 4, l. 104) and all her isolation. What the speaker feels reviving "within my brest" is "The swete accord" and memory of "such slepes as yet delight, / The pleasaunt dreames, the quyet bedd of rest." In that bed together, these two boys, at the center of violent court intrigue, give themselves to each other, from the deepest centers of their own being in "frendshipp sworne, eche promyse kept so juste." In this way, as in the very text of the poem, the boys passed "the winter nightes awaye," the winter of mutability and violence that never left them and now comes back to the speaker destroying his happy memory: "And with this thought the blood forsakes my face." Tears fall down his cheeks "of dedlye hewe" and as soon as he has "Upsupped" his sobs and sighs, he renews his "playnt."

This "playnt" is a second *apostrophe* to Windsor Castle and, as the Petrarchan description of this distraught lover might suggest, the deliberate inset of this speech, emphasizing its outburst, derives from Troilus. Surrey's first line ironically reverses Chaucer's " 'O cause of wo, that cause hast ben of lisse!' " (bk. 5, l. 550) with " 'O place of blisse, renewer of my woos.' " The speaker then turns to the logical center of his elegy: " 'Geve me accompt wher is my noble fere,' " he says to the walls. They once enclosed the young duke, " 'lief' " to his sister, whom Richmond had married, but " 'unto me most dere.' " The bare stone walls echo his words like

a forlorn Petrarchan landscape; there is no other human response in this prison (and significantly there is no Christian consolation or any consolation at all in this prison). This carefully rendered realistic and psychological scene has thus become, by the end of dramatic progression of the elegy, an emblem for all human existence: "Thus I alone, where all my fredome grew, / In pryson pyne with bondage and restraynt." The speaker's only freedom is inside himself; he is transformed once more into his beloved: "And with remembraunce of the greater greif, / To bannishe the lesse I fynde my chief releif." However it may have actually occurred in 1537, this transformation establishes a new figure in the history of the structure of the elegy; the poem rises through music of language to a new reading of human experience. It takes its place among literary texts as a new text, as new myth.

Chapter Seven
Blank Verse: Translations from the *Aeneid*

In the Renaissance, Vergil's *Aeneid* exemplified how invented literary text establishes universal myth. Vergil's special language and music had transformed his text, almost from the beginning, into a communal and theological work. In new Renaissance readings of Vergil, it was probably inevitable that Surrey the humanist poet would seek to translate into his own Tudor world and its developing language this greatest (at least for the Renaissance) of all literary texts. Surrey never completed more than two books of his translation, books 2 and 4. These texts might even be considered as two more separate poems in Surrey's canon, for both of these poems in Surrey's new meter of blank verse develop themes and motifs familiar in Surrey's songs, elegies, sonnets, and poems in Poulter's measure. Foremost among these are nostalgia and the loneliness of the isolated observer, Surrey's special variation on the love complaint. In both of Surrey's Vergil poems, especially in his translation of book 2, nostalgia and loss predominate; similarly the single figure is surrounded by violence in the first Vergil poem and, in the second, becomes a rejected lonely lover. Thus, in both cases Surrey endeavors to imitate archetypal literary subtexts for the purpose of representing his own insistent centers of reality.

The key to this endeavor is translation in its widest and most classic sense, which had always been the formal basis of Surrey's poetry. For any sustained effort in formal translation, certainly in the late 1530s when Surrey likely began his translation, Vergil and the *Aeneid* were natural challenges.[1] They were the classical loci for all that the humanist masters such as Cheke and Ascham had been writing and teaching. Thus in the first fifty years of the sixteenth century, all over Europe, translations of the *Aeneid* into the vernacular began to appear with the timing of buds and flowers in spring, especially in texts from France, Italy, and Scotland that may have influenced Surrey.[2] The Italian translations, the most inventive

in structure of all the sixteenth-century translations that came to Surrey, generally used a new meter, *versi sciolti*, hendecasyllabic (eleven-syllabled) lines without rhyme. It was a meter Surrey had probably read in the eclogues and other poems of Luigi Alamanni, texts that he likely knew when both Surrey and Alamanni were at the court of Francis I, Alamanni's *Opere toscane* with blank verse first appearing in Paris in autumn 1532.

Without question, the use of blank verse in Italy and France as the humanists' formal answer to the question of classical heroic verse acted as an energizing catalyst for Surrey.[3] Nothing survives, however, to tell us of specific influences or just how or when Surrey started his translation. The works themselves, except for a printer's dedication in one of the texts of book 4, reveal nothing. Just as we have no holograph of any of Surrey's poems, so there is no record or notebook from Surrey. Surrey may indeed have made other translations of Vergil's epic, even drafts of other books. Yet in the ruthless sacking by Southwell and Seymour's men of Kenninghall and of Surrey House at Norwich, all Surrey's manuscripts and papers were seized as evidence for his trial and probably later destroyed. The result is that there is no original text by which to compare later versions.

A few days after Tottel had brought out his *Miscellany* in June 1557 entitled as Surrey's lyrics, he published both texts of Surrey's translations of books 2 and 4 of the *Aeneid*. Tottel's is the only text we have of book 2. There are three of Surrey's Book 4: Tottel's published in 1557; an earlier version printed probably earlier in 1554 by John Day from a text edited by William Owen; and a manuscript version (Hargrave MS 205) probably dating from 1568. The three texts diverge greatly in a number of passages, and from none can there be deduced a simple original text or anything like a holograph.[4] Only in those passages where all three agree can a modern reader with any certainty accept the reading as what Surrey likely intended. If the subsequent history of these texts demonstrates uncertainty, the actual dates of composition are also not clear. Modern readers can set, with Ridley, the *terminus a quo* of Surrey's beginning his Vergil project with his reading of the Italian *Aeneid* in its exciting new meter in 1539 and then inventing his own blank verse.[5] Yet the choice of Vergil's epic also rose from Surrey's perspectives on the whole nature of poetic structure, whatever the date of inception. As we have seen, Surrey's poetic forms—the sonnet,

the songs, Poulter's measure—all involved epic qualities such as thematic directness, allusion, dignity of subject (even in an ironic context), and narration. The leap from these, however, to a major translation called for a sustained bravura performance. Surrey might have spent the rest of his life making such a text, writing between his courtly and military obligations as successor to the Duke of Norfolk and the leading peer of the realm—had he lived.

Surrey's Translations from the *Aeneid*

Method.   Book 2, beginning "They whisted all, with fixed face attent," is a retrospective narration in Aeneas's voice about the last night of Troy; book 4, beginning "But now the wounded quene with hevy care," depicts the central figure of "infelix Dido," the unfortunate lover. Both Roman texts are masterpieces of Vergilian pathos. Inventing structures to convey this pathos of nostalgia and of infidelity powerful enough for a contemporary Tudor audience demanded Surrey's fullest talents of translation and the widest range of his poetic art. The translation also demanded Surrey's conceiving of a classic, within a received tradition or "anthology," which would permit the renewal of a perennial form. To turn an inherited text into contemporary Tudor Enlgish, circa 1539–46, meant work that could only be entirely new and original, if it were to be anything. Thus what Surrey achieved "translated into English, and drawn into a straunge metre," according to the title-page of the Day-Owen 1554 text, were two long poems for which, as Thomson remarks, "there is nothing quite like it" in any literature in English before it.[6] Whatever the confluence of texts and sources, which Berdan sees as significant in Surrey's invention of blank verse,[7] and despite attempts to give Chaucer and Grimald the honor, Surrey's blank verse in the composition of these two poems is one of the great moments in the development of literature and language in English.

Surrey's creation of what became a classic form in English—blank verse—sprang specifically from his attempt to appropriate the classical structure of Vergil for his time. Kermode's definition of a classic, by its very nature a model or criterion, "entails, in some form, the assumption," (a premise only possible in a cohesive social context like Renaissance humanism) that the past work "can be more or less immediately relevant and available, in a sense contemporaneous with modern." For Kermode, the "nature" of the new

text "is such that it can, by strategies of accommodation, be made so" that "the classic is an essence available to us under our dispositions, in the aspect of time," that is, in a world of experientially relevant texts.[8] Determining whether a text is authentic and relevant, rarely easy under the best of circumstances, is the central problem, in Kermode's view, for any literary artist but, one may argue, especially for a poet like Surrey who is essentially a translator whose new text always involves subtexts.

Therefore after the probable decision during the late 1530s to attempt a translation of Vergil, the young Henry Howard (in his early twenties and already structuring the story of Troy into his elegies and songs such as "When ragyng love") had to determine strategies for such accommodation. There must have seemed to be three central possibilities: the strategy of rhyme or lack of it; the strategy of marked accents per line; and the strategy of syllabic organization or feet. Despite the precise technical nature of these questions, Surrey's actual problem in composition, as he dared to invent a new English form only later called blank verse, was how to retain "fidelity to the syntactical and rhetorical forms of Virgil."[9] Such faithfulness to the original subtext involved perceiving that dialectic, described by Kermode, between original essence and relevant text. But fidelity to an ancient text like Vergil's had also been prescribed in the teaching of humanists like Petrarch and, less than a hundred years before Surrey, Lorenzo da Valla who had held that usage and idiom in the great texts should be the main objects for imitation (rather than abstract rules formulated from such texts). Lorenzo's conception of fidelity to original texts became the method used in comprehensive humanist documents, such as, in Surrey's time, a work like Erasmus's *Adagia,* which culled texts for their usages and idioms. This method also led to the structural control used by both Wyatt and Surrey; it taught them, in fact, how to invent textures of nuance and subtlety through control of usage and idiom. The Italian translations of the classics had all emphasized such textures and for this reason they had developed a special musicality. The invention of *versi sciolti,* which specifically imitated Vergil's line, was posited on just such control of texture.[10]

Thus the problem for Surrey was to find a metrical structure in a noninflected language like English that would be faithful to the ancient hexameter of the classical epic. This faithfulness demanded clear answers to various questions of strategy. Only with the problem

solved could a poet renew in his own time and place the highest of all Renaissance literary forms, the heroic epic. Surrey wished to recreate Vergil's epic for his time, within his own talents, within his own perceptions of human existence. In this task of translation and faithful renewal Surrey accomplished the best translation of his time by means of three central solutions: a line without rhyme; a line with no more than five stresses or accents (pentameter); and a line with feet, generally with regularity of ten syllables per line.

A line without rhyme.   Such a line had long been the dream of the humanists. Rhyme did not exist in the classical texts. Surrey here, as Ascham recognized when he read the 1554 edition of Surrey's book 4 of the *Aeneid,* was "first of all English men, in translating the fourth booke of Virgill" because he had "by good judgement, auoyed the fault of Ryming." In the *Scholemaster* written around 1560 Ascham also noted that "This mislikyng of Ryming" was not something of "newfangle singularitie" but had been "misliked of many, and that of men, of greatest learning and deepest judgement," although he cites Surrey, despite his praiseworthy "copie," as too content, like Chaucer and Wyatt, with time and custom and use of rhyme in his other poems.[11] Surrey did not use rhyme that frequently, however, and in fact tended in his poetic structures to avoid it, at least in comparison with most of his other contemporaries.[12] This tendency resulted from his desire, like other innovating humanists, to reproduce in the vernacular the enduring texts he had read in classical verse. Surrey was not only part of a revolution in prosody but one of the leaders in bringing aesthetic change into the epic, a social and communal form.

One of the ironies of the humanist revolution followed from its own lessons of imitation; it was the vernacular that paradoxically absorbed the lessons of structure found in classroom rhetorical strategies in Latin and Greek and used in humanist experiments in Neo-Latin prose and poetry. For example, Petrarch, the vernacular master of structure for Wyatt and Surrey continued the Vergilian mode of composition not only in his Latin compositions like *Africa* but in his Italian texts where he integrated multileveled sound and sense.[13] One immediate result of these structural lessons was that the vernacular long line could be seen in a musical texture, with or without rhyme. It was a lesson Surrey absorbed, and the majority of lines in all Surrey's poems represent an experiment toward the long line, more often pentameter, hexameter, or heptameter, with couplets or

cross-rhymes, although Surrey could certainly produce an original and intricate short-line *frottola* like "O happy dames." Surrey's long lines have rhythmic and rhyme patterns that demonstrate how an inherent sense of musicality does not depend on effects of rhyme or any other single device but rather derives from what we have seen in the lyrics as the Petrarchan system of total structure. Within such structure, each word counted, not merely last words that echoed each other. Thus the diligent effort to preserve the syllabic purity of each word in Surrey's long lines, even within his own extraordinary accentual strategies, characterized Surrey's invention of blank verse in English, and his sense of harmonic tones found in the regularity of metrical feet also derived from the Italian synthesis of music and total structure. The result of Surrey's experimentation with musical effects in a long line within a total poetic structure was the regularizing, as countless critics have shown, of iambic pentameter and the English line in general. The imitators who followed Surrey in his regularizing did not understand, with some major exceptions, the musical base for Surrey's regularity of long line until the advent of Marlowe. It is Marlowe's unrhymed "mighty line" that echoes the complex prosodic and rhetorical strategies of Surrey, not least in a probably early tragedy *Dido,* which has lines that clearly reflect Surrey's own text. [14]

Thus the influence of the Italians in the development of blank verse was not limited to the actual texts that used *versi sciolti,* or unrhymed hendecasyllabic lines, to translate the Roman epic. To develop his long line for his vernacular epic, Surrey turned to all the musical influences of the Italians, especially their new technical devices of language and music, which derived in great part from the Neo-Latin experiments of the Renaissance. From them and his own enhanced reading of the Latin originals, Surrey learned how to compose a regular line of iambic pentameter with a music other than rhyme. The results are immediately evident: approximately seventy-five percent of all the lines of Surrey's blank verse are end-stopped with strong masculine endings. In Surrey's total musical structure, this final decided pause balances a strong caesura within the line itself; generally fifty per cent of the lines have a caesura after the second foot; in thirty, after the fourth. [15] Only later when blank verse as a form evolved did the use of enjambment emerge as a major device to develop a verse paragraph, and then only as a means of emphasizing the Italian principle of total musical structure.

Although Surrey also developed his own kind of verse paragraph in blank verse, his deliberate and obviously self-conscious omission of rhyme enabled strategies of sound other than frequent enjambment to enhance the heroic effect. Besides the use of end-stopped lines and frequent caesura, Surrey also found, as a means of heightening the heroic effect in his new vernacular epic without rhyme, two other major strategies: the special manipulation of the pentameter beat and the handling of regular feet within accentual patterns.

A pentameter line.   One of the attacks on Surrey's originality in inventing blank verse has been that he simply took Chaucer's pentameter line in the rhyme-royal stanzas of *Troilus and Criseyde* and in the heroic couplets of *Canterbury Tales* and dropped the rhyme. There is hardly any doubt that Surrey did just that, on one level. But such attacks assume that Surrey did only that in developing a long line without rhyme and that the rest of the verse imitated the structures of Chaucerian verse. As Emrys Jones has fully argued, "the structural unit in Surrey's unrhyming verse is not the line," the syntactical focus in the rhyming designs of *Troilus* and *Canterbury Tales*, "but the phrase or clause."[16] This kind of emphasis directly resulted from following injunctions like Lorenzo da Valla's to imitate the idiom and usage of the original classical text, a kind of imitatio generally unknown to Chaucer and the generation of poets that followed him in England. Such syntactical emphasis on phrasal and clausal units, a characteristic we have noted from the beginning of our discussion of Surrey's poetry, allows in the larger development of Surrey's narrative from Vergil a special "sense of mass and momentum."[17] In fact, before Surrey, there is nothing in English quite like his handling of such objective blocks of action and description.

In this humanist conception of imitation lies the essential difference between Surrey's two poems based on Vergil and Gavin Douglas's *Eneados*. Douglas, an aristocratic bishop, rendered the whole of Vergil's *Aeneid* (and of the thirteenth book added by the Renaissance Italian poet Mapheus Vegius) into lowland Scottish. The bishop's epic was probably finished in 1513 but existed in manuscript until its publication in 1553, six years after Surrey's death. Douglas's intention, as he affirms in his prologue, is also fidelity to Vergil but a Vergil read by the late medieval English mind that viewed the whole action of the Roman "knychtis" as a romance. It is not that Surrey did not also read the *Aeneid* as a chivalric romance; if we judge by his poetic allusions to the story

of Troilus and the classical world, we find the same sense of romance in historical continuity that Douglas intended to convey. But for Surrey the humanist at the court of Henry VIII, the *Aeneid* could be considered not only as perennial romance but as a national epic, for Aeneas was the grand progenitor of Brute, the founder of Albion. Later in the development of the Tudor myth both Spenser in his new Vergilian epic and Shakespeare would see Aeneas as England's great ancestor. This humanist civic purpose, in addition to the linguistic and musical influence of Petrarch and the Italians, marks the difference between these two versions of the *Aeneid* in the first half of the sixteenth century.

Nevertheless, Surrey was deeply impressed by Douglas's powerful pentameter line, if we judge by his extensive borrowing in diction and phrasing from the Scottish poet (estimated at about forty per cent). Although Surrey eschewed Douglas's unhumanist solution of strong end-stopped rhyming couplets for the Vergilian lines, the younger English poet clearly responded to the heavy accentual beats in Douglas's pentameter line. Such accentual strategies mark Surrey's own meter. He may have seen Douglas's solution of the pentameter—generally ten syllables with varied accentual stress—as one way to deal with what Saintsbury identified as the devastating effect of the great vowel shift on the long line in English poetry, the short medieval lyric not suffering as much.[18] Whatever the legacies from the older Scottish poet to the younger "courtly maker,"[19] the essential difference and relationship between the two poets of heroic narrative lies in Surrey's particular uses in his own text of Douglas's achievement.

A specific example will illustrate. In his transcription of the Scottish "scaithful gyft," Surrey found a means to enhance his own device of the phrasal unit out of the martial coloring of Douglas's diction. This typically northern phrase from Douglas is taken over whole but in a specially set context in Surrey almost light years away from his Scottish subtext. In a narrative scene early in Vergil's book 2, Douglas's phrase "scaithful gyft" describes the Trojan horse. The Trojans had first ventured out from their walls, so recalls Aeneas, to see where the Greeks had encamped and what they had supposedly left behind. Instead of confronting the irony of the situation (the audience knowing what these Trojans do not) Douglas plunges ahead with his vivid narrative, even turning Vergil's indirect discourse into full conversation and elaborating Vergil's eighteen lines into

thirty or more (Vergil ends his paragraph where Douglas continues). Surrey, on the other hand, uses the fuller text not so much to enlarge but, by concision and reduction of context, to focus on particulars in phrasal and clausal units. The result is that Surrey even reduces the Vergilian original text to sixteen lines, an economy characteristic of his general method in translation.[20] The pentameter line that emerges from this method contains its own narrative drive. Still retaining the Douglas sweep, it builds through the verse paragraph to its own closure in the gigantic figure of the horse.

Instead of Douglas's rhyme in this passage, Surrey constructs a laconic system of assonantal, consonantal, and alliterative patterns. With the interacting hard consonants of Douglas's Scottish phrase this sound-system is so adapted that patterns of diction play against antithetical syntax (in figures of *chiasmus* and *anaphora*) and inverted language (in figures of *hyperbaton* and *anastrophe*). The effects of concision that Douglas gains by rhyme, Surrey gains by syntax and the insistent caesura after the second strong accent in each line, usually the fourth syllable. Because of persistent use of caesura throughout Surrey's two poems from Vergil, the device appears as if it were a deliberate attempt to place as closely as possible, within a generally regular iambic line, the archaic medial caesura of *Piers Plowman*, *Sir Gawain*, and, beyond Surrey's knowledge, ancient Anglo-Saxon texts like *Beowulf*. Such carefully shaped contextual structures as Surrey is inventing here are a deliberate attempt to be faithful to the complexity of Vergil in Surrey's own English pentameters. Thus using Douglas's Scottish phrase in his own new text, Surrey conveys the sinister music and psychological drama of the opening foreboding scene of Aeneas's narrative to Dido and her court:

> The gates cast up, we issued out to play,
> The Grekish camp desirous to behold,
> The places void and the foresaken costes.
> Here Pyrrhus band, there ferce Achilles pight,
> Here rode their shippes, there did their battells joyne
> Astonnied some the scathefull gift beheld,
> Behight by vow unto the chast Minerve,
> All wondring at the hugenesse of the horse.
>
> (bk. 2, ll. 37–44)

Douglas's text was Surrey's only contemporary Tudor translation of Vergil and no doubt suggested how a medieval and even an Arthurian mentality might adapt the *Aeneid* into Surrey's world. Yet Surrey's court of 1539 (and later) was more modern; it had become the court of Sardanapalus. To define that broken reality (at least from the perspective of a Howard), Surrey needed the psychologically more complex strategies emanating from Italy and, although he might use the older English methods like alliteration, Surrey's use remained rhetorical, fitting old methods into new speech rhythms and new conceptions of poetic structure.[21] To revert to the certainties of Douglas's heroic structures would have been only an act of nostalgia. It would have showed a reverence for full rich language but language no longer appropriate for Surrey's time, except when it offered rhetorical devices like alliteration that could shape new—and to Surrey—truer heroic structures.

From such sources and resources Surrey developed his own method for his pentameters, and although he might miss what Lewis calls Vergil's "lavishness" and appear "lapidary and laconic,"[22] Surrey could write the longer and fuller lines suited to Tudor English. He had in fact written hexameters and his Poulter's measure, as Evans points out, may be an attempt to discover "an English equivalent of quantitative verse,"[23] or what was then considered classical epic form. Indeed, Surrey's pentameters in his truncated *Aeneid* show a new method of expressing the perennial classic. Manipulating a line of five accents or sometimes four plus one weak accent, Surrey gave his time a daring new classic statement, in new form restating the perennial Vergilian themes of communal and personal loss and fidelity.

A line with feet. Perhaps the most obvious legacy of Surrey's work for the later writers of the English Renaissance was the exact syllabic count in the poetic line, especially as it appeared in the influential *Tottel's Miscellany* in 1557. In the case of blank verse, the tendency toward regularity in the lines of his translation of Vergil, printed in the same summer, made a profound impact as the form underwent its metamorphosis into the line basis for English drama. Thomas Sackville, one of Surrey's earliest admirers, not only incorporated much of Surrey's *Aeneid* into his Induction to the *Mirror for Magistrates* but coauthored the first English tragedy and the first English drama in blank verse, *Gorboduc,* itself a synthesis of Vergilian themes and motifs. The relationship of Sackville's dramatic verse to

Surrey's epic line reveals the tendency toward a controlled speech suited to and even demanded by the court and its intellectual and political networks in the universities and churches. Regularity in spoken drama at court or university merely reproduced Surrey's successful experiment with language for his court audience, the result of his attempt to find a common elevated language suited to the court and to the nation it epitomized.

It was the Italians who had taught Surrey the structural value of regularity, of keeping exact iambs, not only in the *versi sciolti* of Vergil translations with their exact eleven-syllabled lines but also in the language of the musician-poets of *petrarchismo*. The Italian translators of Vergil had given Surrey "a standard of accuracy," as Florence Ridley remarks,[24] and this meant not only as literal a translation as possible, avoiding the provincial prolixity of a Douglas, for example, but also a whole system of "echoes," to use Ant Oras's term, which rendered the more stylish concision better suited to Vergil's original Latin. Thus borrowing, a very natural phenomenon in the literature of that day, meant for Surrey, simply discovering in the Italian translations a holistic system of sound and sense. It was a system Surrey not only had discovered earlier in Petrarch but, tutored by humanists, had learned to interpret in the Roman texts he had known since his childhood. Reading blank verse in the plays of Trissino and Rucellai, in translations by Alamanni and Rucellai, and then in various *Aeneid* translations by Liburnio and the circle of Cardinal de Medici, Surrey developed in his own text what Chaucer and Douglas had not taught him, as Oras remarks: "such copious and vigorous use of echoes as almost to abolish the distinction between blank verse and rhymed verse."[25] It was a matter of linking, intensifying, contrasting, and highlighting so as to give greater unity to a whole succession of lines. Such a technical control produced, at its best, the unity of coherently organized wholes both of verse paragraphs and of major sections—an intricately but clearly orchestrated correspondence of part to whole.

It would be simplistic to attribute Surrey's music only to this obvious Italian influence.[26] Surrey used the common sources available to all readers of Vergil in this period, including all the commentaries from Donatus and Servius on, many of them incorporated into each page of Renaissance texts of Vergil.[27] Such common sources deflect the idea of any absolute influence on Surrey by either the Italians or Douglas. Any lover of Vergil would no doubt see the

Latin texts of commentary as essential to interpretation. In these too, as well as the original text, Surrey found a system of "echoes" to reinforce his syllabic regularity. In his own lines, therefore, Surrey strived for a regularity of stress (often with forced results although with exactly counted syllables), and these "echoes," from whatever origin, surround and enlarge this regularity. In the text, such "echoes" often take strained rhetoric and make it into believable and controlled discourse because of contextual effects. These "echoes" operate everywhere in Surrey's Vergil—in the speeches, considered by some as his best translations,[28] as well as in the more abstract descriptive pieces such as the elaborate similes. The following examples will illustrate.

Laocoon's speech, a mini-oration concluding one of Vergil's most quoted lines, is constructed in Surrey's translation as a verse-paragraph with a logical strategy. The speech moves from rhetorical questions to a disjunctive proposition (stated in language where typically Surrey so strains for concision that he becomes ambiguous through figures of *hyperbaton*) and then to the orator's frank injunction:

> O wreched citezens,
> What so great kind of frensie freteth you?
> Deme ye the Grekes our enemies to be gone?
> Or any Grekish giftes can you suppose
> Devoid of guile? Is so Ulysses known?
> Either the Grekes ar in this timber hid,
> Or this an engin is to anoy our walles,
> To view our tours, and overwhelme our towne.
> Here lurkes some craft. Good Troyans, geve no trust
> Unto this horse, for what so ever it be,
> I dred the Grekes, yea, when they offer gyftes.
>   (bk. 2, ll. 56–66)

Here Surrey is succinct, even more than Vergil, through a system of alliteration and carefully placed caesuras that recall romances like *Sir Gawain*. Surrey's text moves from this base to the highly polished interplay of assonance and near rhyme (terminal and internal) and oratorical artifice. The result is a powerful moment in his translated narrative, with its own credibility for its Tudor audience.

Similar is Surrey's interpretative translation of another important moment in book 2, the actual and psychological awakening of Aeneas

to the horror around him. Vergil's pastoral epic simile ironically
distances the violence of this awakening.

> I waked; therwith to the house top I clambe,
> And harkning stood I: like as when the flame
> Lightes in the corne by drift of boisteous winde,
> Or the swift stream that driveth from the hill
> Rootes up the feldes and presseth the ripe corne
> And plowed ground, and overwhelmes the grove,
> The silly herdman all astonnied standes,
> From the hye rock while he doth here the sound.
>
> (ll. 386–93)

This passage has so much actual rhyme, near rhyme, and assonance
that it defies, as Oras remarks, any "customary notion of blank
verse."[29] Once more, a basic pattern of caesuras (more shifting here)
and consonantal repetition, especially alliteration, builds a controlled context for these syllabic "echoes." All of them, particularly
the vowels, reinforce the regular steady movement of the iambs
(varied but not broken by two initial trochees, by spondees, and
other metrical contrasts). The result is not only dramatic action in
the syntax but participation by the reader in the terrible moment
of Aeneas's awakening.

In book 4 Surrey establishes this same context of sounds and
regular feet within the same dominant rhythm of shifting caesuras
and heavily marked accents. In his description of the dawn hunting
party of Dido and Aeneas before their encounter in the cave, Surrey
takes on one of the most famous scenes in Western culture and gives
his own version of imperial splendor:

> And at the threshold of her chaumber dore
> The Carthage lords did on the quene attend.
> The trampling steede with gold and purple trapt,
> Chawing the fomie bit, there fercely stood.
> Then issued she, awayted with great train,
> Clad in a cloke of Tyre embradred riche.
> Her quyver hung behinde her backe, her tresse
> Knotted in gold, her purple vesture eke
> Butned with gold.
>
> (bk. 4, ll. 170–78)

Such a static scene demonstrates Surrey's power to render an iconic presence, a portrait in words, as well as to dramatize the narrative scenes more typical of book 2. His ability to trace in his system of "echoes" the rhythms of the human voice confirms itself as well in book 4 as in the protracted arguments in book 2 of Laocoon and Sinon. In fact, interior monologues dominate Vergil's fourth book. For example, after being "striken domm, / Well nere bestraught" (ll. 359–60) by his vision of Mercury, Surrey's Aeneas in third-person thus ruminates in a brilliant structure of alliteration and shifting caesura:

> What may he do, alas? or by what words
> Dare he persuade the raging quene in love?
> Or in what sort may he his tale beginne?
> Now here now there his recklesse minde gan run
> And diversly him drawes, discoursing all.
>   (bk. 4, ll. 365–69)

This last line, with its alliteration as clue, reminds us of another structure at work in the handling of feet in Surrey's line. Surrey is using another means to gain his effects of rhythm: an older English system of accentual verse and its use of caesura. For some scholars this rhythmic pattern is the basis of his invention of blank verse, and the Day-Owen text the best because, says Herbert Hartman, it represents, in contrast to the other texts, "the older tradition of accentual pentameter as practised by Surrey and his friend and master Wyatt, rather than the 'olde Iambicke stroake' of strict decasylla-bles."[30] For Berdan this accentual rhythm expresses the freedom implicit in all blank verse, "that, while the number of syllables in the line is normally correct, the placing of stress is such that feet in the classical sense cannot be formed from them."[31] Such a me-dieval heritage does indeed touch on Surrey's very conception of blank verse: his use of alliterative patterns; strong caesuras; generally end-stopped lines with some enjambment; and five and often four accents to a line not always coinciding with the regular syllabic stress (with resultant strained syntax, even more strained when Sur-rey affects the classical inversion in an effort to be literal). It is precisely Surrey's moment in the development of English prosody for him to unite, into his own textual dialectic, Italian patterns and old metrical forms. Ironically, modern readers will understand this

achievement better than the generation of Saintsbury, for it was not
really until Ezra Pound that the full impact of Coleridge's innovation
of accentual meter for "Christabel" reached contemporary audiences.
Accentual meter as a way of controlling syllables and individual
lines has been the basis of a number of profound twentieth-century
poems from Eliot's *Four Quartets* to Merrill's contemporary epic; it
is significantly the metrical basis for Robert Fitzgerald's contemporary translation of the *Aeneid*.

In two cases—two voices from Surrey's texts, one communal and
one private—the accents in Surrey's dialectic of various subtexts tell
Vergil's story in measured formal phrases that have the effects of
Greek tragedy. Panthus, whom Aeneas in book 2 meets in the
streets, is a priest "scapte from the Grekish dartes." Clutching "the
sacred reliques and the vanquisht gods," he pronounces the doom
of Troy: "The later day and fate of Troye is come, / The which no
plaint or prayer may availe. / Troyans we were, and Troye was
sometime . . ." (ll. 406, 408, 414–16). The second line here is
Surrey's translation for one of Vergil's greatest phrases, "ineluctabile
tempus," and like "lacrima rerum" in book 1, a nexus for Vergilian
nostalgia. From Panthus, the bold Aeneas calls his brave young men
about him in the dark streets, reminding them of their hopeless
struggle against the forces of history: " 'O ye yong men, of courage
stout in vaine, / For nought ye strive to save the burning town' "
(ll. 445–46). After their fighting, Aeneas summarizes the whole
night of violence and the downfall of everything he had held honorable and sacred in a famous rhetorical question. The rhythm is
like a chorus from a classical tragedy:

> Who can expresse the slaughter of that night,
> Or tell the nomber of the corpses slaine,
> Or can in teres bewaile them worthely?
> The auncient famous citie falleth down,
> That many yeres did hold such seignorie.
> With senslesse bodies every strete is spred,
> Eche palace, and sacred porch of the gods.
>   (bk. 2, ll. 463–69)

Similarly, in Dido's most furious moment, a passage where Vergil
is echoing his own subtext, Euripides' *Medea,* Surrey's alliterative
and tortuous syntax, with its system of accentual rhythms and
"echoes," catches her desperate fury:

> Faithlesse, forsworn, ne goddesse was thy dam,
> Nor Dardanus beginner of thy race,
>   But of hard rockes mount Caucase monstruous
> Bred thee, and teates of tyger gave thee suck.
> But what should I dissemble now my chere,
> Or me reserve to hope of greater things?
> Mindes he our teares or ever moved his eyen?
> Wept he for ruth, or pitied he our love?
> What shall I set before, or where begin?
> Juno nor Jove with just eyes this beholds.
> Faith is no where in suretie to be found.
>   (bk. 4, ll. 477–87)

Given Surrey's own solutions to his technical problems, it is no wonder that his text of blank verse readily adapted itself to the great compositions of theater and drama in the rest of the English Renaissance.

   Conclusion.   Finally, there are two death scenes in Surrey's translations from the *Aeneid* that as high drama set a rhetorical standard for the rest of the century. Here Surrey's own technical standards of a line without rhyme, a pentameter line, and a line fixed in syllables within medieval accentual rhythms draw on all his musical resources. The first is the death of Priam, in whose beheading by Pyrrhus both Vergil and Surrey obviously intended an emblem for the death of a civilization. This severed head also expresses another emblem, the loss of language by which a culture can name and honor the highest levels of communal life.

> Of Priamus this was the fatal fine,
> The wofull end that was alotted him.
> When he had seen his palace all on flame,
> With ruine of his Troyan turrets eke,
> That royal prince of Asie, which of late
> Reignd over so many peoples and realmes,
> Like a great stock now lieth on the shore;
> His hed and sholders parted ben in twaine,
> A body now without renome and fame.
>   (bk. 2, ll. 721–29)

   The second scene, Surrey's depiction of the death of Dido, gains its dramatic effect from extraordinarily concise and objective physical narration and understatement. This portrayal, like that of Priam's

death, represents Surrey's elegiac art at its highest. Dido's death, a famous classical and even Christian (certainly for Saint Augustine) source of pathos, must have presented the young Englishman in his middle twenties with the dangers of melodrama for which his conception of epic syntax did not always prepare him well. Surrey had understood the forces of eros that had brought Dido to her end, having dramatized them before in his own lyrics depicting the isolated lover. In his own translation of Vergil's famous description of the power of love destroying Dido, "Improbe amor, quid non mortalia pectora cogis?" Surrey had underscored the importance of this line by setting it, although in strained syntax, in a rare heroic couplet: "O witlesse love, what thing is that to do / A mortal minde thou canst not force thereto!" (bk. 4, ll. 540–41). To dramatize the end of such faithful driven love, Surrey needed to utilize all his profound technical resources. As the lines in this final passage show, he focuses his syntactical strategies on phrases and subordinate clauses contrapuntally playing them against strong Anglo-Saxon verbs of main clauses, most of them monosyllabic like the diction in most of the passage. The whole strategy of this "first English classical poet" leads to the irony of the final physical detail. Dido's last act as a living human being is an act emblematic of her whole character, the response of her being to the fate that in Vergil's fiction destroyed her:

> But Dido striveth to lift up againe
> Her heavy eyen, and hath no power thereto:
> Deepe in her brest that fixed wound doth gape.
> Thrise leaning on her elbow gan she raise
> Her self upward, and thrise she overthrewe
> Upon the bed, ranging with wandring eyes
> The skies for light, and wept when she it found.
> (bk. 4, ll. 917–23)

These death scenes mark the quintessential nature of Surrey's art, the product of his brief ten years before his own severed head and body, the last of Henry VIII's bloody corpses, ended an era. Elegiac at its most profound, Surrey's poetry offers death-differences, loss, and absence that paradoxically herald new art, new presences, beginnings. Such representation as these two death scenes translated from the *Aeneid* offer combines all the forces of eros that Surrey so

fervently found in Chaucer with the recognition of thanatos as their completion but not their end. In Surrey's language these forces of love and death do not disappear, either into each other or from reality. They exist in a kind of relationship or tension, a dialectic that modern masters of these terms like Freud, Jaspers, and Marcuse would understand well. Priam's head may be severed, but the communal eros that defined the civilization of Troy passed on into the language of Vergil and that of the perennial classic, where, through erotic strategies, absence engenders presence, difference breeds new art. No less the personal destruction of Dido's "improbe amor" restates this same dialectic. Nowhere in book 4 does Surrey's Vergil "translated into English, and drawn into a straunge metre" allow the reader of this fiction to forget the glorious achievements of love, not least those of syntax and diction. At no point in the language is such eros forgotten, even and especially at the very moment of its disappearing before tear-filled "wandring eyes" of countless Renaissance readers, including Shakespeare and Sidney, and beyond, of generations of English readers. These eyes, in fact, have searched "the skies for light" in the text and have found it even at the price of recognition and tears at its very mutability.

Such dialectic within form was the great intention of the humanists. The English humanists, particularly with their native tradition of mutability as poetic theme, sought such translation. Both Wyatt and Surrey understood the dimensions of this Vergilian task in the court of Henry VIII and, if melancholy generally predominates in their texts, ranging from bitterness to nostalgia, it is only that they have understood the integrity of such dialectic within their texts, an integrity of self, eros and thanatos, revealed in the text itself. Theirs is "twice man" Hippolytus, reborn through translation, through language as action, self, in Giammati's terms, as humanist activity moving from old texts to new. In this sense Henry Howard, the Earl of Surrey, is "the first English classical poet," as Warton noted, for with Wyatt he introduces an old form, an old theme, in a new language, a new text. Absence and loss, Surrey's dominant elegiac mode, marks the most glorious Renaissance texts from *Il cortegiano* to *The Fairie Queene, Hamlet, Lycidas*. The enormous presences in these texts arose from the recognition of loss and death, the difference demanded by time and mutability. Yet in the forms of these texts, as with Surrey's (progenitors of so much in the English Renaissance), the severed head does not cease its singing;

death-difference reemerges as continuing text. In the same way the head of Orpheus, itself severed by Maenads, floated down the swift Hebrus to the island of Lesbos. Even there in its cave it never ceased to sing.

Notes and References

Chapter One

1. Edwin Casady, *Henry Howard, Earl of Surrey* (New York: Modern Language Association, 1938), 21–23. The story of Surrey's last portrait also appears in George Frederick Nott, ed. *The Works of Henry Howard, Earl of Surrey, and of Sir Thomas Wyatt the Elder,* 2 vols. (London: Longman, Hurst, Rees, Orme, and Brown, 1815), 1:ix–x; John Martin Robinson, *The Dukes of Norfolk: A Quincentennial History* (Oxford: Oxford University Press, 1982), 49.

2. Robinson, *Dukes,* 2.

3. Nott, *Works,* lxvi–lxxv.

4. Casady, *Howard,* 19.

5. Nan Cooke Carpenter, *John Skelton* (New York: Twayne Publishers, 1967), 102–7. There is still debate, however, over the exact identity of Skelton's Countess of Surrey.

6. Robinson, *Dukes,* 37, and Michael Friend Serpell, *Kenninghall History and Saint Mary's Church* (Norfolk: Breckland Print, 1982), 29–33.

7. Casady, *Howard,* 3.

8. Robinson, *Dukes,* 21–22.

9. Nott, *Works,* xv–xviii (see n. *a,* p. xviii); Carpenter, *Skelton,* 103 (see n. 137); *DNB,* 10:23, and 7:7. See also Sergio Baldi, "The Secretary of the Duke of Norfolk and the First Italian Grammar in England," *Studies in English Language and Literature Presented to Professor Dr. Karl Brunner on the Occasion of His Seventieth Birthday,* ed. Siegfried Korninger. Weiner Beiträge zur Englische Philologie, no. 65 (Vienna: Wilhelm Braumueller, 1957), *passim.*

10. Casady, *Howard,* 31–32.

11. Stephen Merriam Foley, "The Honorable Style of Henry Howard, Earl of Surrey: A Critical Reading of Surrey's Poetry" (Ph.D. diss., Yale University, 1979), 27.

12. Bent-Einer Juel-Jensen, "The Poet Earl of Surrey's Library," *The Book Collector,* 5 (1960): 172. According to this description of Surrey's copy of Castiglione's *Cortegiano,* Surrey "has his name on the title, and very numerous annotations, also in his autograph." (This may be the only autograph we have of Surrey's.) These markings are opposite "literary passages" and are in both Italian and Latin, "all in a very lovely Italic hand." These markings prove Surrey read Petrarch and others in the

original and did not have the lack of linguistic or literary sophistication some modern critics have attributed to him. Another interesting aspect of these annotations, further proof of Surrey's humanist training, is that "he frequently refers by page to an edition of Cicero which he must have had by him."

13. Casady, *Howard*, 31–32. See also Sidney Lee, *The French Renaissance in England* (Oxford: Clarendon Press, 1910), 109–26.

14. Casady, *Howard*, 36–37.

15. Hester W. Chapman, *Two Tudor Portraits: Henry Howard, Earl of Surrey, and Lady Catherine Gray* (London: Jonathan Cape, 1960), 36.

16. Nott, *Works*, lix.

17. Edmond Bapst, *Deux gentilshommes-poètes de la cour de Henry VIII* (Paris: Librairie Plon, 1891), pp. 225–29.

18. Casady, *Howard*, 64.

19. Ibid., 76–79.

20. Nott, *Works*, cxx–cxxiv. This catalogue, "An Account of the Earl of Surrey's Furniture at St. Leonards," gives the scope of the furnishings Surrey had begun for his mansion, with elaborately designed tapestries and cushions and "Turkey carpets" in addition to many other items, all dispersed either to debtors or to Seymour and his henchmen.

21. Casady, *Howard*, 88.

22. Nott, *Works*, 167–69. The council, so Surrey argues, should "impute this error to the fury of rechless youth" and "so gentle a warning" would teach him "how to bridle my heady will: which in youth is rarely attained without adversity." Indeed Surrey feels he can lay before the council "the quiet conversation of my passed life," which has been "unstained with any unhonest touch" as a promise of his amendment; such examination "during my affliction (in which time malice is most ready to slander the innocent)" may allow them to take him out of "this noisome prison, whose pestilent airs are not unlike to bring some alteration of health." If he cannot have the presence of the king's majesty (for "every loving subject, specially unto me, from a Prince cannot be less than a living death"), then perhaps "some place of open air, with like restraint of liberty, there to abide his Grace's pleasure," in other words, a place like Windsor where he had been imprisoned first.

23. Casady, *Howard*, 95–100.

24. Ibid., 103–4. On his first day, according to Wallop's dispatches, Surrey daringly examined the enemy fortifications and was "somewhat saluted" by the firepower of the French, which included a new technological breakthrough of "artificial bullets": "a strange and dreadful sight to see the bullet fly into the air sprouting fire on every side" and then leaping from place to place, also "casting out fire."

25. Ibid., 104–6.

26. Ibid., 112–5. Casady has a seventeenth-century description of this position, which held enormous responsibilities.

27. Ibid., 130.

28. Nott, *Works,* 172–231.

29. M. Bryn Davies, "Surrey at Boulogne," *Huntington Library Quarterly* 23 (1960): 339–48. Although the portrait of a passionate Surrey is probably accurate, the intensely Protestant bias of this account by a Welsh officer betrays a tendentiousness against Surrey. There is no objectivity toward the intent of Surrey's actions or his initial strategy, which was ingenious and typical of Surrey's generally flexible maneuvering and use of cavalry. Consider Surrey's own rather odd explanation for the debacle in his letter to the Privy Council: "and a sudden flight the let of a full victory. And if any disorder there were, we assure your Majesty there were no default in the rulers, nor lack of courage to be given them, but a humour that reigneth in Englishmen" (Nott, *Works,* 201).

30. Casady, *Howard,* 180.

31. Gerald Brenan and Edwards Phillips Statham, *The House of Howard* 2 vols. (London: Hutchinson & Co., 1907), 2:248; Robinson, *Dukes,* 243.

32. After the king himself, the Earl of Surrey had more portraits and drawings of himself than any other member of the Tudor court, according to Sir Roy Strong, *Tudor and Jacobean Portraits,* 2 vols. (London: H. M. Stationery Office, 1969), 1:370.

33. Erna Auerbach, "Holbein's Followers in England," *Burlington Magazine* 93 (1951):49.

34. Arthur B. Ferguson, *The Indian Summer of English Chivalry: Studies in the Decline and Transformation of Chivalric Idealism* (Durham, N.C.: Duke University Press, 1960), 93–94.

35. Casady, *Howard,* 191.

36. Edward Lord Herbert of Cherbury, *Autobiography* and *The History of England under Henry VIII* (London: Alexander Murray, 1870), 737.

37. Casady, *Howard,* 186–88.

38. Chapman, *Portraits,* 121.

39. J. G. Nichols, ed., *Chronicle of the Grey Friars,* Camden Society Publications, no. 53 (London, 1852), 52; see also Chapman, *Portraits,* 122, and Casady, *Howard,* 193–94.

40. Lord Herbert, *Autobiography,* 737.

41. Casady, *Howard,* 198–99.

42. Ibid., 201–2, n. 43.

43. Nott, *Works,* cii.

44. Lord Herbert, *Autobiography,* 739.

45. Chapman, *Portraits,* 138–39.

Chapter Two

1. Richard Foster Jones, *The Triumph of the English Language* (London: Oxford University Press, 1953), 7.

2. A. Bartlett Giamatti, "Hippolytus among the Exiles: The Romance of Early Humanism," in *Poetic Traditions of the English Renaissance,* ed. Maynard Mack and George deForest Lord (New Haven and London: Yale University Press, 1982), 17.

3. Ruth Hughey, ed., *The Arundel Harington Manuscript of Tudor Poetry* 2 vols. (Columbus: Ohio State University Press, 1960), 2:428–30.

4. Hughey, *Tudor Poetry,* 1:322 (ll. 3–4, 23–24). Ascham praises Cheke as "the best master, that euer I had or heard in learning" in *The Scholemaster,* ed. Edward Arber (Westminster: A. Constable & Co., 1895), 297.

5. John M. Berdan, *Early Tudor Poetry, 1485–1547* (New York: MacMillan & Co., 1920), 359.

6. Hughey, *Tudor Poetry,* 2:429.

7. Vere Rubel, *Poetic Diction in the English Renaissance* (New York: Modern Language Association, 1941), 59–67.

8. Charles W. Eckert, ed. "The Poetry of Henry Howard, Earl of Surrey" (Ph.D. diss., Washington University, 1960), 89 ff. Eckert's discussion of Surrey's text is the best analysis to date of the problems of establishing an adequate text for Surrey's work.

9. Hyder Edward Rollins, ed., *Tottel's Miscellany (1557–1587),* 2 vols. (Cambridge, Mass.: Harvard University Press, 1966), 1:2.

10. Ibid., 1:1.

11. Thomas Warton, *The History of English Poetry, from the Close of the Eleventh to the Commencement of the Eighteenth Century* (London: Tegg, 1824), 645.

12. A. R. Ammons, *Sphere: The Form of a Motion* (New York: W. W. Norton & Co., 1974), sec. 16, p. 4.

13. Frank Kermode, *The Classic* (London: Faber & Faber, 1975), 15–16.

14. H. A. Mason, *Humanism and Poetry in the Early Tudor Period* (London: Routledge & Kegan Paul, 1959), 179 ff.

15. Arber, ed., *Scholemaster,* 92–96.

16. Mason, *Humanism,* 236–54.

17. Patricia Thomson, "Wyatt and Surrey," in *English Poetry and Prose, 1540 to 1674,* ed. Christopher Ricks (London: Barrie & Jenkins, 1975), 23–25; *Sir Thomas Wyatt and His Background* (Stanford: Stanford University Press, 1964), 152 ff.

18. C. S. Lewis, *English Literature in the Sixteenth Century Excluding Drama* (Oxford: Clarendon Press, 1954), 231.

19. Nott, *Works,* xlvi.

20. Ben Jonson, *Works,* ed. G. H. Hereford and Percy Simpson 11 vols. (Oxford: Clarendon Press, 1925–52), 8:591.

21. Berdan, *Tudor Poetry,* 523, 542. Berdan sees Surrey as representative of the second generation of Henry VIII's court when, for the first time since Chaucer, the forms of language were relatively settled because the forces of native tradition, medieval Latin, and humanism had begun to coalesce.

22. E. M. W. Tillyard, *The Poetry of Sir Thomas Wyatt* (London: Chatto & Windus, 1949), 35.

23. Thomson, "Wyatt," 154.

24. Kermode, *Classic,* 139.

25. See the discussion of *frottola* and its relationship to literary forms like the *capitolo,* the sonnet, and the *strambotto,* all forms used by Surrey, in Alfred Einstein, *The Italian Madrigal,* 3 vols. (Princeton: Princeton University Press, 1949), 1:34 ff. Although Surrey's poetic text cannot strictly be called a *frottola* because there is no accompanying music, it borrows from the general musical form for its own specific form.

26. Eckert, "Poetry," 16; Rollins, *Tottel's Miscellany,* 2:143.

27. George Puttenham, *The Arte of English Poesie,* ed. Gladys Doidge Willcock and Alice Walker (Cambridge: Cambridge University Press, 1936; reprint ed., 1970), xlv; references to Surrey on pp. 72, 123, and 132 (quotation from the last).

28. Eckert, "Poetry," 17. See here the reference to the musical training suggested by Sir Thomas Elyot in his *Boke of the Govenour,* a work contemporary with Surrey. For Surrey as possible composer, see Nott, *Works,* cvii.

29. Ivy L. Mumford, "Petrarchism in Early Tudor England," *Italian Studies* 19 (1964): 56–59; Eckert, "Poetry," 12: an Italian representative by 1515 had written from London to Venice for new *frottole* for the English nobility who wanted more.

30. Eckert, "Poetry," 14. The dauphin's own Almoner and lute-teacher was Mellin de Saint-Gelais, one of the best poets and musicians of the first half of the sixteenth century in France. He was also the nephew or possibly the illegitimate son of the literary Bishop of Angoulême, Octavien Saint-Gelais, who in 1529 had translated the *Aeneid* into French rhyming couplets. Mellin de Saint-Gelais was also famed for his innovative poetic forms and it is a question of who introduced the Italian sonnet form first into France, Saint-Gelais or Marot. Saint-Gelais was also the most important French exponent of Serafino, a famous Italian imitator of Petrarch and generally considered an influence on the development of Surrey's own poetry. Vying against the medieval rhetoricians at court, Saint-Gelais became as Italianate in dress and manners as Surrey was later accused of being. All these influences reached Surrey in one manner or another during

1532–33 at a very impressionable age. If we judge by Surrey's later reference to Francis I's mistress at this time, Surrey never forgot the contacts and impressions of his fifteenth and sixteenth years.

31. Einstein, *Madrigal,* 1:69.

32. Lewis, *English Literature,* 231.

33. Maurice Evans, *English Poetry in the Sixteenth Century* (New York: W. W. Norton & Co., 1967), 81–82.

34. Baldesar Castiglione, *The Book of the Courtier,* trans. Charles S. Singleton (Garden City, N. Y.,: Doubleday & Co., 1959), 43.

35. Rollins, *Tottel's Miscellany,* 2:143.

36. Puttenham, *Arte,* 132.

37. Richardo J. Quinones, *The Renaissance Discovery of Time* (Cambridge, Mass.: Harvard University Press, 1972), 106–71; Thomas M. Greene, *The Light in Troy: Imitation and Discovery in Renaissance Poetry* (New Haven and London: Yale University Press, 1982), 81–146. Both sections show how Petrarch's texts build from his various subtexts.

38. Berdan, *Early Tudor,* 530.

39. Castiglione, *Courtier,* 47.

40. Jones's punctuation is arbitrary at the end of stanza two. In Emrys Jones, ed. *Henry Howard, Earl of Surrey: Poems* Clarendon Medieval and Tudor Series, ed. J. A. W. Bennett (Oxford: Clarendon Press, 1964).

41. Walter R. Davis, "Contexts in Surrey's Poetry," *English Literary Renaissance* 4 (1974): 47.

42. C. W. Jentoft, "Rhetoric and Structure in the Poetry of Henry Howard, Earl of Surrey" (Ph.D. diss., Ohio State University, 1970), 54–56.

43. Davis, "Contexts," 46.

44. For a discussion of the use of this kind of syllogism in seventeenth-century poetry, see S. L. Bethell, "The Nature of Metaphysical Wit," *Northern Miscellany of Literary Criticism* 1 (1953): 19–40.

45. Tillyard, *Poetry,* 35.

46. Cf. Aeneas's advice to his men in the *Aeneid,* ed. A. Sidgwick (Cambridge: Cambridge University Press, 1934), bk. 1, l. 207: "Durate, et vosmet rebus servate secundis."

Chapter Three

1. Thomson, "Wyatt," 152–66.

2. Raymond Southall, *The Courtly Maker: An Essay on the Poetry of Wyatt and His Contemporaries* (Oxford: Basil Blackwell, 1964), 29. Italics his.

3. Rollins, *Tottel's Miscellany,* 1:2. Cf. Thomson's discussion of how Wyatt and Surrey dealt with the problem of Chaucer's expansion of Petrarch in "Wyatt," 158 and 171–73.

4. Puttenham, *Arte,* 61–62.

5. Thomson, "Wyatt," chap. 7.

6. Berdan, *Early Tudor,* 523.

7. William O. Harris, " 'Love That Doth Reign': Surrey's Creative Imitation," *Modern Philology* 66:298–305.

8. Ovid *Amores* 2. 10, itself a parody of Vergil *Georgica* 2. 490–91.

9. Cf. Surrey's own translation of the Vergilian subtext, bk. 2, ll. 864–66.

10. Frederick Morgan Padelford, *The Poems of Henry Howard Earl of Surrey,* University of Washington Publications in Language and Literature, no. 5 rev. ed. (Seattle: University of Washington Press, 1928; reprint ed., 1966), 49.

11. Thomson, "Wyatt," 176.

12. Puttenham, *Arte,* 223.

13. Foley, "Style," 46–47.

14. Richard S. Silvester, ed., *The Anchor Anthology of Sixteenth-Century Verse* (New York: Doubleday, 1974), xxvi.

15. Ariosto, *Orlando Furioso,* bk. 1, ll. 78 ff.; Boiardo, *Orlando Immorato,* bk. 1, stanza 3; Cicero *De natura deorum* 3. 26.

16. J. W. Lever, *The Elizabethan Love Sonnet* (London: Methuen, 1956), 31.

17. Rubel, *Poetic Diction,* 57.

18. Cf. Thomas Wilson, *Wilson's Arte of Rhetorique, 1560,* ed. G. H. Mair (Oxford: Oxford University Press, 1909), 99 ff.

19. Padelford, *Poems,* 207.

20. Davis, "Contexts," 41.

21. Alastair Fowler, *Conceitful Thought: The Interpretation of Renaissance Poems* (Edinburgh: Edinburgh University Press, 1975), 25.

22. Padelford, *Poems,* 207.

23. Evans, *English Poetry,* 77.

24. Lewis, *English Literature,* 231.

25. Thomson, "Wyatt," chap. 5. Cf. Douglas Peterson, *The English Lyric from Wyatt to Donne: A History of the Plain and Eloquent Styles* (Princeton: Princeton University Press, 1967), chap. 1.

26. Cf. Bert C. Bach, William A. Sessions, and William Walling, *The Liberating Form: A Handbook-Anthology of English and American Poetry* (New York and Toronto: Dodd, Mead & Co. 1972), chap. 3.

27. Peterson, *English Lyric,* 53.

28. Cf. Casady, *Howard,* Appendix II, 244–50.

29. Hughey, *Tudor Poetry,* 2:78–83.

30. Ibid. and Nott, *Works,* 277.

Chapter Four

1. Johannes Huizinga, *The Waning of the Middle Ages* (New York: St. Martin's Press, 1949), 96.
2. Lewis, *English Literature,* 230.
3. Eckert, "Poetry," 53.
4. C. W. Jentoft, "Surrey's Four 'Orations' and the Influence of Rhetoric on Dramatic Effect," *Papers on Language and Literature* 9 (1973): 256.
5. Puttenham, *Arte,* 192.
6. Thomson, "Wyatt," 122.
7. Rollins, *Tottel's Miscellany,* 2:206.
8. Jones, *Surrey Poems,* 115, quotes a *rondeau* by Marot, although the *strambotto* form suggests the influence of Seraphino, who also combined classical allusions and licentious punning.
9. Ivy Mumford, "Musical Settings to the Poems of Surrey," *English Miscellany* 16 (1965): 10.
10. Eckert, "Poetry," 56.
11. Berdan, *Early Tudor,* p. 530.
12. Eckert, "Poetry," 83.
13. These quatrains are separated in Eckert's superior text, "Poetry," 131–32.
14. In fact, in the textual history of this poem the name changes from "Marshall" to "my frende" to "Warner," possibly a reference to Sir Edward Warner, as Eckert notes, "Poetry," 86.
15. Mumford, "Musical Settings," 14.
16. Ibid., 16.
17. Peterson, *English Lyric,* 73.
18. Jentoft, "Surrey's Four 'Orations,' " 253–55.
19. Cf. Rubel, *Poetic Diction,* 57–82: it is one of several words in Chaucer that Surrey renewed for his time.
20. Eckert, "Poetry," 75.
21. "Sink" in Tottel and Jones; "suck" in Nott and Hughey.
22. Jentoft, "Surrey's Four 'Orations,' " 257–62.
23. Cf. Bapst, "Gentilshommes-poètes," 268 ff., and Casady, *Howard,* 99.
24. Hughey, *Tudor Poetry,* 2:90.
25. Cf. Jones's reading of "hast" in line 49, *Surrey Poems,* 128.

Chapter Five

1. George Gascoigne, *Works,* ed. John W. Cunliffe 2 vols. (Cambridge: Cambridge University Press, 1907–10), 1:472.

2. Eckert, "Poetry," 19–33.

3. Jentoft, "Rhetoric and Structure," 138.

4. When imitated in 1591 in *Brittons Bowre of Delights,* for example, the long lines were broken down into the ballad form that would be transformed into the "short meter" of Anglican church-hymns. Cf. Mumford, "Musical Settings," 10–15, and Bruce Pattison, *Music and Poetry of the English Renaissance* (London: Methuen & Co., 1948), 165.

5. Padelford, *Poems,* 217. For the Renaissance tradition of winter landscapes, see Alan T. Bradford, "Mirrors of Mutability: Winter Landscapes in Tudor Poetry," *English Literary Renaissance* 4 (1974): 3–39.

6. Eckert, "Poetry," 103–6.

7. Hughey, *Tudor Poetry,* 2:76–84.

8. Rollins, *Tottel's Miscellany,* 2:299.

9. Bapst, "Gentilshommes-poètes," 370, and Michael Drayton, *Works* 5 vols. (Oxford: Basil Blackwell, 1961), 1:277–94, where the allusion appears in the Geraldine epistle. Cf. also Hughey, *Tudor Poetry,* 2:97.

10. Foley, "Style," 178–79.

11. Hughey, *Tudor Poetry,* 2:98–99.

12. Eckert, "Poetry," 54.

13. Nott, *Works,* 377.

14. Mason, *Humanism,* 244.

15. Puttenham, *Arte,* 73.

16. Hughey, *Tudor Poetry,* 2:118.

17. Ibid., 102. The Psalms were the only music Calvin allowed into his liturgy; in France a major poet like Marot undertook translations into the vernacular, followed by Beza and others, the whole enterprise encouraged by Protestant members of the royal family like Marguerite of Navarre. It should be noted that there were no English Catholic translations, if such a term as "Catholic" (as opposed to Protestant) would in fact have any meaning at this time. Not until the second year of the Council of Trent in 1546 was there even agreement on the correct Latin text to be used for any Psalm translation.

18. Hughey, Tudor Poetry, 2:107. This is a significant shift in subtext.

19. Eckert, "Poetry," 56.

20. Blage, a friend of Wyatt's, figures strongly in the last days of Surrey (cf. Casady, *Howard,* 186–88).

21. Jones, *Surrey Poems,* 130–31.

22. *Aeneid,* bk. 1, l. 203: "forsan et haec olim meminisse iuvabit" (perhaps it will also be a pleasure one day to remember these things).

23. Peterson, *English Lyric,* 76–78.

Chapter Six

1. A. L. Bennett, "The Prinicipal Rhetorical Conventions of the Renaissance Personal Elegy," *Studies in Philology* 51 (1943): 109–23.
2. Rollins, *Tudor Poetry*, 2:156.
3. Cf. O. B. Hardison, Jr., *The Enduring Monument: A Study of the Idea of Praise in Renaissance Literary Theory and Practice* (Chapel Hill: University of North Carolina Press, 1962).
4. Castiglione, *Courtier*, 239.
5. Fowler, *Conceitful Thought*, 26–29.
6. Peterson, *English Lyric*, 53.
7. Tibullus, *Poems*, in *Catullus Tibullus and Pervigilium Veneris* (Cambridge and London: William Heineman, and Harvard University Press, 1939), 3.6.43–44: "Felix, quicumque dolore / alterius disces posse cavere tuom" (Blessed are you who learn by the sorrow of another how to care for your own). Cf. also *Troilus*, bk. 3, l. 329.
8. Davis, "Contexts," 53–54.
9. Cf. Rollins, *Tottel's Miscellany*, 2:311; Jentoft, "Surrey's Five Elegies: Rhetoric, Structure, and the Poetry of Praise," *PMLA* 91 (1976): 28–30; Anthony Low, "Reply," *PMLA* 91 (1976): 914–15; Edgar F. Daniels, "Surrey's 'In the Rude Age,' " *Notes and Queries* (1956): 14–15.
10. Nott, *Works*, lxxxviii.
11. Cf. S. P. Zitner, "Truth and Mourning in a Sonnet by Surrey," *English Literary History* 50, no. 3 (Fall 1983):583.
12. Ibid., 517–22. Cf. Casady, *Howard*, 123–24.
13. Lever, *Love Sonnet*, 50.
14. Davis, "Contexts," 50.
15. As the Duke of Norfolk wrote in 1537, "[My] son of Surrey is very weak, his nature running from him abundantly. 'He was in that case a great part of last year, [which] . . . came to him for thought of [the death] my lord of Richmond' " (Casady, *Howard*, 57).
16. As Eckert notes ("Poetry," 116), the original text reflects the suicidal ambiguity with textual blurring of an original "have" to "half."
17. W. J. Courthope, *A History of English Poetry* 6 vols. (London: MacMillan & Co., 1897), 2:85.
18. John Stevens, *Music in Poetry in the Early Tudor Court* (Lincoln: University of Nebraska Press, 1961), 156–57.
19. Lewis, *English Literature*, 232.

Chapter Seven

1. Berdan, *Early Tudor*, 534.
2. The *Aeneid* was turned into French rhymed couplets by Bishop Octavien de Saint-Gelais, uncle (probably father) of Mellin the poet and musician whom Surrey may have actually known at the court of Francis

I. The Scottish bishop Gawain Douglas completed in manuscript by 1513 his *Aeneid* in lowland Scottish; it was accessible and read by courtiers although its publication in 1553 was after Surrey's beheading. In Italy there were translations from the circle of Cardinal Hippolito de Medici. Book 2 by Molza appeared in 1539 but existed before Molza's death in 1535; Book 4 by Piccolomini, in 1544.

3. Florence Ridley, ed., *The Aeneid of Henry Howard, Earl of Surrey*, University of California Publications, English Studies, no. 26 (Berkeley: University of California Press, 1963), 4.

4. Ibid., 8. For the problems in Tottel's text, see Rubel, *Poetic Diction*, and Henry Burrowes Lathrop, *Translations from the Classics in English from Caxton to Chapman, 1477–1620* (New York: Octagon Books, 1967), 98.

5. Ridley, *Aeneid*, 4–5.

6. Thomson, "Wyatt," 35.

7. Berdan, *Early Tudor*, 541–42.

8. Kermode, *Classic*, 15–16.

9. Jones, *Surrey Poems*, xiv.

10. Surrey may have read Trissino's dedication in his blank-verse tragedy *Sofonisba* in 1515 and quite likely Alamanni's statements on blank verse. See Henri Hauvette, *Luigi Alamanni: sa vie et son oeuvre* (Paris: Librairie Hachette, 1903), 215.

11. Ascham, *Scholemaster*, 144–49.

12. Eckert, "Poetry," 48–50.

13. Ant Oras, "Surrey's Technique of Verbal Echoes: A Method and its Background," *Journal of English and German Philology* 50 (1951): 305–6.

14. Ibid., 301.

15. Eckert, "Poetry," 51.

16. Jones, *Surrey Poems*, xv.

17. Ibid., xiii.

18. George Saintsbury, *A History of English Prosody from the Twelfth Century to the Present Day*, 3 vols. (London: MacMillan and Co., 1906), 1:288.

19. These legacies have been fully investigated by Ridley, *Aeneid*, 13–30, and Priscilla Bawcutt, "Douglas and Surrey: Translators of Virgil," *Essays and Studies by Members of the English Association* 27:52–67.

20. David A. Richardson, "Humanistic Intent in Surrey's *Aeneid*," *English Literary Renaissance* 6 (1976):211.

21. Jones, *Surrey Poems*, 134.

22. Lewis, *English Literature*, 234.

23. Evans, *English Poetry*, 79.

24. Ridley, *Aeneid*, 32.

25. Oras, "Surrey's Technique," 26.

26. This argument is a result of German scholarship at the turn of the century as summarized in Berdan, Ridley, and Hartman, *Surrey's "Fourth Boke of Virgill"* (Purchase, N. Y.: privately printed [by John Johnson at the Oxford University Press] for Carl H. Pforzheimer, 1933), ix–xxvii.

27. Berdan, *Early Tudor,* 536–39, and Hartman, *"Fourth Boke"* xxii–xxv.

28. Jones, *Surrey Poems,* 29.

29. Oras, "Surrey's Technique," 294.

30. Hartman, *"Fourth Boke,"* xvi.

31. Berdan, *Early Tudor,* 341.

Selected Bibliography

PRIMARY SOURCES

The Aeneid of Henry Howard Earl of Surrey. Edited by Florence H. Ridley. Berkeley and Los Angeles: University of California Press, 1963.

The Arundel Harington Manuscript of Tudor Poetry. Edited by Ruth Hughey. 2 vols. Columbus: Ohio State University Press, 1960.

Certain Bokes of Virgiles Aenis turned into English meter, by Henry Earle of Surrey. London: Richard Tottel, 1557 [STC 24798].

Certayn Chapters of the prouerbes of Salomon drawen into metre by Thomas sterneholde [Surrey's paraphrases——STC 2760].

The Fourth Boke of Virgill . . . drawne into a strange metre by Henrye, late Earle of Surrey. London: John Day for William Owen, 1554.

Henry Howard, Earl of Surrey: Poems. Edited by Emrys Jones. Clarendon Medieval and Tudor Series, edited by J. A. W. Bennett. Oxford: Clarendon Press, 1964.

Muir, Kenneth. "Surrey Poems in the Blage Manuscript." *Notes and Queries* 20S, n.s. 7, no. 10 (October):368–70.

Nugae Antiquae: Being a Miscellaneous Collection of Original Papers in Prose and Verse . . . by Sir John Harington. 3 vols. London: J. Dodsley and T. Shrimpton, 1769–75, 1779, 1792. Revised edition, edited by Thomas Park. 2 vols. London: J. Wright for Vernor and Hood, Poultry, and Cuthell and Marin, 1804.

Padelford, Frederick Morgan. "The Manuscript Poems by Henry Howard, Earl of Surrey." *Anglia* 29 (1906):273–338.

The Poems of Henry Howard Earl of Surrey. Edited by Frederick Morgan Padelford. University of Washington Publications in Language and Literature, vol. 5. Seattle: University of Washington Press, 1920. Revised edition, 1928. Reprint, 1966.

"The Poetry of Henry Howard, Earl of Surrey." Edited by Charles Willison Eckert. Ph.D. dissertation, Washington University, 1960.

Songes and Sonettes, written by the ryght honorable Lorde Henry Hawarde late Earle of Surrey, and other. London: Richard Tottel, 1557 [STC 13860].

Surrey's Fourth Boke of Virgill. Edited by Herbert Hartman. London: Oxford University Press, John Johnson for Carl H. Pforzheimer, 1933.

Tottel's Miscellany (1557–1587). Edited by Hyder Edward Rollins. 2 vols. Cambridge, Mass.: Harvard University Press, 1929–30.

The Works of Henry Howard Earl of Surrey and of Sir Thomas Wyatt the Elder. Edited by George Frederick Nott. 2 vols. London: T. Bensley for Longman, Hurst, Rees, Orme, and Brown, 1815–16.

SECONDARY SOURCES

Bapst, Edmond. *Deux gentilshommes-poètes de la cour de Henry VIII.* Paris: Librairie Plon, 1891. Still an excellent source for Surrey's biography; even his sometimes bizarre conjectures are perceptive.

Berdan, John M. *Early Tudor Poetry, 1485–1547.* New York: Macmillan & Co., 1920. An early but very valuable survey.

Casady, Edwin. *Henry Howard, Earl of Surrey.* Modern Language Association Revolving Fund Series, no. 8. New York: Modern Language Association, 1938. The standard biography to date, both informative and penetrating in its use of fact and interpretation of fact.

Chapman, Hester W. *Two Tudor Portraits: Henry Howard, Earl of Surrey and Lady Catherine Gray.* London: Jonathan Cape, 1960. Novelistic biography, generally unsympathetic, with good mise-en-scène of Tudor court and period.

Davis, Walter R. "Contexts in Surrey's Poetry." *English Literary Renaissance* 4 (1974): 40–55. A perceptive and pioneering reading of Surrey's achievement.

Einstein, Alfred. *The Italian Madrigal.* 3 vols. Princeton: Princeton University Press, 1949. An essential reference for any understanding of the musical forms Surrey used.

Evans, Maurice. *English Poetry in the Sixteenth Century.* New York: W. W. Norton & Co., 1967. A chapter on Wyatt and Surrey offers an excellent and full introduction to Surrey.

Foley, Stephen Merriam. "The Honorable Style of Henry Howard, Earl of Surrey: A Critical Reading of Surrey's Poetry." Ph.D. dissertation, Yale University, 1979. One of the most perceptive of the recent dissertations on Surrey.

Fowler, Alastair. *Conceitful Thought: The Interpretation of Renaissance Poems.* Edinburgh: Edinburgh University Press, 1975. Powerful if sui generis interpretations of several of Surrey's major sonnets.

Herbert, Lord Edward of Cherbury. *Autobiography and The History of England under Henry VIII.* London: Alexander Murray, 1870. Probably the most valuable document for understanding the last days of Surrey.

Jentoft, Clyde W. *Sir Thomas Wyatt and Henry Howard, Earl of Surrey: A Reference Guide.* Boston: G. K. Hall & Co., 1980. An indispensable tool in any Surrey research and an excellent compilation of many

varied works with a general introduction that masterfully, if suc-
cinctly, charts the critical reputations of both poets.

————. "Surrey's Five Elegies: Rhetoric, Structure, and the Poetry of
Praise." *PMLA* 91 (1976): 23–32.

————. "Surrey's Four 'Orations' and the Influence of Rhetoric on Dramatic Effect." *Papers on Language and Literature* 9 (1973): 250–62.
Both these essays offer new readings of Surrey that build on formal
analysis and open up the humanist background of his poetry as a
means of understanding the works.

Kermode, Frank. *The Classic.* London: Faber & Faber, 1975.

Lewis, C. S. *English Literature in the Sixteenth Century Excluding Drama.*
The Oxford History of English Literature, vol. 3. Oxford: Clarendon
Press, 1954. As in most of of this volume, the passages on Surrey
are tendentious, full of penetrating readings, and eminently quotable.

Mason, H. A. *Humanism and Poetry in the Early Tudor Period.* London:
Routledge & Kegan Paul, 1959. His analyses of Surrey are quarrel-
some but set very well in the context of the period.

Mumford, Ivy L. "Musical Settings to the Poems of Surrey." *English
Miscellany* 8 (1957): 9–20.

————. "Italian Aspects of Surrey's Lyrics." *English Miscellany* 16 (1965):
19–36.

————. "Petrarchism in Early Tudor England." *Italian Studies* 19 (1964):
56–63. All these studies demonstrate the Italian influence on Surrey
and his time, especially in terms of music and musical forms.

Oras, Ants. "Surrey's Technique of Verbal Echoes: A Method and Its
Background." *Journal of English and Germanic Philology* 50 (1951):
289–308. Although directed toward Surrey's translations of the *Aeneid,*
the methodology discussed here demonstrates the precision and for-
mality of Surrey's lyrics as well.

Pattison, Bruce. *Music and Poetry of the English Renaissance.* London: Methuen & Co., 1948. A valuable introduction to the Tudor court music
and entertainments and their close relationship to the poetry of the
period.

Peterson, Douglas L. *The English Lyric from Wyatt to Donne.* Princeton:
Princeton University Press, 1967. Although rather thesis-bound, a
first significant analysis of the formal roots of Surrey's art.

Richardson, David A. "Humanistic Intent in Surrey's *Aeneid.*" *English
Literary Renaissance* 6 (1976): 204–19. A general, insightful discussion
of Surrey's approach to his task of translating Vergil.

Robinson, John M. *The Dukes of Norfolk: A Quincentennial History.* Oxford:
Oxford University Press, 1982. The chapters on Surrey and his father
and ancestors are very useful in this survey of the Howard family.

Southall, Raymond. *The Courtly Maker: An Essay on the Poetry of Wyatt and His Contemporaries.* Oxford: Basil Blackwell, 1964. Good analysis of the influence of Chaucer's *Troilus* in this period.

Thomson, Patricia. *Sir Thomas Wyatt and His Background.* Stanford: Stanford University Press, 1964. Essential study for the period.

————. "Wyatt and Surrey." In *English Poetry and Prose, 1540 to 1674,* edited by Christopher Ricks. London: Barrie & Jenkins, 1975. Although her emphasis is on resuscitating Wyatt, Thomson's profound and wide knowledge of the forms and shape of poetry in the period and of the medieval sub-texts give her work and especially her analyses of Surrey considerable depth.

Zitner, S. P. "Truth and Mourning in a Sonnet by Surrey." *English Literary History* 50 (Fall 1983):509–29. An analysis of Surrey's elegy on Clere that combines various new critical methods and gives a definitive reading to the sonnet.

Index

169